The Uttermost Deep

The Uttermost Deep
The Challenge of
Near-Death Experiences

Gracia Fay Ellwood

Lantern Books ● New York
A Division of Booklight Inc.

2001
Lantern Books
One Union Square West, Suite 201
New York, NY 10003

Printed in the United States of America

Library of Congress Cataloging-in-Publication Data

Ellwood, Gracia Fay.
    The uttermost deep : the challenge of near-death experiences / Gracia Fay Ellwood
        p. cm.
    Includes bibliographical references and index.
    ISBN 1-930051-27-1
    I. Near-death experiences. 2. Future life. I. Title

BF1045.N4 E54 2001
133.9'01'3—dc21

                                                                    2001038046

Where can I go from your Spirit?
Where can I fly from your Presence?
If I ascend to heaven, you are there;
If I make my bed in Sheol, you are there!
If I take the wings of the morning
And dwell in the uttermost . . . deep,
Even there your hand shall lead me,
And your right hand shall hold me.
. . . .
Even the darkness is not dark to you,
The night is bright as the day. . .

—Psalm 139:7–10, 12

For Richard Scott Lancelot Ellwood
in boundless gratitude
for the once and future dream

Acknowledgments ⟡

I ACKNOWLEDGE WITH GRATITUDE THE PERSONS WHO supported me in the writing of this work (though I remain responsible for any failings). Among them are David Ray Griffin, who wrote detailed critiques of each chapter; members of the International Association for Near-Death Studies and others who helped me find materials and/or discussed various topics with me, particularly P. M. H. Atwater, Nancy Evans Bush, Susan Blackmore, Bruce Greyson, John Hutchison, Cynthia Johnson, Raymond Moody, Kenneth Ring, George Ritchie, Michael Sabom, Kimberly Clark Sharp, Steven Smith, Frank Spaeth, and Greg Wilson; the experiencers who told me their stories and pondered my questions; the friends upon whom I relied for psychological as well as intellectual help, especially Mary Gennuso and Doris Robin; my care-full editors, Eugene Gollogly and Martin Rowe; and last but not least my devoted family, Richard Scott Lancelot Ellwood (who also provided crucial technical assistance), Fay Elanor Ellwood, and Robert Scott Ellwood, who kept alive my confidence both in the project and in myself.

Friends, may the wings of your freedom give others the power of flight.

Table of Contents ⌒

Introduction ⤙

THE CHALLENGE OF NDES

M OST NORTH AMERICANS ARE FAMILIAR BY NOW WITH "the Near-Death Experience" (NDE): the experiencer (NDEr) floats out of her body, observes the scene, speeds through a dark tunnel, sees a wonderful bright light, reviews her life, perhaps enters heaven, meets deceased relatives or religious figures, returns, and undergoes great life-changes. More sophisticated listeners notice cultural influences in the experience: the guides and the overall message of the life review tend to manifest democratic ideals; the religious figure is one familiar to the NDEr, usually part of her own religious background.

Then one encounters a case like that of Jer. Four years old and always very afraid of water, Jer fell into the deep end of a swimming pool and was pulled out blue and unconscious. After a week of coma, he revived, apparently undamaged; one of his first actions after returning home was to declare that he intended to jump back into the deep end of the pool. When he emerged, he said "See....I came back again." A year later, with an uncharacteristically mature manner, he said: "Sit down. I have to talk to you, Mother." He told her that when he drowned he had been sitting on the roof, watching the resuscitation attempts; that he had seen something "real pretty in the sky"; had walked down a tunnel, seen a bright light, and reached for the hand of God. When that was withdrawn, he reluctantly returned. "On the way back, I saw the devil. He said if I did what he wanted, I could have anything I want....But I didn't want him bossing me around." His perplexed mother reported that since his experience he had become moody, had "a faraway look," had dreams good and bad, sometimes about "castles in the sky," and had severe behavioral problems after he started school. When she inquired about his moodiness, he said: "I think I'll keep that my business for a while."[1]

The proper explanation for Jer's story is not obvious. One can imagine a four-year-old watching a TV talk show about NDEs and building a vivid sky-castle fantasy around such things. But what do we make of the chilling Mephistophelian offer? Are we to imagine that Jer beguiled his time with Christopher Marlowe's *Doctor Faustus* rather than *Sesame Street*? Could a mere fantasy turn a small child into "a grown-up person in a little body," one who, according to his mother, was unimpressed by pain and apparently without fears?[2]

This four-year-old's encounter with "the devil," while atypical in some ways, may be seen as representing a few of the many difficulties posed by painful near-death experiences. Not all is Good News of love and light; the innocent and the uninitiated may be faced with sinister figures and situations that sophisticates long ago relegated to the realm of dark legend. Reports of such experiences are still comparatively rare, but they issue a challenge even greater than that posed by the more usual peaceful or radiant NDEs.

I hold that in trying to meet this challenge, we may learn something important about human destiny and about the world. Thus, in this book I will try to answer certain basic questions: What are NDEs? How do painful NDEs relate to peaceful and radiant ones? What is the relationship of painful NDEs to the experiencer's cultural and individual life and to actual death? What does it mean to say that NDEs are (or are not) real? I will present various perspectives in the search for a hopeful interpretation of painful NDEs.

Provisional Definition of NDEs

Authorities differ as to the best definition of NDEs, leading to uncertainty as to whether certain borderline cases should be included or not. I suggest the following: an NDE is an event in which a person is threatened by imminent death, or perceives such a threat, or is clinically dead; rather abruptly enters an altered state of consciousness; and finally returns to (relatively) normal consciousness as she or he revives or the threat recedes. After giving illustrations of experiences in Part I, I give a fuller descriptive definition.

Principles and Terminology

Principles of the Study of NDEs

The fundamental building blocks of NDE studies are stories of experiences. If I am to interpret this complex material I must of course do more than tell stories; I must trace out patterns and suggest ways that the material might be fitted into reasonably coherent worldviews. Some scientific investigators distrust stories, calling them "anecdotes," implying that they cannot give us significant truth (as repeatable experiments can). Their ideal is to leave them behind. I avoid using the term "anecdote," because I hold that stories of experiences are crucial in the search to understand the universe. They hint at what is possible; they show up cultural conditioning, but also suggest, or even claim, the mind's transcendence of the body. It is important to be cautious about these claims. But to dismiss them may be to lose profound and liberating insights into the nature of the world.

This is not to say that all NDE stories are equally reliable. The motivations of NDErs and writers retelling their tales may be a desire to find truth, or perhaps to evangelize or entertain; thus embroidery or bias may enter. Most NDErs are clearly sincere, but a few are careless to the point of dishonesty. Most (not all) seem to have very sharp memories of the event.

Certain basic concerns of science, particularly psychical research (parapsychology), can help bring understanding. Those parts of NDEs in which the experiencer perceives herself to be out of her body, or encounters deceased persons, or enjoys vast knowledge, appear to be paranormal; that is, they violate some basic assumptions underlying the modern worldview, especially the belief that the mind cannot gain knowledge or act upon the world except through hearing, sight, and the body's other senses (and various instruments). Since the study of NDEs, therefore, overlaps with parapsychology, it will be helpful to summarize some of parapsychology's central principles for the study of spontaneous paranormal events.

In essence, we need to investigate the material with care, for if stories of experiences are seriously inaccurate or even false, our theories will obviously go astray. The nineteenth-century pioneers of the Society for Psychical Research (SPR) and the American Society for Psychical Research (ASPR) set guidelines for sifting fact from error and fraud in regard to paranormal events. Parapsychologist G. N. M. Tyrrell pointed out that the methods employed are partly those of the historian and partly those of the law-courts. As in the field of law, witnesses must wherever possible be cross-examined, and matters of fact must be verified (without the atmosphere of conflict found in many courtrooms). Details of persons, times, and places should be included; secondary witnesses must be asked for confirming (or discounting) accounts whenever possible.[3] The character of the witness (though often unknown) is also a matter of concern, as is the character of the investigator.[4] The possibility of chance or coincidence is often relevant. As in historiography, experiences that have been told to others, recorded, or acted upon soon after the event will usually carry more weight than accounts based on the old memories of a single witness or experiencer.

A central issue in psychical research's study of apparently paranormal events is whether or not they are veridical, or "truth-telling." If someone claims to have known telepathically of an event in a distant place, it is important that the investigator confirm both the account and the distant event. Veridicality of this sort is sometimes present in NDEs, and is important; but an NDE may contain significant truth even though confirming testimony may not be possible. In any case, however, care should be taken that the documentation of NDEs is as accurate and detailed as possible.

The pioneers of psychical research aimed to deal with their data scientifically; the methods they used were primarily those of the social sciences, recommended by parapsychologist Rhea White as the most fruitful for contemporary investigators. These methods include surveys, individual case studies, and experiential studies (i.e. studies by the experiencer).[5] In my opinion these are the basic methods for investigating NDEs as well. But this does not mean that informal collections or unsophisticated first-person narratives are not valuable. Such stories and collections of stories that are written with reasonable care, and whose writers show a genuine desire for knowledge and understanding, I will call "proto-scientific" studies; they present us with the basic data. It is, after all, with puzzling observations and experiences that science began. Stories clearly told to entertain, inspire, or evangelize may have value as well, but caution is required, as the writer may be tempted to improve the story or omit inconvenient parts.

Belief and Skepticism

The meanings of the terms "believers" and "skeptics" seem obvious, but they warrant a closer look. Persons who interpret the out-of-body and other-worldly elements of NDEs as delusory creations of the human body or mind in the face of death call themselves skeptics. They may receive some abuse in the popular media, but among educated persons, especially in the sciences, the term "skeptic" has prestige; it suggests that such persons are rational, scientific, hardheaded. To be a "believer," on the other hand, suggests credulity, romantic fantasy, and superstition.

Before accepting this use of "skeptic" and "believer," we would do well to look more closely at just what it is the self-styled skeptic is skeptical about. We should notice that neither the "believer" nor the "skeptic" listening to an NDE account can claim to *know* with certainty exactly what went on, or its true explanation; neither shared the experience, neither is omniscient. The skeptic's "I don't believe that story" is in fact equivalent to "I *believe* that that story is not true," or, further, "I *believe* that what really happened is nothing but X." So whether our skeptical believer is truly hardheaded depends not on the gratifying prestige associated with the word, but on the bases for her or his belief. These bases will involve (a) the strength or weakness of the evidence, as well as of any other evidence like it, and (b) the nature of the skeptic's worldview into which the evidence must be fitted. We have seen above some of the characteristics of strong and weak evidence. If the skeptic is aware of these characteristics, is knowledgeable about similar evidence, judges in an emotionally disciplined way that this particular narrative is not strong enough to be convincing, and leaves the matter open, he or she is indeed hardheaded. But in many instances self-styled skeptics pay little or no attention to the evidence; they dismiss it with a contemptuous word ("anecdote," "anomaly") simply because it is incompatible with their materialistic worldview, a worldview they have no wish to challenge.[6] (More of this later.) Here they are not skeptical at all. They *believe* their worldview; they *believe* the evidence is, therefore, not worth examining. This is not hardheadedness but credulity turned upside down. In this study I will reserve the term "skeptic" for the cautious and open thinker I have described, while those who engage in "dogmatic denial at long range,"[7] as William James put it, I will call *anti believers.*

Remembering and Forgetting

How accurate are NDE accounts? One of the most knowledgeable critics, Susan Blackmore, who considers herself a skeptic, takes her signals about NDEs and other (claimed) paranormal events from the fallibility of memory. She points out that accounts of experiences are reconstructions, and are affected by emotions:

And, since we are all human, the version we tell is likely to be just that little bit more interesting or poignant than it might have been. Also, when we tell stories to others together with a friend...social pressures act to encourage both people to tell the same story...friends and couples may talk about the bits they agree on and often forget to mention the bits they don't.[8]

Blackmore does not deny that NDEs happen, but she holds that seemingly paranormal elements in these and other extraordinary experiences can best be explained by the human tendency to make unconscious changes in the story (together with little-appreciated ways in which perception misleads us).

We may grant that accounts of spontaneous cases are reconstructions and thus may not always be accurate. It is also true that some persons who have psychic experiences do like them, enjoy telling them, and may improve them. But there is another side. Some experiencers are uncomfortable and even frightened by psychic experiences. They want an ordinary explanation, and, as they retell the event, begin to tone down its extraordinary features. Do most unconscious changes lie in the direction of embroidering the event or streamlining and demystifying it?

Light may be cast on the issue by one feature of an early study. The pioneers of the (English) Society for Psychical Research who carried out the 1894 Census of Hallucinations (involving 17,000 persons) found that there were many more recent cases of apparitions than old cases, suggesting a human tendency to forget such experiences. "It was decided that the number of visual hallucinations reported must be multiplied by four to allow for those obviously forgotten."[9] This apparent tendency to suppress memories of hallucinations and visions suggests that more people tone down their experiences than embroider them. Walter Franklin Prince, an experienced investigator with the American Society for Psychical Research, found this to be the case in his own work; he says that when he examined later versions of a case and then looked at the original account, generally he found that the original was more detailed and more evidential.[10] Other researchers, asking experiencers or witnesses to retell their stories at intervals of weeks or years, have found little difference.[11] In contrast, I know of at least one NDEr whose story is noticeably "improving" with later retellings.

Thus, memory is indeed imperfect. But it is not clear how this fact affects the message of many NDEs and other extraordinary experiences that suggest that human beings can transcend their ordinary bodily limitations. Many NDErs claim that the memory of their long-past experience remains as vivid as yesterday, whereas others assert that they have forgotten important parts.

Reports of NDEs and other psychic and spiritual experiences have stunning implications for the existence of a spiritual world, or a spiritual dimension to this world, but the knowledge we need to evaluate the stories with confidence is often is not available to us. In these cases, we must decide whether to believe that the stories are probably largely true, and reflect upon their implications for such a larger world; to believe they are largely false, and affirm a narrower world; or leave them up in the air. If we take the last position, we are unlikely to spend much energy reflecting on the spiritual world they imply. Both a wider-world position and a narrower-world position have their risks; one could be wrong, even disastrously wrong. In this book I have chosen to take the risks of a wider-world position, while considering the cases with as much honesty and self-discipline as I can.

PART I

WHAT ARE NEAR-DEATH EXPERIENCES?

One ⁀

MOODY'S WORK: "THE NDE"

W HAT ARE NEAR-DEATH EXPERIENCES? IN THIS CHAPTER
I begin to answer this question with a summary of the
characteristics of NDEs as given in Raymond Moody's
groundbreaking 1975 book, *Life After Life,* and its 1978 continuation,
Reflections on Life After Life.

Moody's Analysis

Moody's interest in the phenomena he terms "near-death experiences"
began when, as an undergraduate at the University of Virginia, he
encountered a professor of warm and kindly personality (George Ritchie)
who related an extraordinary experience he had had during a period when
he was clinically dead. Later, when as a professor of philosophy Moody
sympathetically presented material on survival of death, he found that in
nearly every class at least one student would come up afterwards to relate a
personal NDE. His files grew. Moody began to give presentations to the
general public, and by the time he wrote *Life After Life* he had collected
about 150 cases.

Moody placed his experiencers in three categories: those who were
resuscitated from apparent death; those who in the course of accidents or
illnesses came very close to physical death; and those who while dying (not
to revive) told their experience to others.[1] I will refer to cases in the final
category by the older term, "deathbed visions."

In his analysis, Moody identified fifteen typical elements. Early in the
experience the NDEr may undergo the following: "Hearing the News," that
is, hearing a doctor or bystander pronouncing that death has taken place.
"Feelings of peace and quiet": fear or physical pain give way to serenity,
warmth, and comfort. "The Noise": the person hears unusual sounds, such

16

as a buzzing, ringing, roaring, whistling, chiming. "The Dark Tunnel": the person seems to be moving rapidly through a dark space such as a cave, valley, or tunnel. "Out of the Body": the person finds herself separated from her body, often viewing it from above; the experiencer may be a point of consciousness, or a cloudy shape, or a body like the physical. She can see, hear, and think clearly, but other (physical) persons cannot perceive her.[2]

The middle parts of an NDE may include the following: "Meeting Others": at some point the person encounters spiritual beings who have apparently come to welcome her, or tell her that it is not her time. These may be deceased family members or friends; they may be unrecognized. "The Light": the experiencer sees a marvelous, brilliant light. Typically it begins dim and rapidly brightens, but despite its intensity it does not hurt her "eyes." It is felt to be a personal being, radiating enormous love and warmth. Christians tend to identify the being as Christ, while people of other or no religious persuasion may refer to the being as an angel. Communicating mind to mind, the being asks the person a question such as "What have you done with your life to show me?" The questioner is not seeking information or implying any condemnation but intends to draw the person out. "The Review": at this point the experiencer undergoes a review of her life in vivid, detailed images, presented in rapid succession or all at once. For example, a driver of a large semi-trailer truck lost control of his vehicle, which turned on its side and skidded toward a bridge. His life review, from age two onward, took place during this skid, a matter of a "split second."[3] (Because some reviews include scenes pertaining to the future, I will use F. Gordon Greene and Stanley Krippner's suggested term "Life Overview" instead of "Life Review.)[4]

Moving toward its end, the NDE may include the following: "The Border or Limit": a few NDErs approach some kind of border—a fence, a shoreline, a door—which they usually do not succeed in crossing. "Coming Back": reluctantly the experiencer decides to return, perhaps because of children to raise, or other unfinished business. Or she may simply awaken in her body.[5]

The aftermath of the experience may be characterized by the following: "Ineffability": NDErs find that words can't express the experience. "Telling Others": nonetheless, returned experiencers try to tell their stories to friends or medical caretakers, but find in nearly all cases that they are rebuffed, and so tend to fall silent. "Effects on Lives": many experiencers feel that their lives have been deepened; they live in the present more; they feel it is important to love others and to gain knowledge. Some gain telepathic abilities. "New Views of Death": experiencers are no longer afraid of death, for they are confident that it is only a transition to a better form of life. However, they are not seeking death, for they know they have tasks to perform before then. "Corroboration": in quite a few cases, there is corroboration of experiencers' accounts of what they saw while out of body, such as relatives in other rooms in the hospital.[6]

The rest of Moody's book presents some historical parallels to his findings and answers typical questions and comments that he has heard. The author concludes on a restrained note, acknowledging that he is quite aware that his book is not a scientific study and that it does not prove that there is life after death.[7]

Moody continued to gather NDE cases after the publication of *Life After Life*, and published a second informal book, *Reflections on Life After Life*, in 1978. Here he furthered his analysis of NDE phenomena with four new elements that he encountered in his further research. They are: "The Vision of Knowledge," a state in which the experiencer seems to know all realities, co-existing in timelessness.

> It seemed that all of a sudden...for a second I knew all the secrets of all ages....But after I chose to return, this knowledge escaped.... [8]

Some experiencers encounter this vision of knowledge in the form of a university or library in which any question they ask is immediately answered. "Cities of Light": numerous experiencers describe scenes suggesting Biblical ideas of heaven: a paradisal meadow, a gleaming city. "A Realm of Bewildered Spirits": several NDErs tell of seeing spirits who appear to be trapped in an unhappy state. In one case the experiencer (Ritchie) saw a dulled female spirit hovering above a living man as he walked down the street; she was trying to tell him what to do, but he was oblivious of her.[9] "Supernatural Rescues": some persons have reported NDEs of a somewhat different pattern—a life-threatening situation in which they receive guidance in the form of a voice (and in one case, a light also) telling them how to escape.[10]

4

Moody also presents in *Reflections* important further information about the life review, citing the case of a man who not only saw all the events of his life but also saw their consequences for others, and was profoundly ashamed and repentant. "And it wasn't like I was looking at a movie... because I could *feel* these things...."[11] Moody suggests that this self-judgment, if it comes to persons such as the Nazis who perpetrated great horrors, is as terrible a hell as can be imagined. (Following David Lorimer's analysis of "empathic resonance" as the central characteristic of mystical union and the deep life review,[12] I will refer to this element as the "empathic life overview." It will be discussed further in Chapter Four.)

Life After Life was immensely successful, partly as a result of earlier work by well-known psychologist and thanatologist Elisabeth Kübler-Ross. The book was followed a few years later by social-scientific studies that confirmed that Moody's descriptions were essentially accurate. The early 1980s were an expansive period. Some leading lights, who in their published studies made it clear that survival had not been scientifically proven, acknowledged informally that they personally were convinced of its reality, suggesting that the peaceful and radiant NDE provided a picture of what life after death was like.

However, as often happens, what at first seems to be a relatively clear and consistent matter turns out to be complex and untidy. Some NDE accounts appeared that did not fit the Moody scenario well. Furthermore, some experiences that *did* fit it—including tunnel, light, religious figures, and other elements—were unrelated to death. (These have sometimes been termed Not-Close-to-Death-Experiences, or NCDEs.) Some persons have experienced such states when they thought themselves to be facing immediate death, though in fact they were not in danger. One pilot about to crash had an experience of brightness and apparent precognition immediately *after* he regained partial control;[13] some Near-Death Experiencers (NDErs) have continued to see the light for a time after their return[14] or to have other forms of ongoing mystical consciousness.[15] And, crucially, some NDEs surfaced that were terrifying and painful. For these reasons, I shall generally avoid the phrase "the Near-Death Experience," which implies a single pattern, but keep the term in the plural.

Two ~

PRECURSORS IN MODERN TIMES

NEAR-DEATH EXPERIENCES HAVE BEEN DESCRIBED AND discussed for more than two thousand years. However, the first attempt at scientific documentation is in the late nineteenth-century studies of NDEs and NCDEs, including the extensive out-of-body explorations of several pioneers. Several major themes in this early material are in agreement with Moody's findings, others differing somewhat or not dealt with by Moody's two basic studies.

Serenity and Paradisal Beauty

The first attempt to deal with what are now called Near-Death Experiences social-scientifically is the essay "Notizen über den Tod durch Absturz" ("Remarks on Fatal Falls") by Swiss geologist Albert Heim. One of the two issues Heim emphasizes is the peaceful, serene state of mind of the person facing death. Heim's interest was sparked by his own experience of a fall of more than sixty-six feet during a mountain-climbing expedition. During the fall Heim was vividly aware of the contrast between the great shock and distress his watching companions were undergoing and his own state of peace, especially toward the end of the fall. His description of his serenity is inseparable from the beauty he perceived: "like magnificent music a divine calm swept through my soul. I became ever more surrounded by a splendid blue heaven with delicate roseate and violet cloudlets."[1]

Heim collected accounts of other persons who came close to death in accidents, especially alpine falls. Nearly ninety-five percent, he reports, experienced such a calm state. Interestingly, many of these experiencers heard beautiful music and, like Heim, saw themselves surrounded by a wonderful blue heaven with rosy cloudlets.[2] An example of serenity amid beautiful cloud scenes occurs in the cross-cultural study of deathbed visions by Karlis Osis and Erlendur Haraldsson (discussed later in this chapter). A dying woman found herself gazing at a beautiful sunset with clouds that suddenly looked like gates; she felt she was being called or drawn to the gates. The vision resulted in great serenity.[3]

More often than clouds, the images of heavenly beauty that appear in NDEs are of wonderful gardens and landscapes with intense, saturated colors. Such paradises made up sixteen percent of Osis and Haraldsson's cases.[4] Beautiful buildings also appear (though less frequently), reflecting the Christian Heavenly City.

Heim considers the feeling of deep peace and enjoyment of celestial beauty, in a situation that would normally arouse terror, to be the most remarkable factor of the experience. Although these feelings suggest that the mind transcends the limitations of the body, survives death, and enters heaven, Heim does not conclude that this near-death pattern points to survival. In fact he asserts that what accompanies actual death is painless extinction. He does not call dying persons' feelings of peace delusory, but seems to regard them as a fortunate human potential that can soften the grief of survivors.[5]

non local mind
Atwater

Music

These features of peace and beautiful music described above anticipate two of Moody's fifteen elements, "feelings of peace" and "noise" or music. Music deserves a category to itself, because some of its pre-1975 instances are much more significant than Moody's description suggests. The two-part study of D. Scott Rogo (himself a musician) uncovered some instances that are quite extensive, even evidential. Music is heard not only by NDErs but by those who actually die, by attendants at deathbeds, even persons at a distance from the death scene. The music may be instrumental, choral, or both.[6] In most death-related instances, the hearers connect the music with spirit welcomers.[7]

A notable characteristic is that the music begins faint, crescendos, continues at the louder pitch (rarely does it become really loud), and dies away.[8] As nearly all these cases are independent of one another, Rogo considers this little-known but frequent factor to indicate that the music is real and not a mere hallucination.

An example of music heard at a distance from the deathbed, by more than one person, is the following:

> My grandfather... William Stephens, lived in Bridgeport, in Dorsetshire. His eldest son ... lived on the Island of Guernsey. One night he [the son] and his wife were awakened by strains of exquisitely beautiful music .... Shortly afterward they heard that my grandfather had died that same night and, as they afterward found, at the same hour that they awoke from their sleep.[9]

Such collective cases, says Rogo, are evidential. But the collectiveness does not mean that the music is "objective" in the sense that it is heard through the ears, as the following case shows. Deafmute John Britton, close to death from rheumatic fever, after a partial recovery reported that at his crisis he "had been allowed to see into Heaven and to hear most beautiful music." At the time, his fingers swollen, he was unable to converse freely in the sign language to which he was limited. His sister and his sister's husband, Mr. S. Allen, who were in a room below, heard music coming from his room; Mr. Allen described the music as like an aeolian harp, while Mrs. Allen called it very sweet wordless vocal music. Running up to investigate, they found John looking upward and smiling blissfully. By mouthing words he managed to convey "Heaven" and "beautiful." (He also showed telepathic knowledge about the coming of two relatives, who soon appeared.) Mr. Allen supplied a plan of the house and grounds to show why the music could not have come from a normal source outside.[10] But what Britton heard could not in any case have been from an ordinary source, since he was deaf.[11]

Rogo holds that the death-related music cases are part of the evidence for survival of death. One reason for this conclusion is that much evidential spiritualistic communication, especially through the mediums Leonora Piper and Gladys Osborne Leonard (see Chapter Ten, pages 172–175), also tells of wonderful music accompanying the death process. These cases cannot be reductionistically explained by cultural expectations of heavenly angelic choirs, says Rogo, because of the frequent crescendo–diminuendo effect, not expected by the percipients, and because some of the cases are collective.[12] Rogo acknowledges, however, that the minds of the experiencers do affect what they perceive.

Other forms of psychic experience such as poltergeist phenomena and apparitions also tend to cluster around death, says Rogo, and he theorizes that the death experience causes an opening to the "psychic ether," so that "any properties of the 'other world' such as celestial music may become perceivable."[13] In the case of music heard by a distant person at the time of a loved one's death, this openness to the other world occurs at both places. (Rogo points out that hearing extraordinary music in many cases is linked not only to death but also to mystical experience[14] (compare the mystical elements, particularly associated with the light, in NDEs).

Welcomers

Moody's analysis of spiritual beings—relatives, friends, or unknowns—meeting NDErs is abundantly supported by earlier accounts, some of which are evidential. One important type of evidential case was first discussed by social activist Frances Power Cobbe in her pioneering 1882 essay "The Peak in Darien: The Riddle of Death." Cobbe relates that a dying woman in joyful surprise spoke of seeing her three deceased brothers, then saw a fourth thought to be alive in India. This "excited such awe and horror in the mind of one of the persons present, that she rushed from the room." In time the news came that the brother had in fact died before this date.[15]

Cobbe's term "Peak in Darien," taken from John Keats' sonnet "On First Looking Into Chapman's Homer," has come into common use for this kind of evidential case in which the dying or near-dying person sees a welcomer whom she or he did not know had died. But Cobbe was not referring to evidence when she used the term. For her, the Peak in Darien is the symbolic mountain "which we must all ascend in our turn—the apex of the two worlds, whence the soul may possibly descry the horizonless Pacific of eternity."[16] Cobbe was not primarily interested in the investigation of survival by scientific means; in fact, she asserts that belief in immortality must be based on "altogether different ground,"[17] namely, religious faith in Divine Love.[18]

Another evidential type of welcomer case tells of welcomers being seen not only by the dying but by one or more deathbed attendants. The most dramatic instance of this type is reported by Englishwoman Emma Pearson, who together with her cousin, her niece, and the housekeeper Eliza Quinton were caring for Miss Harriet Pearson, Emma Pearson's aunt, as she lay dying. On the night of December 22, 1864, Emma and her cousin were lying in an adjoining room but not sleeping when they saw a short figure dressed in an old-fashioned wig, shawl, and cap pass their open door. The cousin called out that it was Aunt Ann (Harriet Pearson's beloved deceased sister), and the two quickly got up. At the same time the niece, who was in another room, came out saying that she had seen Aunt Ann, but did not know where she had gone. Eliza Quinton was awakened and the house searched, but no one was found. A supporting account of these events was provided by Eliza Quinton, who added that Harriet Pearson told all of her attendants, before her death the following evening, that she had seen and recognized her sister, who had come for her. The accounts, reported to the Society for Psychical Research (SPR), were written in 1888. The case is significant in that no fewer than three attendants were reported as seeing the welcomer, with two persons giving accounts, but is weakened by the twenty-four-year gap before the accounts were written.[19]

There are a few other such cases of welcomers being seen by attendants. One in which the experiencer wrote her account very soon after the event is that of Mary Wilson, a professional nurse, who was caring for a dying Mrs. Rogers. Mrs. Rogers had spoken of her eagerness to see her second husband, Mr. Rogers, and her children again, which made the nurse rather nervous. About 2:30 A.M. Mrs. Wilson was sitting up with her patient (Mrs. Wilson's daughter also being present, asleep) when she happened to look toward the door to an adjoining room and saw a red-bearded, florid-faced man standing in the doorway looking at her and then at the unconscious Mrs. Rogers. Mrs. Wilson took him for a living person until his motionlessness made him seem uncanny and frightened her. She turned to awaken her daughter; when she looked back, the figure had disappeared as silently as he had come. An investigation of the house showed no way that he could have come in. The next morning Mrs. Wilson inquired of Mrs. Rogers' niece, who told her that the apparition did not at all look like Mr. Rogers, but exactly resembled Mrs. Rogers' first husband, Mr. Tisdale, thirty-five years deceased, who was quite unknown to Mrs. Wilson and others in the vicinity.[20] Cases such as these in which the welcomer is seen by an attendant are comparatively rare, but strongly suggest that some welcomers, at least, are more than mere images.

Veridical Perceptions

Moody's element of "Corroboration" is supported by deathbed visions in which the dying person told of being out-of-body and seeing events (on earth) that she or he could not have seen ordinarily. An example: In 1739 an

English Quaker, a Mrs. Birkbeck, lay near death in the house of some friends. After expressing a longing to see her children once again, she went into an apparent sleep, awakening after ten minutes to announce that she had been at home and had seen them. Shortly thereafter she died.

At the same time, the three children announced excitedly to their caretakers that their mother had been there; Esther, the youngest, said that her mother had called her to come. Esther did in fact die not long thereafter. Despite being old, this case is a strong one because the events were recorded soon after by the caretakers of both parties.[21] Among NDE cases, it is rare for an apparition of a dying person to be seen by living persons. It is even more unusual that a still-living person serves virtually as a welcomer to a person soon to die.

Light, Union, and Transformation

Of pre-1975 NDE cases centering upon light and leading to transformation, the most significant is the clinical death of George Ritchie, whose experience launched Moody's interest, and part of whose story was told in the magazine *Guideposts* in 1963. This article tells that Ritchie was ill with pneumonia in the hospital at Camp Barkeley, Texas, where he was undergoing basic training in December 1943. He had just received orders to go to Richmond, Virginia, where he was to attend medical school as part of the army's doctor-training program. But his illness grew worse, and on December 19 he collapsed while an X-ray was being taken.[22]

He awoke to find himself lying in a tiny room lit only by a nightlight. Desperately anxious that he would miss the train to Richmond, he sprang out of bed. He was disturbed to see a body lying in the bed he had just vacated; wanting to avoid probing this mystery, he ran out into the hall. An orderly coming down the hall ran right through him. Ritchie was perplexed by this and by the fact that he went through a closed door to the outside, then found himself speeding eastward through the night air. But he could not escape his fear regarding the strangeness of these events. He stopped in a town by a river and asked for information, but was again unseen. Realizing that he was no longer solid, he decided he had to return to the camp and try to rejoin his body.[23]

He returned to the base and, with some difficulty, found his body, which was covered by a sheet. Realizing that he was dead brought a moment of despair. But almost at once the room began to fill with a marvelous light.

"[A] thought was put deep within me. 'You are in the presence of the Son of God." The light was also an intense, joyous, compassionate love: "I wanted to lose myself forever in the wonder of It.... [I]t has affected every moment of my life since then." At the same time as the light, simultaneous scenes of every episode in his whole life appeared, each one asking him what he had done with his time on earth. Watching the scenes, he felt his life had been trivial and irrelevant.[24] After the experience he found himself back (in his body) in the small room, the light he had seen now fading.[25]

His medical chart included an entry stating that he had died on December 20, 1943. At the suggestion of an orderly, nine minutes later the attending physician had given him a shot of adrenaline in the heart, and he had revived. Ritchie concludes by saying that now, as a physician, he feels that each time he has been able to help some suffering person, that "He [Christ] was there beside me again."[26] In later writings Ritchie explains more fully the process of transformation initiated by his encounter with the Light that was Christ. We may note that this crucial part of his experience (though not some other parts, to be discussed below) essentially fits the evangelical Protestant beliefs of his family.

There is a handful of cases in which perception of light is potentially evidential: i.e., the light is seen by one or more attendants at a deathbed or NDE sickbed. Frances Cobbe gives one such case:

> At the last moment so bright a light seemed suddenly to shine from the face of the dying man, that the clergyman and another friend who were attending him actually turned simultaneously to the window to seek for the cause.[27]

The nurse attending C.G. Jung during his NDE in 1944 also saw his body glowing with light (as she had with earlier dying patients).[28] It is not reported whether the light the nurse saw had the same blue color as that which Jung saw in his vision.

As with the music and the welcomers, the perception of light by attendants suggests that these elements are not reducible to the private imagery of the dying or nearly dying persons.

For a few Out-of-Body Experiencers (OBErs), notably mathematician J. H. M. Whiteman (1906–) and "Yram" (Marcel Louis Forhan, 1884–1917), the central focus of OBE exploration, shaping their entire lives, is movement toward mystical union with the Divine, sometimes perceived as light. Whiteman had a pivotal mystical experience at age twenty-four: during a walk (while embodied) he chanced to look up at the sun, and perceived the divine "Source," which he continued to see when he looked away. A transformation of personality already underway was reinforced, with a commitment to Total Obedience to the divine. He felt tremendous power flooding through him giving feelings of spiritual intoxication and of great love for others, especially helpless creatures such as children and animals.[29]

Whiteman's spiritual discipline has involved techniques of Recollection, that is, overcoming tendencies to diffuseness and self-indulgence, and learning rather to focus closely on specific objects and to maintain a continual openness to the divine.[30] Another prerequisite for the mystical life, according to Whiteman, is overcoming of Fixation (tension, wishful thinking, attachments to physical things), and achieving Obedience to the divine[31] in order to unify the self in unity with the divine. In accordance with Christian Neoplatonic theory, Whiteman holds that at the core of the self is the Scintilla or divine spark, the apex of the soul. (More about this concept in Chapter Fifteen.) From the Scintilla flows a stream of consciousness, the Hidden Child. When the Fixations that hide the Child are removed, one becomes an expression of Universal Humanity; one is enabled to love one's neighbor as oneself because one can *be* the neighbor via empathy.[32] (Here is a potential overlap with the Empathic Life Overview.) When separated from the body, such a person may perceive the divine light. The following experience, dated November 1932, closely parallels the Moody-type NDE:

>...During the night I became fully awake to...Obedience, now stronger....Almost immediately, the separated form was drawn upwards, quickly...Above and in front, yet in me, of me, and around, was the Glory of the Archetypal Light...streaming forth in Love and Understanding, and forming all other lives out of its substance....[T]he contemplating soul...was...poised through the adoration of love and total submission....[33]

Whiteman has had such visions of the divine light on more than twenty-five occasions; some of these times he also experienced wonderful warmth.[34]

As with Whiteman, Yram's central concern was the quest, involving years of disciplined striving, to rise to higher levels of consciousness until one is united with the Infinite. For Yram, a Theosophist, this mystical union is impersonal. He recommends that the seeker choose a single selfless Ideal and concentrate upon it, relax, and learn to suspend all thought.[35] (This principle finds support in Kenneth Ring's observation in *The Omega Project* that NDErs tend to have a greater capacity than average for dissociation and absorption. See Chapter Three.) One must give up egotism and gain the capacity for altruistic love.[36] Yram summarizes the process of rising to cosmic consciousness as moving from a plane of oppressive density and opacity (the physical) to a thinner plane of gray mist, and thence into a "luminous clarity" like the sun at midday.[37] In the highest state of perfect multiplicity in unity, "we can feel, think...with an ease which is nothing short of prodigious." There is a melting down in divine love for the world, an awareness of an ocean of perfect harmony, a willingness for any sacrifice that this love may require.[38]

Powers of the Mind

Several researchers present evidence that the mind exhibits expanded powers in NDEs or OBEs. Frequently experiencers claim to be able to read the thoughts of those they encounter, whether incarnates or discarnates. Here is a typical account by a Mrs. H. W. Jeffrey: "You hear what people are saying to each other, and what their brains are thinking at the same time. It is amusing, for they do not say what they think."[39]

Another extraordinary power sometimes claimed is greatly enhanced capacity for thought (mentioned above by Yram). Albert Heim laid stress on this capacity. During the ten seconds or so of his alpine fall, his mind produced a torrent of clear and coherent thoughts, which he remembered in detail. Among these thoughts: He assessed his chances of surviving as depending upon whether or not there was a border of snow at the base caused by melting on the cliff face. He planned if he survived to take a drop from his flask of spirits of vinegar; he decided his alpenstock might still be useful to him, and grasped it firmly; he tried to take off his glasses to guard against fragments of glass damaging his eyes. He planned to call out to his brother and friends that he was all right whether he was well or not. He considered the effect of the news of his death on his family, mentally consoling them; he realized that he would not be able to give a university lecture scheduled for five days hence. This flood of thought included "my whole past life ... in many images," united in "elevated and harmonious thoughts...."[40]

The issue of speeded and clear thoughts was investigated in a survey by Russell Noyes, Jr. and Roy Kletti, the rediscoverers of Heim's study, who gathered accounts of NDEs chiefly due to accidents. Some of Noyes' work is reported in Chapter Five.

Another of the mental powers that has been reported in NDEs and OBEs is the creative ability to shape the experience. Pioneer OBE explorer Sylvan Muldoon asserts that parts of OBE visions are purely "thought-forms" (a Theosophical term): namely, figures that seem to exist on their own, but in fact are only dynamic images created by the thinker.[41] Reflecting on his own many OBEs, Muldoon makes the significant point that his rather solitary manner of life in the flesh (he was an invalid much of the time) was reflected in his out-of-body travels; he seldom encountered others.[42] He noticed that in this state his thought instantaneously produced the thing thought of, sometimes consciously, sometimes on a level beyond consciousness. For example, while out-of-body he often found himself wearing the same clothes as his physical body. These products of the mind are usually experienced as just as firm and three-dimensional as ordinary physical things.[43]

It is Muldoon's conviction that in certain of these cases "*projections are controlled by a seeming superior intelligence which appears to be innate in or directed to the subject.*"[44] Muldoon's language suggests that this intelligence is a transcendent self of greater power than the ego. Though operating unconsciously from the viewpoint of the limited out-of-body mind, from its own perspective this intelligence might better be described as superconscious.

Whiteman is another who observes that the OBEr influences, via "fantasy," what he or she sees, but for Whiteman this influence operates largely in unhealthy states, marked by Fixation (tension, attachment). He does not consider that the whole scene is created by fantasy, but features of the scene may be altered or created by fantasy's unconscious workings.[45]

Jung made a similar comment about a temple with a lamp-encircled door he saw in his NDE; it resembled some he had seen in his earlier travels.[46]

The "Astral Body" and the Silver Cord

Yram's writing is part of an early twentieth-century flowering of work supported by English editor and publisher Ralph Shirley, focussing on "astral projection" or out-of-body experiences (OBEs). The writings are largely of two kinds: books of personal experience, with "how-to" instructions, and casebooks that include NDEs. Both include occult theory typical of Spiritualist and Theosophical circles. Using a modified form of the typology of parapsychologist Charles T. Tart, I will class the how-to books as psychic or spiritual technologies; the casebooks I categorize either as popular (or religious) in intent, or as proto-scientific studies.[47]

An important characteristic of the early OBE studies is the fact that the explorers tended to experience their consciousness not as a point but as lodged in the "astral body." This second body was understood to be ordinarily merged with the physical, emerging from it during OBEs. Able to glide through the air, move through walls, and visit other planes, normally it was linked to the physical body by a line called the "silver cord."

The pioneer who gave most extensive attention to this matter, Sylvan Muldoon, observed that his connecting cord, a white or grayish cable, varied in thickness depending on the distance of the astral body from the physical. He saw the cord pulsate with each heartbeat as it conveyed energy from the astral to the physical body, keeping the physical alive. Thus the definition of death for Muldoon and other early writers is simple: the severing of the cord.[48]

Other accounts describe the connecting line variously as a ribbon of light, as a smoky string,[49] or "like an arm."[50] The prominence of the topic makes it likely that suggestion was a factor in its appearance for some, but unquestionably there were persons who knew nothing either of out-of-body experiences or cords, but found at their first experience that the cord was there.[51]

That unconscious wishes affect the astral body appears from the 1889 case of Dr. Wiltse, who succumbed to typhoid fever. He found his consciousness retreating upward from the feet to the head: "I...peeped out between the sutures of the skull....I appeared to myself something like a jelly-fish..." He expected to appear as a naked spiritual body standing beside his bed, and that is in fact what soon happened. With some embarrassment he scuttled past the various people in the sickroom to the door, but found at the door that he was now clothed. No one could see or hear him. He could distinguish the sex of each person but could not identify individuals, even family members—a curious fact that will become significant later when NDEs in persons born blind are considered. He passed out through the door, looking at the rainwashed street, which seemed vividly clear. A short man in physical life, he noticed that he was now taller, which also pleased him. He was able to see his back as well as his front, which he thought was due to using his bodily eyes; he perceived a fine cord from his spiritual body to the physical one.[52] In this case, then, although some expectations were fulfilled, one element was a surprise, prompting a rather far-fetched explanation.

The next case shows that not only unconscious but also deliberate mental activity can affect the out-of-body form. Explorer Robert Monroe, during one of his many OBEs, found that while standing in the center of his room, he was able to stretch out his arm and touch the wall some eight feet away; when he relaxed, the arm resumed normal size. He speculates that one can take any shape one intends, including animal shape, and that when left alone the second body will revert to normal human shape.[53]

The issue of whether the out-of-body consciousness necessarily perceives itself in a second body at all was one of the issues investigated in three OBE studies. In a 1960 study, English parapsychologist Robert Crookall, in response to a questionnaire he sent to OBErs, reported that about twice as many reported seeing or feeling a silver cord as did not,[54] suggesting that about two-thirds had an apparitional body. However, parapsychologist Hornell Hart in his 1954 North American survey of 155 cases (ninety-nine of which contained veridical elements) found that of those who reported seeing their bodies from outside positions, only a little more than one-fourth found themselves in an apparitional body.[55]

English investigator Celia Green in her 1968 survey found a situation similar to Hart's. She categorized her cases as either "parasomatic," meaning that the experiencer was "associated with a seemingly spatial entity,"[56] which in some cases closely resembled the physical body, and in other cases was a mere shape,[57] or "asomatic," meaning that the person was "temporarily unaware of being associated with any body or spatial entity at all." While some cases were ambiguous, the large majority—eighty percent—were asomatic.[58] This finding contrasts both with Crookall's findings and with the general impression given by the (unsystematic) early reports.[59]

Furthermore, among Green's respondents only a minute percentage—about three and a half percent—reported perceiving something like a cord when asked if they felt any kind of connection to their physical body.[60] My impression from reading many contemporary NDE cases is that, here too, cords are very rarely reported. This discrepancy may be partly because NDE researchers seldom ask. However, because most out-of-body NDErs found themselves floating above their bodies, a cord would have been conspicuous. According to traditional theory, those who "came back" should still have had an intact cord. The concept of morphic resonance, to be discussed in Chapter Seven, may cast light on this perplexing situation.

There are a few exceptions to the general pattern that those who perceive themselves in second bodies find that they resemble their physical bodies. In a few cases, middle-aged OBErs have looked in mirrors and found their second bodies to be youthful.[61] Even more remarkable is the situation of Whiteman, who has kept careful records of his thousands of OBEs. He finds that his spiritual body differs from one "separation" to another depending on his spiritual condition; when in his highest spiritual state his second body, which he calls the Mystical Form, is transfigured. This Mystical Form is female. He perceives her to be his true self: unutterably beautiful, unimaginably real and fulfilling. She sings in a soprano voice; she is conscious of female internal organs, and has experienced childbirth. At one point Whiteman suggests that this state is what is meant by the Resurrection.[62]

Cultural Influence

That not only individual but also cultural creativity is at work in NDEs was firmly established by Karlis Osis and Erlendur Haraldsson's cross-cultural study of deathbed visions in the United States and India in the mid-1970s. Although the second study was first published in 1977 after Moody's book appeared and therefore strictly speaking comes under Chapter Three, I present it here because the research was done before 1975. The inspiration for the study was not Moody's work but William Barrett's 1926 study *Death-Bed Visions*.

In the U.S. portion of the study, twenty-five hundred physicians and twenty-five hundred nurses were sent questionnaires, to which 1,004 replied, with about half reporting cases of deathbed visions. Telephone interviews followed. Of the total number of cases, the authors selected 216 for close study. The inquiries in India were carried out face to face, so nearly all the medical personnel they asked did fill in the questionnaires. Of the 704 usable responses, 255 cases were selected for close study.[63]

The authors categorized the visions from both studies into otherworldly phenomena and this-worldly phenomena, finding that eighty-three percent of U.S. cases and seventy-nine percent of Indian cases were afterlife-related. These afterlife figures were chiefly deceased relatives and religious figures. At this point, however, a difference emerged: the majority of U.S. patients saw deceased relatives, whereas the majority of Indian patients saw religious figures.[64] Religious figures seen in India were (among Christians) principally Jesus, the Virgin Mary, and angels; Hindus saw devas (celestial beings), Krishna, Shiva, demons, Yama (the God of death), or one of his messengers, the Yamdoots.[65] The majority of the apparitional figures presented their purpose as coming to take the dying person to the next world, even in cases in which death was not expected by anyone.[66] The responses of the patients also differed between the two countries. In only one U.S. case did the patient refuse to go; all the other U.S. patients responded with serenity or elation. However, in the Indian cases, a full thirty-four percent responded with depression or fear, and tried to resist the summons. This was especially true when the apparition was a Yamdoot.[67] Among Indian Christians, fourteen percent resisted.[68] Another difference between the two countries had to do with the gender of the deceased human welcomers. In the United States, sixty-one percent of those apparitions were women, whereas in India female apparitions made up only twenty-three percent.

Still another cultural difference surfaced in regard to patients who were sent back: in India, but not in the U.S., the reason sometimes given was mistaken identity.[69] To Western ears this explanation sounds bizarre, but not necessarily to Indians, who popularly think of the afterlife as run largely by lesser spirits.[70]

Although descriptions of paradisal scenes did not differ overall between the two countries, in one Indian case the experiencer rode to paradise and back on a cow[71]—not surprising given that for Hindus the cow is a symbol of divine nurturance.

It is clear that the creative influence of culture on NDEs is potentially very great: what is the experiencer projecting, what is she actually encountering? Furthermore, the discovery that certain elements are projections does not mean they cannot be part of a real afterlife, tending to differ for different cultures. But obviously not all persons in a culture have similar experiences; can the mind of the NDEr transcend her culture as it seems to do her body? Later chapters will present cases that suggest it can.

Three

STUDIES CONFIRMING
AND EXPLORING "THE NDE"

T HE HUGE SUCCESS OF *LIFE AFTER LIFE* ATTRACTED THE attention of a few persons with training in the sciences and humanities. This was exactly what Moody had hoped for. He had candidly acknowledged that his book did not qualify as a scientific study, and that he hoped to see it stimulate studies that were.[1] As we have seen, he put interested physicians, scientists, and scholars in touch with one another. The result was the founding in 1981 of what was to become the International Association for Near-Death Studies (IANDS), at first headquartered at the University of Connecticut under the leadership of Kenneth Ring. IANDS produces the quarterly *Journal for Near-Death Studies* (at first called *Anabiosis*). Most of the scholarly and scientific work presented below is by persons affiliated with IANDS.

Definitions and Basic Descriptions of NDEs

One of the first questions NDE researchers have sought to answer is: How exactly is an NDE to be defined or described? On the basis of his "Connecticut Study" of 102 persons, in which he found Moody's account largely confirmed, Ring judged that the heart of the NDE is what he terms the "core experience": an unusually powerful or deep NDE, typically including tremendous peace, a sense of being separate from the body, of moving through a dark space toward a beautiful light, a panoramic life review, and a decision or command to return to the body.[2] Ring proposed a "weighted core experience index" to judge the depth of the experience; that is, the various elements were assigned scores depending on their presence and intensity, so that an individual's total score could range from zero to twenty-nine.[3] This core experience "tend[ed] to unfold in a characteristic way. In general, the earlier stages of the experience [were] more common."[4]

Ring breaks this pattern down into five stages, the later ones appearing with systematically decreasing frequency in his study. The stages are: peace and quiet (reported by sixty percent of those who had the core experience), separation from the body (reported by thirty-seven percent), entering the darkness (twenty-three percent), seeing the light (sixteen percent), and entering the light (ten percent).[5] Ring considers these five the main stages. The appearance of deceased relatives or friends, the encounter with a numinous presence, and the life review are factors related to the decision to return, which may break off the experience at any of the five stages.[6]

It should be noted that Ring does not insist on his five-stage model. In an early (co-authored) study of NDEs brought on by suicide attempts, he presents the alternative that those NDEs chiefly featuring the OBE, or the (peaceful) dark void, or the tunnel and light and other world, may follow essentially separate, distinctive patterns.[7]

English experiencer/researcher Margot Grey, taking Ring's Core Experience model as her guide, found that the same five-stage pattern and the same aftereffects generally prevailed among her own cases.[8] There was one important contrast to Ring's Connecticut Study: Grey found a number of painful cases (about one eighth of her total), manifesting the same five stages but with opposite values[9] (see Chapter Four).

Cardiologist Michael Sabom, whose 1982 study of 116 survivors of near-death crises also found Moody's picture confirmed, defined NDEs as any experience undergone during an episode of unconsciousness associated with physical near-death.[10] (Cases such as Heim's alpine fall would thus be excluded.) Sabom classed NDEs in two categories: the autoscopic (referring to the viewing of oneself in the OBE), and the transcendental or otherworldly. He acknowledged that some NDEs had both elements. Sabom concentrated on the autoscopic, since these experiences offered a potential for confirming some perceptions as veridical.[11]

Seeking descriptive criteria for NDEs, Bruce Greyson in a 1983 essay offered his NDE Scale based on results of a questionnaire. It presented and grouped the many NDE elements into four clusters: Cognitive Component, Affective Component, Paranormal Component, and Transcendental Component. The Affective and Transcendental Component items were the most frequently reported. Greyson's approach avoids the implication of Ring's Core Experience model that there is a traceable scenario, "the NDE."[12]

Effects of Prior Religious Convictions on NDEs

The prior convictions of NDErs, religious or nonreligious, that may influence their experiences involve both cultural and individual dimensions. We have already noted that the OBE explorers of the early twentieth century tended to experience the spiritual world as they expected to find it, though there were some surprises. To what extent did expectations fostered by prior beliefs cause some recent NDErs to see angels, or Jesus, or paradise? A remarkable 1982 NDE suggests that expectations have an enormous effect. Artist Mellen-Thomas Benedict, a seeker who had no commitment to any particular religion, perceived the light as taking various forms one after the other: "Jesus, Buddha, Krishna, mandalas, archetypal images, and signs." In response to the questions Benedict asked the light, he learned that "your beliefs shape the kind of feedback you are getting..." and that visionary experience in connection with the light gives one an opportunity to evaluate those beliefs.[13]

A study that supports such a position on a cultural level is Carol Zaleski's *Otherworld Journeys*, which compares early medieval and contemporary NDEs. Zaleski shows that in medieval cases certain themes appear that are in keeping with beliefs of the times, such as emphasis on punishment for sin. She points out that in modern NDEs, however, little is said about punishment; human wrongdoing is seen as a learning process; hell is gone.[14] She is wrong that hell has disappeared, as we shall see in Chapter Four. But her point is helpful in evaluating the influence of a culture's religious ideas on present-day NDEs, which will be further discussed in Part II.

On an individual level, however, expectations arising from religious beliefs clearly are not the whole story. Christians do see Jesus, but so do certain atheists and agnostics who had not only rejected religious beliefs but were certain there was no survival of death. One finds no shortage of articulate NDErs who give accounts of their astonishment when, instead of the extinction they were fully expecting, they found themselves fully conscious and gazing at light, spirit welcomers, or religious figures; a profound change of heart usually followed.

This informal finding is supported by statistical analysis. Ring's Connecticut Study determined that among his three main religious categories—Catholic, Protestants, and no affiliation—there was not a higher representation of core experiencers in the first two. Ring found the same in regard to degree of religiousness, so far as he was able to measure it; those who professed prior belief in God, in life after death, heaven, etc., were no more likely to have core experiences than those who did not profess such beliefs.[15] (Ring did give his opinion that religiousness affected the *interpretation* of the experiences.[16])

Sabom's 1982 findings were no different. Out of the seventy-eight persons he interviewed, of the thirty-three who had NDEs, eighty-two percent had religious (mostly Christian) affiliations; thirty-six percent went to church often. Of the forty-five patients who did not have NDEs, eighty-nine percent had religious (mostly Christian) affiliations, and fifty-one percent attended church often. He comments that there were no significant differences between the two groups, but in fact his figures show a decidedly greater percentage of frequent church attendees among the *non*experiencers.[17] It is true that religious beliefs and feelings are hard to reduce to statistics, but it seems clear that on an individual level, expectation based on beliefs and degree of religious fervor cannot be presented as the sole explanation for the contents of NDEs.

Other potential contributions of NDErs to their experiences will be discussed below.

NDEs Among Children

The issue of NDEs among children also received early attention, since it seems evident that if the experiences of children, especially the very young, do not differ crucially from those of adults, culture is not all-determining. In a 1983 essay subtitled "Shades of the Prison House Reopening" (from which came the Faustian experience of Jer cited on page 8), Nancy Evans Bush reported on seventeen child experiences, all volunteered cases. Fifteen were narrated by the now-adult NDErs anywhere between eleven and sixty-five years after the event, and two were told by the mothers of the still-young experiencers, each four years old at the time of near-death. One of the accounts came from the adult experiencer's reliving under hypnosis the NDE (consisting chiefly of light and peace) she had at thirteen months of age; the rest remembered them consciously, some claiming great vividness.[18]

Most of the same basic motifs of adult experiencers were represented— OBE, tunnel, peace, welcomers, the light, great wisdom or knowledge, return either by the NDEr's own decision or by being sent back. The light appeared much more frequently than in Ring's and Sabom's first studies, but there were no life reviews, no sense of judgment. A single apparently evidential feature appears in one case, namely a meeting with a deceased sister whom the NDEr had not known about. Evans Bush points out that the supposedly immature experiencers tended to feel enormous wisdom and confidence during their NDEs. A characteristic comment: "I wasn't nine years old, I was eternal." At the same time, Evans Bush acknowledges that some of the adults telling their childhood experiences probably included some adult overlay in their interpretations.[19]

Glen Gabbard and Stuart Twemlow's 1984 book on OBEs, *With the Eyes of the Mind,* has a section on NDEs, including three more volunteered childhood cases—one narrated by the now-adult experiencer and two recent cases told by the children's mothers. In the latter group, one child was two and a half and the other four. All three included the light, in two cases associated with a loving figure. In both these cases the child, like an adult, was given the choice of remaining or returning. In contrast to the relatively simple recent cases, the older case was detailed, with many Moody-type features present. The authors judge that the fact that childhood cases are consistent with adult cases "makes the cultural programming argument untenable."[20]

Pediatrician Melvin Morse reported on a hospital study comparing twenty-six children who had had life-threatening events with a control group consisting of 121 seriously ill children. All the controls had life-threatening conditions but were not near death (though some were mistakenly perceived to be dying). Both groups were treated with the same kinds of medications and underwent the same stresses of the critical-care unit. In response to open-ended questions, twenty-two of the group of twenty-six described NDEs that were consistent with previous collections of adult NDEs. During their periods of apparent unconsciousness they perceived themselves as awake and alert. Some examples: "I was climbing a staircase to heaven. It was long and dark and I could see a light. I came back because my brother had already died and it wouldn't be fair [to my parents]" and "I thought I was floating out of my body. And I could see a light." Religious figures and spiritual guides also appeared in the narratives. In contrast to Evans Bush's findings, some of Morse's child NDErs did see images from their past.[21]

Morse also studied one hundred adults who had NDEs as children, giving them a battery of psychological tests with particular reference to aftereffects. Comparing them with one hundred controls who did not have NDEs, but some of whom had had mystical experiences of light in childhood, Morse found similar psychological profiles among those, whether NDErs or not, who had had mystical experiences of light. They showed low death anxiety, sound health habits, time spent in meditation and in service. Adults who had nearly died in childhood but did not have NDEs had increased death anxiety and evidence of post-traumatic stress. Other controls scored in the normal range of these tests. Morse adds that it is unknown whether these differences were predisposing factors or the consequences of the experience.[22]

Morse holds that the NDE accounts of children are particularly important because of children's lack of cultural sophistication. Certainly toddlers lack cultural sophistication, but since children as young as four and five do absorb religious ideas, his blanket assertion that children are not culturally polluted is questionable.

There are cases of NDEs even in infants. An example is that of Mark Botts, who in his twenties made public an NDE he had had at nine months. At age five he astonished his parents by describing his brush with death from respiratory failure, during which he went out-of-body, saw his (living) grandmother searching anxiously for his mother in a distant part of the hospital, entered a tunnel, and crawled laboriously upward to a distant light. A wind blew him into a beautiful golden world where he went "gliding with God on the golden roads." Reluctantly he accepted the divine instructions that he was to return. His mother Carol Botts supported his account, testifying that he had indeed succumbed at that time for forty-five minutes as a result of tracheal failure. He had never been told of it, and could not have known normally of the grandmother's search for her in the hospital.[23] She also testified that as he grew up he showed several of the typical aftereffects of NDEs.

Reports such as this are likely to arouse resistance in some quarters. The modern worldview dictates that an infant of nine months cannot recall detailed experiences, particularly conversations, because of the lack of ability to conceptualize. Mark would, of course, have acquired concepts by the time he told the story, and it is possible that it altered somewhat in the family's memory. But since what originally impressed his parents was its evidentiality, this NDE should not be dismissed, particularly since it is far from being the only infancy case.

P. M. H. Atwater's study of NDEs among children supports several of the points made above, but also shows patterns, especially in aftereffects, not described by other researchers. The vast majority of her 277 child experiencers did not have deep NDEs with hellish or heavenly or unitive dimensions, but only had the initial elements, such as out-of-body awareness or a sense of deep peace. The range of ages included an important cluster of experiencers between birth and fifteen months. A substantial number of them also recalled other events, some evidential, in connection with and even before their births. An example is Carol Gray of Atlanta, a severely abused child who recalled and recounted to her parents her father's assault against her mother when she was pregnant with Carol, knocking the mother against a table, resulting in her going into labor early. At three days, Carol had her second NDE; she remembered looking through the window of the incubator at the infant body, reporting on the body's abnormal coloration and on the state of her internal organs. An NDE she had at age two included an encounter with a grandfather who showed her [an image of] his pocket watch, chain and knife, which he said he had bequeathed to her, his namesake, in his will. The grandfather had died before her birth, and her family did not believe her account until twenty years later, when her mother found the will with the bequest as Carol had said.[24] (More on the matter of memories from infancy in Chapter Nine.)

Atwater found that patterns of aftereffects among children also tend to differ from those among adult experiencers. A child may feel she is guilty and responsible for the disappearance of the loving otherworldly beings,[25] as well as for the actions of parents who respond to her experience with abuse or abandonment.[26] Furthermore, whereas adult experiencers tend to go into healing and other nurturant work, child experiencers tend to excel in math and physics. But children and adults do have areas in common: development of psychic gifts, electrical sensitivity, sensitivity to light and pharmaceutical drugs, mystical tendencies, and the like.[27]

Even more disturbing, perhaps, than parental abuse as a result of NDEs is the appearance of hellish NDEs among very small children. This topic will be discussed in the following chapter.

Light, Darkness, Union

NDEs with strong light, union, and other-world themes tend to be those with the most extensive aftereffects. These themes will be emphasized also because of their importance to the theories of the meaning of painful NDEs presented in Part IV.

In many cases the experience of union occurs in connection with the light. Kenneth Ring, who explores the aftereffects of deep NDEs in his 1984 *Heading Toward Omega,* cites in detail fourteen cases that emphasize light, profound union, and knowledge. For example, experiencer Joe Geraci says:

> ...I just immediately went into this beautiful bright light.... It's something which becomes you and you become it. I could say, 'I was peace, I was love.' I was the brightness, it was part of me....You're all-knowing—and everything is a part of you....It was eternity. It's like I was always there and I will always be there, and that my existence on earth was just a brief instant.[28]

Another example is Tom Sawyer (his real name), who was in tears as he tried to convey the intense love that he felt in the light, a union that included the "magnificent experience...[in which] you realize that you are suddenly in communications [sic] with absolute, total knowledge....You can think of a question... and *immediately* know the answer to it."[29] Businessman Joseph Dippong first experienced the light as though multiplied into many colors through a diamond, and the core of the light as an immensely loving being. "Everything ... was familiar—as if I had always known of its existence... I felt I knew this being extremely well...for although it was neither my mother nor my father, it was both." Then a magnificent white light shone through this scene. "I became aware that it was part of all living things and that at the same time all living things were part of it."[30] "Darryl" [Dannion Brinkley] experienced the light both as a being and as splendor infusing a city, particularly a cathedral that was "built of knowledge," all knowledge, in which he could participate at will.[31]

For a few NDErs, union occurred in an experience of darkness and/or void. An example is Mellen-Thomas Benedict, mentioned above as having experienced the light as a succession of figures from different religions. For him this light was not ultimate. At its invitation he passed through it and rocketed through the universe. He entered a second light, "a profound stillness...beyond Infinity. I was in the Void." Trying to describe this stunning experience, he speaks of the Void as being full of energy, of

Godhead periodically creating and decreating universes, of Absolute Consciousness, of the Zero-Point studied by science.[32]

Another void case was the 1983 NDE of John Wren-Lewis, involving an immediate movement of consciousness into a "shining darkness" (a term he derived from his studies in mysticism) in which he existed in blissful union with all things. He felt his personal self to be somehow "budding out" from the shining darkness, without ceasing to be the darkness. He had no imagery of any sort, either divine figures or welcoming loved ones, nor did he feel the need for any.[33]

One NDEr who used the term "void" to describe an experience not completely formless is P. M. H. Atwater. At one point in her second NDE she found herself to be a sparkle in "the Void," a "nonplace" in which she existed in perfect bliss and love, not as a body but as a sparkle of pure consciousness along with trillions of other sparkles. She would have been happy to remain there forever, but this state issued in an empathic life review with a good deal of pain[34] (see Chapter Four). Others speak of being suspended in a peaceful darkness without mentioning any sense of ultimacy, totality, or divine source.

Painful void experiences will be discussed in Chapter Four.

Aftereffects

The aftereffects sketched in Moody have been generally confirmed and greatly expanded. Life changes are sometimes are so extensive that the experiencer sees them as dwarfing the experience itself.

1. Value Changes

One of the effects most immediately obvious is a change in personal style and values: persons who were insecure and retiring tend to become assertive; driven personalities are likely to mellow.[35] Ring cites examples: "Stella," very shy and submissive in accordance with her rigid fundamentalist upbringing, became a businesswoman and civic leader;[36] a high-achieving psychologist lost her interest in impressing others with her insights and simply wanted to communicate in gentle ways.[37] Prior values of prestige and material gain tend to give way to a childlike awe at everyday things, love for and connectedness with all living things, and a desire to serve. There is greater orientation toward living in the moment. Boundaries fade; chronological time can lose its meaning.[38] P. M. H. Atwater observes that many experiencers love in a nonattached way.[39] Not only do nearly all NDErs affirm life after death, with greatly reduced fear of death, but many affirm or show interest in reincarnation.[40] Along with a greater appreciation for nature comes increased sensitivity to ecological and planetary issues.[41] As mentioned in connection with child experiencers, in many cases these changes in personal style and values are opposed by NDErs' families and circles of associates, creating pain and stress; divorces are common.

Returned NDErs are not necessarily involved in institutional religion, Ring reports, but tend to be more spiritual in a universalistic way. Some of them declare that they feel at home in any religious service, whereas others feel uncomfortable in virtually all. However, Michael Sabom, in his 1998 study of NDErs in the "Bible Belt" city of Atlanta, found that church attendance tended to increase after the experience, and that very few changed their religious affiliation.[42] Likewise, Arvin Gibson's Utah studies show a tendency for his predominantly Mormon experiencers to have continued or increased commitment to their churches.[43] In either case, however, most experiencers tell of feelings of closeness to God.[44]

Ring cautions in *Heading Toward Omega* that his NDErs were self-chosen, that the changes in question were derived largely from self-reports, and that his findings are thus preliminary.[45] And in fact there is a less attractive side. For example, P. M. H. Atwater during her research made a point of interviewing family members as well as NDErs about aftereffects, and found that some experiencers use the new expanded consciousness to avoid communication and family responsibilities.[46] This unfortunate state could be a stage or a lifelong trap. Atwater emphasizes that the NDE is the first step of a *potential* spiritual journey, and that it includes alienation and loneliness as well as joy and feelings of union.

Some NDErs do not show aftereffects to any great extent. Australian experiencer and researcher Cherie Sutherland gives a helpful analysis of the varying rates and levels of spiritual development following NDEs. Among the two hundred NDErs she studied (fifty intensively), Sutherland observed that the way the experience was integrated into the experiencers' lives depended on whether they were already familiar with spiritual and psychic phenomena, and the kind of reception their stories received. She found four "trajectory types": Accelerated, Steady, Arrested, and Blocked. (Those in the "blocked" category denied that their experience had any real significance.)[47] She also contacted her NDErs eighteen months after the interviews to ask about the effect of her investigation upon their lives. She found that in many cases her interaction with them had been a liberating one, sometimes even enabling them to move on from an arrested state to fuller integration.[48]

2. Psychophysical Changes

The changes in values sketched above tend to be accompanied by significant bodily changes. In *The Omega Project*, Ring reports on his and his colleagues' investigation into the relationship between NDEs and Unidentified Flying Object Experiences (UFOEs), and the aftereffects of each. Comparing NDErs and UFOErs with each other and with controls who were interested but had not had the experiences, they found that both types of experiencers resembled one another in being much more likely than the controls to report several psychophysical changes.

One change reported was increased physical sensitivities to certain things such as bright light and loud sounds (as well as certain foods, alcohol, and pharmaceutical drugs).[49] Another change has been called electrical sensitivity: some experiencers found that their presence caused regular or periodic interference with electrical and electronic equipment. Street lights might blink out as the person walked under them, then come back on; computers would malfunction more frequently than normally. Some experiencers simply could not wear watches. These happenings may mean that distinctive patterns of electromagnetic activity have developed in these persons.[50]

Still another development was the appearance of "the kundalini syndrome," including symptoms such as sensations of energy currents ("rushes") in the body, localized feelings of extreme heat (especially in the hands), migraine headaches, shaking, and the like.[51] Some of these manifestations appeared to be directly correlated with healing gifts; e.g., Barbara Harris tells of a migraine headache stopping and energy flowing from her head into her hands at the moment when she began to lay on hands.[52] Yvonne Kason points out that kundalini manifestations appear, not only after NDEs and UFOEs, but in connection with other forms of spiritual awakenings: mystical experiences, psychic experiences, intense concentration, practice of martial arts, meditation and other spiritual disciplines, spontaneous visions of religious figures, and the like.[53]

3. Psychic Development and Veridicality

Several investigators have found that NDErs "manifest a variety of psychic abilities...[as] an inherent part of their transformation."[54] In *Heading Toward Omega*, Ring tells of a definite increase in reported out-of-body experiences, psychokinesis, healing, precognition, and clairvoyance among his respondents.[55] Telepathy is very common. An example from the past cited by one scholar is the Lakota Sioux shaman Black Elk, who reported that his initiatory NDE resulted in a telepathic awareness of the presence of buffalo or enemies.[56] Some NDErs report visions of deceased persons; these apparitions may appear to give spiritual support and counsel,[57] or make the experiencer aware of a crisis, such as danger to a loved one or the death of the person who appears.[58] Ring's findings were confirmed in studies by Bruce Greyson and Richard Kohr.[59]

In his first study, Michael Sabom paid particular attention to the issue of the verifiability of accounts of out-of-body experiences during NDEs, or, to use his term, the autoscopic NDE. He found six cases in which returned NDErs gave highly detailed accounts of equipment and events they had seen during resuscitations, matters of which they could not have had normal knowledge. He was able to corroborate their accounts by consulting medical records and interviewing medical personnel and family members. Asking controls to imagine such resuscitations, he found major errors in all the accounts of the controls but only a few minor errors in those of the NDErs. In one particularly notable case, a heart patient while out-of-body noticed, among other things, a very obscure detail: two needles on the defibrillator, one fixed and one moving. Sabom's study, while it does not provide proof that there is a mind separable from the body, does make it evident that all the imagery in NDEs is not reducible to fantasy.[60]

An example of verified clairvoyant perception during the OBE phase of the NDE is the celebrated case of "Maria's tennis shoe." The investigator, Kimberly Clark (later Kimberly Clark Sharp), was a medical school instructor and clinical care social worker in 1977 when a patient named Maria told her of having floated near the ceiling of the room while doctors and nurses were attempting to revive her from cardiac arrest. Then, said Maria, she "thought herself" outside the building over the emergency room driveway, eventually thinking herself over to an object on a third floor ledge on the north end of the building. It was a tennis shoe, with a worn place by the little toe; she asked Clark to locate it. Circling the building, Clark could not see it from outside, but eventually, after entering many rooms in the north wing and peering downward through the windows, she located the unlikely shoe, which was exactly as Maria had described it.[61] Another medical professional, nurse Kathy Milne, reports a very similar story of an out-of-body patient spotting an abandoned shoe, this one on a hospital roof.[62]

Particularly important to the issues of evidence and transcendence is Kenneth Ring and Sharon Cooper's *Near-Death and Out-of-Body Experiences in the Blind: A Study of Apparent Eyeless Vision*. The authors investigated thirty-one cases of blind persons who had NDEs, OBEs, or both, of whom fourteen were persons blind from birth. Of the twenty-one who had had NDEs, fifteen declared positively that they could see during the experience, four were not sure ("I've never seen—I can't tell") and one denied being able to see.[63]

Ring's question—"Do blind people have NDEs, and are they the same as those of sighted persons?"—was thus answered with a very definite "Yes." An example: Vicki Umipeg, blinded at birth by excess oxygen in an airlock incubator, had two NDEs, one in 1963 at age twelve and another in 1973 at age twenty-two. Before her NDEs she had had no visual images at all, even in dreams, but she definitely had clear visual-type imagery in both NDEs. During the second one she experienced herself as rising out of her body, seeing her body and the medical attendants, going through the roof, seeing the streets and city lights around the hospital. She found it "disorienting," "very foreign," "overwhelming"; she was not sure whether she saw color. Then she went through a tunnel into another world, where the "feel" of vision was different: not disorienting but "clear," "direct," "the way it's supposed to be." In her life overview she saw the transformed figures of two retarded children whom she had befriended in her childhood in a school for the blind. They had both died in childhood, but appeared to her now as adults, "bright and beautiful."[64]

It should be noted that other blind NDErs who had never seen color were confident that they did see it during their experiences.[65]

Besides the crucial element of the perception of visual-type imagery by the majority of the blind persons, three of the cases turned out to be veridical; in two of them the blind NDErs' reports of what they saw were confirmed in interviews with their associates. One saw a stack of dirty dishes she thought had been washed; the other saw the design on a tie a friend had bought for him.[66]

Of all psychic reports, precognition is often thought to create the most serious problems, because it violates our assumptions that the effect can never come before the cause. There is no space here to deal with this vexed philosophical issue, but because precognition can be particularly evidential, it deserves a close look. As with OBE perceptions, some instances take place in the NDE itself, in the form of what Ring terms the "personal flashforward," a continuation of the life overview that shows what can be expected to happen in the experiencer's life if he or she returns. Some of these flashforwards are quite detailed, and are reported to have been fulfilled years later in detail. In some cases memory of the flashforward later enables the experiencer to act to escape a catastrophe (such as taking a different traffic route to avoid a multiple-vehicle accident).[67]

Another kind of apparent precognition, which Ring calls prophetic visions, deals with the future of the planet. Certain NDErs report an impending scenario of natural and human disasters—earthquakes, volcanic eruptions, economic breakdown, nuclear disasters. Often the experiences do not include dates, but Ring's NDErs tended to interpret them as due around the late 1980s. There was wide agreement that the time of troubles would usher in an age of peace and brotherhood around the turn of the millennium. Some NDErs felt that the events were inevitable, while others felt they might be averted if humanity changed its ways.

In many cases the details were lost after return to normal consciousness, but would re-emerge shortly before being fulfilled in a disaster such as the eruption of Mt. St. Helens in 1980. But despite their potential as evidence, most of these predictions were not on file before the fulfilling event, and thus depend on the experiencer's word. Some that were on file have been right; others wrong. Ring considers a variety of interpretations of these prophetic visions, tending to favor the view that the apocalyptic scenario is one future that may or may not be realized.[68]

Atwater in an account of aftereffects of her own experiences describes what she calls "future memory": occasional altered states of consciousness in which she suddenly becomes largely oblivious of her circumstances while she perceives, in vast detail, images of a short or long series of events that are to be expected in her own life. She records that these foretastes usually are fulfilled precisely, with only a few minor images not accurate.[69] In keeping with the sense of timelessness during many NDEs, Atwater holds that these visions are not foretastes of a possible or even probable future, but a living-out, in anticipation, of events that are eternally real.[70]

4. Changes in Mental Functioning

Some NDErs report that their minds seem to work more efficiently than before their brushes with death; they can absorb information, comprehend basic issues, and solve problems more readily than before. These accounts, while hard to prove,[71] are in keeping with the speed and clarity of thought felt during NDEs (pages 17, 28) and to widespread reports that many NDErs feel a great desire for knowledge, going back to college, devouring books in areas that previously had little interest to them.

Besides the paranormal gifts mentioned above, experiencers have other extraordinary signs of expanded consciousness, which tend to echo elements of NDEs. Some examples: Yvonne Kason has had episodes of "luminosity," when the world seems brightly illuminated; other living things such as plants may seem to glow with inner radiance.[72] Other NDErs describe bright inner light continuing or recurring after their NDEs, in some cases accompanied by energy rushes; occasionally onlookers may see light radiating from the experiencer's face.[73] The feeling of expanded consciousness may take a literal form; almost continuously since John Wren-Lewis' NDE, he has felt as though the back of his head is gone and he is open to the infinity he experienced then.[74]

Not all expressions of expanded consciousness are benign. Some experiencers report alarming episodes in which they are aware of evil forces or presences; they may feel that the presence puts negative thoughts into their minds or attempts to take them over. Prayer and affirmations of the greater power of goodness or of God seem to be helpful in dealing with these menacing experiences.[75]

The Creative Influence of NDErs on their Experiences

Why do some persons who have had brushes with death report NDEs while others remember nothing? Are there characteristics NDErs have that the non-experiencing (or non-remembering) survivors lack, characteristics that perhaps influence the experience? Experiencer Barbara Harris (later Barbara Harris Whitfield) found from informal surveys that a high percentage of those who had had NDEs or other spiritual awakenings had, like herself, been abused as children.[76] This finding was confirmed, for both NDErs and UFOErs, in Ring's Omega Project. (This does not, of course, mean that *all* NDErs or spiritually awakened persons have had traumatic childhoods.) Ring is clear that he does *not* interpret the high percentage of childhood trauma to mean that UFOEs and NDEs are a form of mental disturbance, but that the early stress enables the child to learn to dissociate from his physical situation and become deeply absorbed in other things. A capacity for deep absorption means that later the person would consciously perceive and remember alternate realities during the near-death and abduction incidents, realities others might forget.[77] P. M. H. Atwater, however, does not find a significant rate of childhood trauma among her interviewees.

The fact that features in certain OBE accounts have been confirmed as veridical does not mean that NDErs do not contribute in some ways to what they see while out-of-body. While the out-of-body scenes reported by some of the blind in Ring and Cooper's study appear to be what a sighted person would see from that vantage point, in other instances there are odd omissions or additions. In two cases, for example, the consciousness of the NDEr while hovering overhead perceived her body not in the visual detail one would expect but as a kind of outline.[78] (Recall Dr. Wiltse's NDE in which he could perceive the sex of his attendants but not their identity [page 31]). In one case the (blind) NDEr reported seeing her body *through* the upper bunk above it.[79] Ring and Cooper compare these puzzling perceptions to the ability of certain persons whose ordinary vision is poor but who see extraordinary details in NDEs, even 360-degree perception down to every hair and follicle on an attendant's head. Ring and Cooper call it "transcendental awareness."[80]

In one rare case, the NDEr's creative contribution to her experience is conscious and deliberate. P. M. H. Atwater, while out-of-body during her second NDE, noticed that shimmering pastel figures were appearing around her corresponding to her thoughts and questions. She decided that, since she was apparently creating these, she would experiment with creating something specific; she made a house (it was so real she could open the doors), a tree, and cities with active, moving inhabitants. At the end of the experiment she wished them away and they vanished.[81]

It is clear that there are several ways in which NDErs as individuals contribute to what they experience. These findings are relevant to the larger question already touched on: to what extent do cultural assumptions and attitudes contribute to the body of NDEs in a given culture, a given period? More about this in Part Two.

Laboratory Investigation

Investigating NDEs under laboratory conditions might yield much knowledge and insight, but it is obvious that to bring oneself or another to the brink of death in this search is morally unacceptable. Looking for insight into the element of deceased welcomers (but operating more out of a sense of play than of scientific investigation), Raymond Moody did something like a laboratory study: he created a setting in which one may cultivate an altered state of consciousness in order to seek an encounter with a deceased friend or family member. He derived the idea from the ancient Greek institution of the psychomanteum (oracle of the dead), in which the seeker would spend a prolonged period of time underground, then would engage in scrying (gazing into a glass) in an attempt to establish contact with a deceased person. Moody set up his own psychomanteum, the "Theatre of the Mind," in which a person interested in communicating with a deceased loved one spent a day exploring her intentions in a special environment conducive to altered states of consciousness. Then she relaxed on a low chair in a dimly lit, black-velvet-draped booth with a mirror above eye level, arranged so that only darkness appeared within it.[82]

Moody had expected perhaps ten percent of his participants to have any success, but to his surprise slightly over half of the more than three hundred early participants had encounters—via sight, hearing, or touch—during their first attempt. (A number of those who failed the first time succeeded the second or third times.)[83] There were some surprises. About one-fourth saw not the deceased relative they hoped for but a different one. Sometimes the apparition came out of the mirror into the booth (ten percent of the visions); sometimes the participant, like Lewis Carroll's Alice, seemed to himself to enter the mirror (ten percent).[84] In several instances the apparition appeared, not during the time of scrying, but a few hours later in another place.[85] Although Moody had selected very grounded, reasonable people to participate, all who saw visions were emphatic that they had had a real encounter with the deceased.[86]

As with many NDEs, mirror visions in the psychomanteum tended to have a life-changing effect on the participant. While in most cases these changes were not on the level of a total transformation in outlook as with some NDErs, there was a great deal of healing of grief and, just as important, a new perspective on an unhappy relationship, making forgiveness and renewal possible. Moody himself had tried and failed to have a vision of his cherished maternal grandmother, but after he left the psychomanteum he had an unsought but transforming vision of his once-difficult paternal grandmother.[87]

These early results suggest that at least one element of the NDE can often be induced in a non-life-threatening setting. Moody discourages any hope that evidential information can be gained in this manner,[88] but there seems no reason why psychomanteum experiencers may not occasionally see Peak-in-Darien visions or gain telepathic knowledge.

Shared Deathbed Visions

Moody has also called attention to a phenomenon that is being reported in large numbers: persons at a deathbed who appear to share the experience of the dying person, whether light, out-of-body travel, welcomers, or other elements. As we saw in Chapter Two, such cases have been reported since the nineteenth century, but some of the more recent accounts describe a fuller sharing. Here is an example from Alister Hardy's Religious Experience Research Unit, Manchester College, Oxford:

> I felt he (my dying husband) might be aware of my presence although unconscious, and took his hand and closed my eyes. Immediately my surroundings disappeared from my conscious mind and I was aware of two distinct things at once: reverence for the presence of God on my left hand side, powerful in its effect, and then I was swiftly being propelled into a vast current into space that is almost indescribable. It resembled the ecstasy of a beautiful symphony....Love was its force....I was closer in love and spirit with [my husband] than ever in our actual lives. The energy of this vast stream of upward and outward spatial experience finally frightened me as I was aware that if I held on to my husband's hand too long I should be unable to return. I dropped it and opened my eyes to look for God. But he wasn't there....When I closed my eyes my son was in

the act of putting the telephone back on the receiver: when
I opened them his hand had just placed it there.[89]

Rarely, two or more persons share an NDE and return to tell the same
tale (or overlapping tales). A dramatic instance took place in 1989, when
forty members of a Colorado forest firefighting unit working to contain a
blaze below them on a steep slope were trapped in an inferno when the
wind changed. As the crew boss, "Jake," tells the story to researcher Arvin
Gibson in 1996, he and the others crawled upwards, struggling to breathe.
Finally, they collapsed one by one. Poised above his body, Jake saw his
companions likewise above their bodies, and spoke to one of them. Jake
went on to see the light and, in it, his deceased great-grandfather. Given the
choice to stay or go back, Jake returned to a body still surrounded by the
flames. He was unable to feel the heat, which melted metal tools, or hear the
roar. Protected, he walked up to the relative safety of the hilltop, where the
noise was again audible. All the crew members escaped uninjured. Awed by
their experience, the firefighters knelt in prayer. Comparing notes then and
later, the ethnically and religiously diverse group found that each had had
some sort of NDE, had met with deceased family members, and had been
given the choice to remain or return. Gibson does not give confirming
accounts from any of the others; I unfortunately learned of the case too late
to investigate it further for this book.

Placing NDEs in Context

In *The Final Choice,* "an exercise in the healing imagination" but "based on
matters of fact,"philosopher Michael Grosso reflects on NDEs in the
context of the larger issues of meaning. He points up the bankruptcy of the
materialism of Western culture, its inability to deal with death. The
challenge is to form a new myth of death that will affirm physical life yet see
death as the precursor to transformation. To this end he takes up the
concept of Mind at Large that has been offered by Aldous Huxley and others
to account for certain unexplained facts of biology, evolution, and altered
states of consciousness. He seeks to draw a picture of Mind at Large,
showing its potential relationship to our survival, both here and hereafter.[92]
By Mind at Large Grosso means a transpersonal consciousness, but not
necessarily the omnipotent deity of traditional Western religion.

Speaking from a Jungian perspective, Grosso proposes that NDEs activate what he calls the Archetype of Death and Enlightenment (ADE), a constellation of motifs that "portray...a passage toward greater consciousness of the Self." It is a form of "a death–rebirth process" that manifests in other ways as well.[92] The ensuing transformation of life Grosso refers to by the New Testament term *metanoia*, transformation of mindset (usually translated as repentance),[93] thus emphasizing its nature as a religious conversion. Similarly, Grosso compares the many apparitions of the Blessed Virgin in our century with the Being of Light and suggests that the apparitional Virgins are instances of the Being projected into public space. Both are manifestations of Mind at Large, working to bring about transformation of consciousness in the individual and in society.[94]

In a similar vein, Kenneth Ring gives expression to a theme voiced by John White, John T. Robinson, and other core experiencers in his speculations that we are "heading toward Omega." He suggests that the large number of NDErs postulated in the U.S. alone by the Gallup poll, and many other persons who have undergone mystical transformations, *"[m]ay... collectively represent an evolutionary thrust toward higher consciousness for humanity at large...."*[95] Kundalini, with its powerful effects on the body activating latent spiritual potentials, is the proposed mechanism of this evolutionary development.[96] Ring further suggests that this development may come about through the "morphic resonance" processes hypothesized by Rupert Sheldrake"[97] (see Chapter Seven). Borrowing from the concepts of Teilhard de Chardin, Ring calls this projected evolutionary stage "Omega." (He does not assert it to be the final stage, as Teilhard's expression "Omega Point" implies.)[98]

Ring points out that the proliferation of NDEs and UFOEs appears on a planet in imminent danger from nuclear and/or ecological death. Drawing upon Grosso's thought pointing to the initiatory nature both of NDEs and UFOEs, and comparing them with the shamanic journey, Ring theorizes that at this time the Near-Death and UFO symbols of world catastrophe and a Golden Age represent a kind of collective dream issuing from Mind at Large, giving warning and hope.[99] In later writings Ring, again citing Grosso, makes it clear that the mirage of a Golden Age has beckoned to humanity for centuries, and that he no longer expects it to dawn in our times.[100]

In *Whole in One* David Lorimer explores the moral implications of the life review, linking it to the sense of the underlying unity of all things in mystical NDEs. In the deepest stratum of the life review, one perceives in one's past actions an "empathic resonance" with others[101] (thus my term "empathic life overview"). Lorimer brings to bear on the deep life review various examples of telepathy, focussing especially on the phenomena of psychometry, in which (as in Eugene Osty's studies in the 1920s) a psychically sensitive person holds an object that has been in contact with another, and is able to perceive feelings, actions, and physical circumstances from that person's life. Since in some of Osty's cases the person holding the object perceived events that took place *after* it left the earlier personality, it appears that the process does not necessarily involve traces left on the object, but means that the object may be a link to a vast collective memory that records all things—a super-individual mind.[102] One may see a resemblance to Grosso's Mind at Large.

Lorimer suggests that the deep life review and the phenomena of psychometry and hauntings are particular manifestations of a cosmic empathic resonance, such as is experienced by many mystics and by NDErs who enter the Light. There is a profound sense of the overcoming of the walls of ego, with a melting into universal love, and an awareness of all knowledge.[103]

Summary

The overall effect of these works and others is to confirm the picture of "the NDE" as an event in which the experiencer transcends the limitations of the physical world, probably experiencing, perhaps in symbolic form, a foretaste of goodness to be encountered after death. Although researchers emphasize that we do not have proof, impressive findings such as the transformation of life in many experiencers, and Moody-type NDEs in small children and persons born blind, have the effect of reinforcing Moody's analysis.

However, the picture has never been as monolithic as the phrase "the NDE" implies, even among the researchers cited in this chapter; and besides, from the beginning other voices have expressed opposing viewpoints. Thus, Chapters Four and Five will present two major kinds of challenges to this general picture.

Four

A CHALLENGE TO THE PEACEFUL NDE: PAINFUL NDES

NDES THAT ARE PAINFUL OR HAVE PAINFUL ELEMENTS ARE not new; they have been reported occasionally for decades. Moody mentions them in his second book; they loom large in a 1978 book by Fundamentalist Christian author Maurice Rawlings. But these unpleasant phenomena were neglected in scholarly NDE studies until the middle 1980s. An issue on painful NDEs appeared in the *Journal of Near-Death Studies* in 1994 and another in 1996. It was no longer possible to think of "the NDE" as consisting only of good news of inevitable peace and joy.

Painful NDEs and NCDEs take several forms, with experiencers sometimes being mere witnesses, sometimes being participants. In presenting examples of this material, I begin with the mildest form, and go on to more openly hellish experiences.

Needy Beings

1. Loss of Identity

Some painful NDEs and NCDEs seem to reflect a situation of pathetic, unhappy spirit-beings* apparently attached to the earth-life of their past. Moody gives such a case in *Reflections:* An NDEr (Vi Horton)[1], as she was rising up over the hospital but before she entered the tunnel, saw a dull gray area inhabited by many depressed, confused spirits. They were humanoid in form but not distinct; they shuffled about aimlessly, seemingly unaware of the NDEr and the spiritual world. "They seemed to be caught in between somewhere." However, Horton adds, "They may have some contact with the physical world. Something is tying them down, because they all seemed to

---

*Terms such as "ostensible" or "apparent" qualifying "spirit" or "spirit-beings" are implied throughout this chapter.

be bent over and looking downward....It looks like they have lost any knowledge of who they are...no identity...."[2]

A case from my own files, the 1977 NDE of Los Angeles resident Tom Mace, supports the element of loss of identity of the spirits in Vi Horton's account; in this rare case, the loss of identity is the NDEr's. Mace tells that while sleeping outdoors he rolled over onto a snake and was bitten in the face. Uncertain what to do, he lay back down, but then found he had left his body. He felt he was standing up, but in fact was not embodied, and could not see his physical body. He was very frightened at first and moved about uncontrollably. He rose upward over the night landscape, coming down but going into the ground by mistake (the total darkness disturbed him greatly), then coming up again. Calming himself somewhat, Mace taught himself how to move about. He found he could not feel pain, touch, or pleasure, and could not remember who he was: "A brain can store memories—a soul can't." It was also very lonely. Yet he knew somehow that he had been in this state previously, before incarnating. He wanted embodiment badly enough that he made various attempts to take over the bodies of animals, but found that he did not know how to operate in them, and they soon died. After a time the fear diminished and he became more peaceful. Various other adventures that he chose not to share took place. Eventually he realized that his body was still alive, and returned to it.[3][*]

2. Addiction and Attachment

In some instances, the unhappy, needy spirits appear to be addicted to things and persons in the physical world where they hope for gratification; like Mace, they try to possess, or rather attach themselves to, living beings. George Ritchie, part of whose influential NDE was sketched in Chapter Two (page 25), writes further in *My Life After Dying* of being given a tour of both painful and inspiring afterdeath realms by the figure of Christ. With his guide, Ritchie flew to a large city jammed with people, some (the living) surrounded by auras and others without auras and invisible to the living. The Christ guided him into a tavern where ethereal beings tried repeatedly

---

[*]I have been told by a person who knows Mace well that his word is not always reliable. However, this person has reason to believe that his NDE story, which he has scarcely shared with anyone, is a memory of a real experience.

to pick up glasses of liquor, but to their great anguish their hands would go right through the glass.

From time to time a living person would become totally intoxicated and his aura would split and peel away from head to feet. Quickly an aura-less being sprang in and disappeared, apparently attaching himself to the living person. Ritchie concluded that the disembodied were the surviving spirits of alcoholics, still addicted and seeking vicarious gratification by attaching themselves to living drinkers.[4]

J. H. M. Whiteman also recounts experiences of attachment by unhealthy beings, both when he was in his "separated" body and in the physical. Here is an example from an OBE of March 6, 1954:

> ...I came face to face with an entity of "evil" tendency....[Whiteman kept him at bay for about fifteen seconds.] A momentary...paralysis because of that influence was followed almost at once by the remarkable effect as of a man-spirit entering into me and violently throwing my arms about in order to escape. I seemed to be hurled from that state back to the physical world, returning with a sharp jolt at the solar plexus.[5]

Whiteman did not feel saved by his return to the physical, as he perceived that he had brought the spirit back with him.[6] In fact, he holds that this sort of multiple consciousness caused by spirit attachment is a regular feature of most embodied life.

The entity's efforts to escape suggest that his act of attachment was not really intentional. It also appears that unintended attachment, in this case by the OBEr, happened to Robert Monroe, who tells of three occasions in which he tried to return to his body and found to his alarm that he was apparently in someone else's body, in each case a sick or injured person, and that attendants did not realize it.[7] In a case dated November 11, 1960, after an out-of-body excursion Monroe thought he had returned to his body. But when he awoke he found himself in a strange place where he was told by two women, apparently relatives of the person whose body he had entered, that he had been ill for a long time. Their dress seemed "normal" (apparently meaning contemporary) to him, but when he asked them what year it was he was told it was 1924 "according to the Greek method (?) of calculating time." This oddity suggests some form of retrocognition, but Monroe does not try to interpret it. In two of the three instances Monroe had difficulty getting out of the strange body and, in the "1924" incident with the two women, even after leaving the body he could still feel them trying to hold him back.[8] In another context Monroe mentions that totally unrestrained spirits of the deceased, the "Wild Ones," can and do "piggyback" on (attach themselves to) the living, adding that they can get nasty at times.[9]

It can be seen that Whiteman, Monroe, and Ritchie accept the idea that unhealthy spirits of the deceased can and do enter or attach themselves to living persons, creating problems for them. Traditional ideas of "possession" usually assume that the possessor is a demon. But these experiencers do not use the language of demonology, nor do they suggest that the spirit-attachment concept explains all mental and emotional problems. For contemporary readers, spirit-attachment is hard to take seriously. I suggest, however, that the reader try to keep an open mind on the matter, which is discussed further in Part Three.

Moody gives a case of an earthbound spirit-being who evidently was quite aware of her identity and focussed on particular embodied persons, trying strenuously and unsuccessfully to communicate with them, though not seeking possession:

> One [spirit] seemed to be a woman who was trying so hard to reach through to children and to an older woman in the house. I wondered if...this was the mother of the children...[T]hey continued to play and pay no attention, and the older person seemed to be going about in the kitchen...with no awareness that this person was around...[10]

Ritchie also observed such cases in the crowded city: a young man walking down a sidewalk was accompanied by a spirit being, "trying to tell him how to dress and what to do with his life, but he could neither see nor hear her. I gathered she had been his mother...."[11] It is significant that the idea of earthbound spirits was incompatible with Ritchie's evangelical Christian views at that time.

3. Haunting

The aftermath of the atypical NDE of Sylvan Muldoon suggests another traditional belief about surviving spirits, namely, that they may haunt a place. One day in 1916, the teenaged Muldoon and two other boys set out to survey the damage from a recent violent rainstorm. A power line had snapped and was hanging dangerously. Naively Muldoon took hold of the wire to move it aside. It was live, and he lost consciousness; his friends later told him that he screamed, leaped about ten feet into the street, still holding the wire, his face bulging. He fell, tried twice to rise, and failed. Presently he became conscious, standing outside his fallen body, his spiritual form in the same position as the physical body: slightly curled in the middle, arms rigid as though grasping the wire his body still held, one leg drawn up. Both bodies trembled. His second body could feel the full force of the electricity, which was agonizing in the extreme. His friends, unaware of the second self, were paralyzed with horror. Suddenly they came to their senses and began to call out. Neighbors gathered, one wearing rubber boots; when he picked up Muldoon's physical body, pulling it away from the wire, the second self "seemed to bound right back into it again and was conscious there...." All were astonished that he was still alive after ten minutes in contact with the wire.[12] In this case the out-of-body pain clearly stems from a this-worldly source.

This case is unusual in that Muldoon's pain did not cease when he found himself out of the body. Furthermore, almost every night after that for an unspecified period of time, the unlucky Muldoon re-enacted it exactly in his dreams. Sometimes he would become conscious that it was a dream and would then find himself out of the body, standing beside the bed. On one of these occasions he found himself out of the body and standing at the site where the near-electrocution had happened.[13] Muldoon himself compares this event to the situation of haunting ghosts who re-enact repeatedly the circumstances of a violent death.[14]

P. M. H. Atwater describes a pattern she calls "Haunting" in which disturbing or painful elements from an NDE recur in the NDEr's later life. This pattern seems to be akin to what Muldoon underwent; it differs in that, in all the examples Atwater cites, the NDE elements intrude into waking consciousness. None of them involve later OBEs at the site of the NDE.[15]

In the above cases, NDErs, OBErs, or the spirit-beings they observed were in an unhealthy condition, attached to places, living persons, addictive substances, or physical life in general. Most were trapped and unhappy, but unwilling and/or unable to free themselves. The entities in the following cases are in a similar plight, but do not appear in earth-scenes among the living.

In the following cases, dejected, troubled spirits similar to those seen by Vi Horton appear (page 56), but actually *in* the tunnel, and evidently not in a position to look at earth. If the tunnel represents transition between worlds, the difference may be important. The NDEr in the first case is one Elaine Winner, who recounts:

> It's a dusky, dark, dreary area, and you realize that the area is filled with a lot of lost souls, or beings, that could go the same way I'm going [to the Light] if they would just look up. The feeling I got was that they were all looking downward, and they were kind of shuffling, and there was a kind of moaning. There were hundreds of them, looking very dejected. The amount of confusion I felt coming off of it was tremendous. When I went through this, I felt there was a lot of pain, a lot of confusion, a lot of fear, all meshed into one. It was a very heavy feeling. They weren't turning toward the Light. In fact, they didn't even know the Light existed.[16]

Another NDEr, Reinee Pasarow, described perceiving "individuals who were lost" in the tunnel, which for her was "like a watery, gray area."[17]

It is not said in any of these cases that the spirits had lost their identity, but the general impression is that there is little individuality, with feelings of distress and confusion in the whole group.

A case similar to Elaine Winner's, in which lost beings appear to be in the tunnel region, is that of the medium Elizabeth d'Espérance (Elizabeth Hope, 1855–1919). This case has profound implications. The experiencer tells that she was recuperating from a life-threatening illness and undergoing a period both of collapse of faith and of profound guilt (she feared her mediumship was not a means of divine guidance but that she was deluding herself and others). She was not dying but was longing for death when she had an extraordinary experience, which was to have a transforming effect on her life:

I felt a curiously faint sinking sensation, and the printed pages I had been trying to study became strangely indistinct...Everything became dark....The faintness passed away....I had moved away from the sofa, but somebody else was there holding the book...[I felt] a marvellous sense of health, strength and power.

...I moved towards the window. Strange how curiously dim my surroundings seemed. The walls disappear[ed]...a little distance off, I saw a [spirit] friend whom I recognized...my friend through ages....He spoke, or perhaps he did not use language...'Did I see where I was?'...the sunshine had faded and we were in a narrow road....I held my friend by the hand....Dark gloomy overhanging rocks were on each side...[with] projections which seemed to block up the passage...a pitfall yawned open-mouthed...a long weary way...surrounded by cold mist...yet here and there gleamed out a warm clear light....

Looking back over the way she had come, d'Espérance saw that the gleams of light were diffused over the whole and that she might have saved herself several stumbles, detours, and falls into pits had she been more aware of the light. The path became symbolic of her past life.

I looked farther, and...afar off, a brilliant gleam of light burst out, flooding the road with glory unconceivable. I could not bear it. I was ashamed and hid my face for the light penetrated me....I saw myself as I really was....Who can describe the indescribable? Time had disappeared, space no longer existed....I realised that, mean and poor as I was, I was yet a part of this undying, infinite, indestructible whole....The secrets of life and death were unveiled. The reasons of sin and suffering were evident....I saw...living, radiant creatures...my soul went out to them in love, friendship, and adoration...while there were others for whom I felt an intense compassion....If they would only let me, I could do so much to dispel the shadows in which they were surrounded.

They [the souls in the shadows] had helped me....We had worked together....We were...all members of the great family....The light had entered my soul and I was filled with joy ineffable. It was mine, this new-born fire....It was within their hands, too, but they had not laid hold of it....I would...help them as my friend had helped me into the light....[18]

d'Espérance's strong compassionate desire to share with these once-helpful unfortunates her experience of the light that is also fire impelled her to leave the light for "a misty cloud-like region in which one felt stifled and cramped." There were forms and shapes (apparently souls) in the mist as well as the rocks she had seen earlier, but the rocks were now only vapors she could pass through. All was dim and shadowy. Here, she felt, the "dream-life" was lived. "I saw that...life, which animates all things, is undying...circling for ever through form after form...." d'Espérance controlled the desire to escape back into the light and sought to clothe herself in mist in order to communicate with the blind captives. By this she seems to mean both venturing back into the misty region and returning to her physical body, which she then did, feeling back in prison again.[19]

It is not quite clear whether the "blind ones" for whom d'Espérance feels such compassion are earthbound spirits in the gray realm or incarnate persons; she could be referring to both, in view of the fact that as a practicing medium she saw herself as living in both worlds.

This case is remarkable in that it not only contains elements found in both radiant and painful NDEs, *but sees the realm of the lost and the realm of the light as essentially one*. Guided by a welcomer she has known for ages, the experiencer goes through a dark, dangerous passage (later seen to be part of the gray misty regions) into light, light that in retrospect she can see has been present even in the dark passage, though she scarcely saw it then. She now knows that, as both light and fire, it is also within herself and even within the lost souls, her brothers and sisters in the region of mist and shadows. Her realized inner light arouses in her a compassion which causes her to turn her steps back into the mist, to tell them to open their eyes to what they already have. She is not, like most returnees, sent back by visionary figures or drawn back by duties or ties to particular persons in the flesh, but by detached love fired by the light. This case will be particularly important when we come to interpret the significance of the tunnel and to find an explanation in the form of a scenario that will bring together radiant and painful NDEs.

In a cluster of entity cases with a very different tone, which P. M. H. Atwater encountered in the late 1960s before her own NDEs, the beings were not in the tunnel but at the end of it. A heart-attack patient Atwater had befriended reported that she went through a tunnel toward a bright light, but that when she reached the light she found herself in

> a landscape of barren, rolling hills filled to overflowing with nude, zombie-like people standing elbow to elbow doing nothing but staring straight at her. She was so horrified at what she saw [that] she started screaming. This snapped her back into her body where she continued screaming until sedated.

Amazingly, three other people on the same hospital ward, all unknown to each other at the time, apparently had virtually the same experience.[20] These entities (or perhaps mere images) appeared so dehumanized and identity-less that it is hard to tell if they were even aware of being needy. The case is a distressing mirror-image of radiant NDEs.

Most accounts of dull, spiritless beings in dim realms come from experiencers who only observe them; the account of suicide attempter Angie Fenimore differs in that she found herself on a dim foggy plain as a participant with thousands of other entities who had killed themselves. She was able to read their minds: self-absorbed, self-justifying, or totally empty in despair. In spite of this telepathic contact she felt alone. Release came when a powerful voice and a point of light appeared, expanding to reveal a being of light (apparently God the Father as understood by Mormons) who asked her if this was what she wanted. Fenimore felt permeated with great love and beauty and a sense of recognition of God from pre-earth-life. The other suicidal spirits were clearly unable to see this light, who was giving her vast insights into her life and the soon-to-follow effects of her intended death. She began to see that she was not only a victim of mistreatment but was responsible for her life. She also felt the presence of Jesus, his deep compassion and empathy with her pain. After a time her perception shifted, and she began to see beings of light all around, whom she felt were helping people on earth. Finally, with a rushing sensation, "the darkness sped past" and she found herself back in her body.[21]

Robert Monroe also describes a dark area with needy beings; he calls it "the inner ring," a plane close to the earth's surface (he does not mention a tunnel or passageway). The chief difference from the above cases is that the unhappy beings become aware of him and pull or grab at him. Most of the entities that give him trouble seem to be subhuman and animal-like, though some can change their shape to that of children. Two even take the form, momentarily, of Monroe's two daughters, apparently showing access to his memories (or else projection on his part). In the majority of these cases the attacks are not vicious but merely a sucking attachment that frightens him greatly at first. He finds that mere movement seems to attract the beings in this area, whereas if he waits, motionless, they drift away.[22] He remarks that if one moved violently and fought back against the "fish," "then more excited entities came rushing in to bite, pull, push, shove,"[23] a pattern suggesting the principle of "like attracts like."

In summarizing his observations, Monroe calls spirits attached to earth situations "the locked-ins," and describes them as ignorant that they are deceased, compulsively preoccupied with earth-life, and having no interest in spiritual realities. Other denizens of "the inner ring" are "the dreamers," apparently the out-of-body minds of sleeping persons repeating their daylight activities or trying to act out fantasies and wishes. They are given to disappearing suddenly, presumably as they awaken. The third class, the "wild ones," are spirits who are in fact aware that they are in a strange situation, but have no wish to understand it. Totally out of control, they throw themselves into replicas of physical activity, especially bizarre sexual activity. Monroe describes seeing a huge heap of writhing spirit-bodies, obsessed with getting sexual gratification, oblivious to all else.[24] Monroe also sees animal spirits in "the inner ring."[25] It may be noted that according to Monroe's categories, the distinction between those bound to earth and those in a dim, formless setting is a relative one. They are ignorant, consumed with their needs, and lacking in any real caring or respect for others.

The images of hell described by visionary Marietta Davis after her nine-day coma (probably an NDE) in 1848 are more like the above cases than like the views of her evangelical Christian circle, in which hell is the expression of divine wrath against sinners. In her experience the sufferings of the lost, largely spiritual in nature, are self-created. Addictions loom large. For example, those given to social pleasures, preoccupied with impressing others through jewels and fine dress, are drawn to a place where they are able to parade about splendidly clad, attend banquets, and engage in witty repartee. They find, however, that satisfaction merely whets their desires unbearably.[26]

Threatening Beings

There is no sharp line between entities who seek to satisfy their acute needs by sucking at the OBE or NDE traveler in annoying ways, and those whose clutching becomes a serious threat. As we saw with Monroe, who learned to deal with certain situations by controlling his fear, the OBEr's emotional reaction is an important factor. The following case is ambivalent: Luisa Vazquez, a battered wife, attempted suicide in an attempt to escape her violent marriage. In the hospital, she found herself not above but below her physical body, descending by stages. After a period of total blackness, she found herself trying to climb up a slimy stone wall, but periodically pulled downward by a strong force. Luisa felt increasing pressure. Finally she hit bottom, where she found a greenish-gray being who gestured toward the left in the direction of another being, whom she perceived to be her deceased father, positioned in a kind of spotlight along with another being. Her father reproachfully asked her if she were a "quitter" and gave her to understand that she had a choice. A vision of the burial soon to take place made her realize she wanted to live. She was now determined to go back, but a vast number of the greenish-gray beings around and below the small platform on which she stood clutched at her ankles, "trying to convince me to stay. 'You wanted this! Come down! This is a new dimension, a new world!' " Luisa kicked one foot free, then felt her father's hand below her pushing her upward. She found herself again on the wall, climbing. The ascent was very hard, as though she were battling a gigantic wind. Listening intently she heard faraway human voices; climbing, she felt the pressure lessen.

Luisa's mind was now working a thousand times faster than in life. At some point during this climb a small sparkler-like light appeared to her right. "It moved around me in awesome patterns, even occasionally traveling through the wall. It radiated a great feeling of companionship and trust. Later, I asked it if it had come to light my path, and it seemed to respond joyfully." Re-entering her body, she perceived with joy that the light was still visible near her waist and so bright that she could not see her legs. It expanded until it filled the room, communicated "You're safe," and disappeared.[27]

In the case of Cathy Baker, an elderly woman who had suffered from depression after her husband's death, many of the same features appear but the sense of menace is greatly sharpened. During surgery for an ulcer, Baker left her body and entered a twilit tunnel with a narrow raised pathway and a powerful headwind. She was greeted by hideous laughter and moaning from her right, where she could feel and dimly see a vast pit filled with people. Their skin was bluish gray and their arms reached out to grab her. On her left she could see nothing, but was almost paralyzed with terror by an intensely malevolent presence watching her.

At this point Baker sensed a strong, benevolent woman, dressed in a blue gown, at her back urging her to go to the end of the tunnel. "Don't look at them. Stay on the path." The guide communicated a patience and kindness that strengthened the NDEr. About halfway down the long tunnel the evil entities on either side disappeared, leaving only the wind. After a tremendous struggle she arrived. The guiding presence disappeared as she experienced a wonderful golden light and encountered St. Peter and Jesus.[28] This case will figure prominently in discussions in later chapters.

The opposing headwind in these cases stands in vivid contrast to the more frequent cases in which a power draws NDErs down the tunnel with tremendous speed. The "hideous laughter" of the needy, clutching beings in Cathy Baker's tunnel suggests insanity or sadism or both, and the benevolent guide offers not only an encouraging push, as with Luisa Vazquez, but crucial protection both from the clutching beings and from the demonic malevolence on her left.

In *Life At Death* Kenneth Ring presents the idea that the tunnel may sometimes be a construct intended to give the NDEr passage through a danger zone lying between the physical world and the dimension of light.[29] A similar idea is reflected in Monroe's "inner ring." The several cases with needy beings in the tunnel, especially that of Elizabeth d'Espérance in which the passageway was perceived as formed and definite on her journey outward but permeable and inhabited by needy beings on the journey back, offer confirmation for this idea.

Threatening figures sometimes take the form of beasts, monsters, or grotesque humanoids. In a case reported by Margot Grey, a woman working in the kitchens of a nursing home was overcome by heat. She rushed outside feeling faint and sick:

> I found myself in a place surrounded by mist. I felt I was in hell. There was a big pit with vapour coming out and there were arms and hands coming out trying to grab mine....I was terrified....[A]n enormous lion bounded towards me from the other side [of the pit] and I let out a scream. I was not afraid of the lion, but I felt somehow he would unsettle me and push me into that dreadful pit....[30]

Apparently the lion did not in fact cause her to fall into the pit; we are not told how the experience ended. Grey offers an interpretation for this experience based on its similarity to a Not-Close-to-Death Experience (NCDE) of a young man, a student of the Mother (Mira Alfassa Richard, colleague of Aurobindo) of the Pondicherry ashram in India. In an altered state the subject was walking through a jungle when he saw a huge tiger about to spring on him. Remembering the Mother's counsel to show no fear and stand his ground, he confronted the tiger, who began to shrink until, at the size of a domestic cat, it walked away.[31] In both of these cases the experiencer had been abandoned by a spouse who had gone off with someone else, and both were filled with rage. The Mother interpreted the tiger as a "thought form" of this rage, which would have destroyed the visionary had he not responded courageously.[32] It seems clear that in some cases the apparitions are projections of the emotions of the subject.

An example of an NDE with threatening figures happening to a small child is reported by P. M. H. Atwater: a five-year-old after going out-of-body found herself trapped in a large black cube, with dark clawlike hands everywhere trying to grab her. Although this scene was transmuted into a sea of opalescent light in which she floated pleasantly, the effect on the child's life was negative, as the frightening part of the experience overwhelmed the pleasant part. [33]

A monster-figure whose form seemed to come from a primitive level of consciousness was perceived by Oliver Fox in an NCDE of February 6, 1916. As he passed into trance, Fox perceived "great forces...straining the atmosphere," and blue-green flashes in all parts of the room. He then saw a filmy shapeless monster, "spreading out in snake-like protuberances," with enormous blue-fiery eyes. Fox was terrified but gained control over his fear, turning away from the monster. When he turned back, it was gone.[34]

That the disappearance of the figure was partly due to Fox's gaining control of his fear is suggested by his earlier experiences. In his youth he had a series of dreams of intense beauty, a "seemingly divine atmosphere," and also dreams of intense ugliness, suggesting heavenly and hellish NCDEs. He makes the point that, in the painful dreams, "if the shape of horror was faced boldly it would either be dissipated or actually changed into a thing of beauty, and the latter always happened when my compassion was aroused and conquered my aversion."[35] Both the tiger in the student's vision and the frightening figures in Oliver Fox's hellish dreams of adolescence are rendered harmless by a courageous, affirmative response.

Like Fox, Whiteman in an experience with animal-figures was also able to transform a situation of threat by controlling his consciousness. Whiteman's separations sometimes begin in the dream state. In one such instance he found himself in a pit with wild animals, one a lion reaching out to maul him. He was afraid, but

> I recollected the Lord, with the knowledge that putting forth of love would conquer all. A wave of love flowed through me, though not sufficient to raise me completely. I seemed to emerge from the pit...a lion, or perhaps a large dog (for now there was no fear) suddenly appeared. Reaching out to stroke this animal, I became still more liberated....[36]

Thus Whiteman, like Fox, holds the ideal of responding to threats with love, and at times has been able to realize it.

Sometimes there is no explanation for the withdrawal of a threatening figure. In one instance, a woman whose NDE was triggered by a heart attack reported entering a gloomy room where she "saw in one of the windows this huge giant with a grotesque face that was watching me." This "welcomer" beckoned her to come with him, which she did through a "tunnel or cave" amid moving things at her feet and moaning voices. She was in increasing distress, crying, when the giant inexplicably freed her and sent her back.[37] Similarly, in the case of Arvin Gibson's child NDEr Mike, the terrifying snarl he heard when he reached out and touched something in the darkness was later followed by a light and a loving presence.[38] But nothing is said to suggest that it was by controlling fear or responding with love that the happy ending in these cases was brought about.

The Mirror-Image Pattern

It will be helpful to consider some typologies of painful NDEs that have been offered. Margot Grey points out that there is a significant analogy between the five-stage sequence of events in Ring's "core experience" and the hellish NDEs. These two patterns form a kind of mirror-image whose negative side can be summarized as follows:

1. Fear and a feeling of panic
2. Out-of-the-body experience
3. Entering a black void
4. Sensing an evil force
5. Entering a hell-like environment[39]

Grey divides her painful cases into two phases. The first phase is composed of "Negative NDEs," in which the experiencer feels fearful, lost, and desolate. The atmosphere is gloomy; the experiencer may feel on the brink of an abyss. The second phase she calls "Hellish NDEs;" they are more intensely painful and are often characterized by the presence of evil beings who threaten or taunt or attack. The cries of souls in torment may be heard; occasionally hellfire and the devil are encountered.[40] An example of a hellish NDE:

> I felt an inner struggle going on between myself and some evil force. At the last moment I suddenly felt an inner explosion and seemed to be enveloped in a blue flame which felt cold. At this point I found myself floating about six inches above my body. The next thing I remember is being sucked down a vast black vortex like a whirlpool and I found myself in a place that I can only describe as being like Dante's *Inferno*. I saw a lot of other people who seemed grey and dreary and there was a musty smell of decay. There was an overwhelming feeling of loneliness....[41]

This case has two elements of traditional Western hell imagery, namely, downward movement and fire. But the flame is experienced at the moment of going out-of-body, it is cold, and the actual situation in hell is one of gray, dreary crowds rather than torment. Thus though the imagery is hellish at the beginning, the case actually seems to fit in Grey's category of dreary "negative" experiences rather than being one of horror.

Nancy Evans Bush and Bruce Greyson also find a resemblance in structure between certain painful and radiant NDEs. Their collection of fifty cases falls into three categories. The first group, although they have the same features as the prototypical radiant NDEs, are perceived by the NDErs as terrifying. Kenneth Ring has aptly named this class "Inverted NDEs."[42] An example:

> As I looked under me...a strong wind was pulling me into what seemed to be a funnel shaped like a cornucopia, only opened at both ends. I was flying, and drawn directly into the vortex or funnel. At the end the lights were blinding, and crystal flashing was unbearable. As I neared the very end, I was reaching for the sides, trying to stop myself from falling off the end into the flashing crystal....I vividly remember screaming, "God, I'm not ready; please help me."...[W]hen I screamed, an arm shot out of the sky and grabbed my hand and at the last second I was kept from falling off the end of the funnel...and the heat was really something.[43]

As with radiant NDEs, the experiencer moves rapidly through the dark passageway; at its end is light, but it is a blinding, flashing crystal rather than a loving Being; the light gives off intense heat instead of pleasant warmth. The heat and the downward direction are ominous, but perhaps it is chiefly the soullessness of the destination that makes it terrifying. Of this more later.

Vortices

A type of usually distressing NDE that might be put in the "Inverted" category (though Bush and Greyson do not call attention to it) is the vortex image seen in the above case and in Grey's case. William Serdehely reports several vortex-type NDE cases: "One person experienced a 'clockwise spinning vortex' of blacks, whites and grays; one reported an 'all gray whirlpool'...."[44] Funnel images are not always terrifying; author William D. Pelley in an NDE in 1928 finds himself whirling out of control, although he is soon reassured by two welcomers; later he is conveyed back to his body in a swirling motion by a blue vapor.[45]

The vortex seems to appear particularly in cases involving anesthetics, but is obviously not limited to them. The massive whirling energy that carries one away like a leaf in a storm suggests a giant impersonal energy or power, painful for the experiencer but quite different both from the masses of needy, clutching beings and from the malevolent presence of Cathy Baker's NDE (and others below).

However, the power of the vortex is not irresistible. Gloria Hipple of Blakeslee, Pennsylvania, when hospitalized for a miscarriage, was placed at a forty-five degree angle and neglected for a long period. As in an earlier experience, she found herself pulled down a spinning vortex. In panic she tried to grab at the sides, but there was nothing to hold. A dark curtain appeared ahead, then a white spot which became a grinning skull hurtled toward her.

> With a bellowing yell, I screamed: 'No! damn it, no! Let me go. My babies need me! No! No! No! No!' The skull shattered into fragments and I slowed in movement. A white light, the brightest light I have ever known...was in place of the skull....It was a welcome, calming light.

Then she felt herself floating upward in great peace and heard the voice of her husband, who was now present.[46] She damned hell to hell, and found that it turned into the light.

Another experiencer who was successful in resisting a vortex and an evil being associated with it was Yram. "I had not been feeling well....I was sucked up by a whirlwind which carried me up in an unknown direction." He managed to stand upright in the "magnetic stream" and soon found "an individual of menacing aspect coming towards me...." Dismissing his momentary fear, Yram awaited his approach with a smile and, when the aggressor lifted his arm to strike, Yram called upon his guides, an action that stopped the attacker. Yram then pointed a finger at him and made him vanish.[47] Clearly it it is possible to regain poise and become proactive even in the midst of such a huge whirling force.

Rarely, the vortex has been associated with a life overview. Raynor Johnson tells of a drowning man who saw the scenes of his life, the final ones in extraordinary, vivid detail, whirling about him. Crowds of people were present, even in scenes unconnected with them; the whole was suffused with golden light.[48] This feature is like P. M. H. Atwater's third NDE: after entering a blissful light, she perceived two vortices in an hourglass-like shape, with an intense radiant energy where the center should have been. These were not terrifying, but did give her a sense of great awe. She did not feel herself to be drawn into the vortices during the experience but instead saw her entire life, all her past and future lives, and those of her associates, present in both vortices.[49]

The way in which Gloria Hipple apparently changed her experience from a painful to a radiant one—aggressive resistance motivated by altruism—is rare. More often it is after NDErs have accepted the experience that their terror resolves itself into peace, so that the remainder of the experience more or less fits the Moody-type pattern. For example, Bush and Greyson cite the case of a nurse suffering from a high fever after an operation who found herself no longer a body in the hospital but a consciousness surrounded by a misty substance. Lights flashing in a circular shape repeatedly and rapidly advanced toward her and retreated. She was extremely frightened, but after a time she began to reassure herself—"You can handle this; you're strong; you'll be okay"—and to pray to God. Suddenly the fear gave way to "*complete peace*." She felt at one with all and surrounded by profound love.[50] It seems that the frightening and painful aspects are sometimes caused by, or strongly linked to, the experiencer's resistance.

Meaningless Void

According to Bush and Greyson's typology, the second group is made up of cases in which the experiencer finds herself desolate in a dark void which seems to be everlasting. Here is an example (Nancy Evans Bush's own experience, given anonymously[51]):

> [During childbirth, while she was given anesthetic] First there was only unconsciousness....I was aware...of moving

rapidly upward into darkness...with immense speed and great distance.

A small group of circles appeared ahead of me....The circles were black-and-white and made a clicking sound as they snapped black to white, white to black. They were jeering and tormenting—not evil, exactly, but more mocking and mechanistic. The message in their clicking was: Your life never existed. The world never existed....You were allowed to imagine it....There was never anything there. [I]t was all a joke.

There was much laughter on their parts, malicious. I remember brilliant argumentation on my part, [summoning up various memories,] trying to prove that the world—and I—existed....They just kept jeering.

"This is eternity," they kept mocking. This is all there ever was, and all there ever will be, just this despair. It was empty, except for me and them, and dark....It seemed to go on forever. I was debating and simultaneously grieving....I knew no one could bear that much grief....

Time was forever, endless rather than all at once. The remembering of events had no sense of life review....[The experience] was more than real: absolute reality. There's a cosmic terror we have never addressed....It wouldn't matter how I died or when; damnation was out there, just waiting.[52]

It was only years later that she saw, to her terror, a picture of one of the circles, and still later learned that they represented the yin/yang symbol of Taoism.

Several elements make this experience a grim mirror of radiant NDEs: The experiencer rises upward, but into nothingness rather than an unfolding of ultimate meaning; instead of eternity there is everlastingness; instead of an insightful life overview shown by a being of unconditional love, there is a desperate recall of past events to defend oneself in a losing argument with mocking, mechanistic entities.

Another remarkable feature of the case is the appearance of a symbol borrowed from Taoism in the visions of a culture-bound North American.

Nancy Evans Bush declares that she was quite unfamiliar with Eastern religion at this time. While one cannot prove that she had never seen and forgotten a yin/yang symbol before her NDE, the point is that neither the symbol nor its message that all is meaningless illusion come from her own unexamined mainline Protestant experience. (Nor does the symbol have the meaning it has in Taoism.)

Pamela Kircher recounts a similar case of a young man whose NDE was brought on by a drug overdose leading to seizures. He found himself in a gray "Void" (his term) facing a circle that turned slowly from one side to the other, black to white to black, with a clicking sound. Painfully lonely, he reflected that his empty drug-centered life had led him to this situation. He cried out desperately to God for help and found himself back in his body.[53]

The two cases are obviously alike in having been sparked by a drug, involving a gray-black void and clicking circle(s), and agonizing feelings of isolation. But Nancy Evans Bush's experience lacked the cause-and-effect significance of the other; she was not an addict but a devout person trying her best to live a good life. Her release did not come as a result of prayer; her experience and its message of cosmic meaninglessness remained unresolved for years afterwards.

An NCDE void experience clearly analogous to Bush's is that of Peggy Holladay. In an automobile accident in 1973, Holladay seems to have had an NDE, though she remembered very little of it. In 1986 she had a powerful, radiant NCDE, which she interpreted as an emergence into consciousness of her 1973 experience. Later in 1986, while looking into a mirror at a time when she was in grief she asked herself, "What am I really upset about?" Suddenly she found herself

> floating in space. Almost simultaneously the deep Realization..."hit" me that I had died and I was completely ALONE, never to be with any loved ones, or for that matter, [any] living thing....Even though this experience only lasted about ten seconds...to me it was for all eternity. [C]onjure up...the greatest amount of fear and terror [you] could imagine and then multiply it by 5 billion [—] it still wouldn't equal what I felt.
>
> As this horrible feeling overtook me I started screaming, saying, "NO, NO!" I could see my body on the

other side of the mirror and, as hard as I tried to pull myself back into it it, was as if some huge force was pulling me back out into space. I finally, with the hardest struggle, made it back into my body, which was just standing there at the sink....

Holladay interpreted this looking-glass experience as a "Total Aloneness energy" at the core of every person, causing each of us to do all the fear-based things we do. This awareness made it possible for her to feel compassion for herself, for a relative with whom she had a bad relationship, for everyone.

One of the cases in Greyson and Bush's article, which may be classed as in the "everlasting void" category, began very differently. The experiencer, a woman in childbirth, found herself floating peacefully down a narrow river toward a beautiful arched bridge. She was eager to get into the shadow of the bridge, for she knew that would mean death. When she entered it she found herself a small ball of light in the heavens, but the peace was gone, and she was spinning around and screaming soundlessly. She was united with all humanity but terribly alone in the vastness of the universe, convinced that it would be forever.[54, 55] The arched bridge may be an image of a gateway into another dimension, but there is no explanation for the unnerving movement from peace to anguish. The experiencer's assertion that she was simultaneously united to all humanity resembles Peggy Holladay's interpretation of her pain in the Void as the "total aloneness energy" present in all persons.

Hellish Experiences

Bush and Greyson's third category, smaller than the other two, involves "more graphic hellish symbolism, such as threatening demons or falling into a dark pit." (In Barbara Rommer's study, this third category was the largest, nearly forty-two percent.) The cases above involving arms reaching out of a pit, earthbound or "inner ring" entities, and spirit attachment differ from this third category not in kind but in degree. The following cases give genuine meaning to the word "demonic." (Admittedly, the case of Cathy Baker [page 67] is also in this league.) Bush and Greyson do not mention hellfire, but I propose to subdivide hellish cases into entity-centered and fire-centered (although there are a few that involve both).

1. Entity-Centered Hellish Cases

Two of the examples Bush and Greyson give show frightened NDErs tormented or finding themselves among tormented beings. In the third case, an attempted suicide, the experiencer reports:

> I hung in the rope and strangled....I saw my body hanging in the rope; it looked awful. I was terrified....Demons were all around me: I could hear them but could not see them. They chattered like blackbirds. It was as if they knew they had me, and had all eternity to drag me down into hell, to torment me...trapped hopeless between two worlds...for all eternity.
>
> I had to get back into my body....I ran to the house, went in through the door without opening it, cried out to my wife but she could not hear me, so I went right into her body. I could see and hear with her eyes and ears. Then I made contact, heard her say, "Oh, my God!"
>
> She grabbed a knife...and ran out to where I was hanging and got up on an old chair and cut me down....[56]

The hell which the experiencer in his panic anticipated is like the gray existence of the needy beings in that it was "between two worlds," but much worse in that it involved tormenting demons. This case also involves attachment. It is potentially more evidential than the possession by alcoholic spirits witnessed by Ritchie (pages 57–58) and Monroe's possession of sick persons, in that we have not only the word of the NDEr but might be able to get an account from the person invaded, the wife, as well. Evidentiality is strengthened by the fact that the takeover led to direct action, that is, rescue.

In an OBE in 1923 Muldoon was violently attacked by the apparition of a recently deceased man whom he calls F. D. An hour or two earlier, Muldoon had heard the new widow recounting dreadful stories of her husband's deeds, and Muldoon recounts that his "blood boiled with rage" against F. D. By the time Muldoon lay down to go out of body he had forgotten the conversation. But no sooner was he out than he saw the figure of F. D. "glaring at me like a maniac....I knew instinctively that he meant revenge." The F. D.-figure took advantage of Muldoon's terror by leaping on him and beating him ferociously. Muldoon was rescued, he reports, by his "controlling power"; F. D. was unable to hold on as Muldoon rose to a horizontal position above his body and was "slammed" back in.[57] Muldoon interprets this rescue as the work of his own higher mind. His mention of "revenge" makes it clear that he believed the attack was the surviving F. D.'s reaction to his own earlier feelings of hostility.

Robert Monroe experienced violent encounters during his movements through certain areas of the "inner ring." Upon one occasion, Monroe was attacked by an extremely vicious entity who knew how to move in on his nerve centers and seemed bent on truly destroying his consciousness. After a long, terrifying fight Monroe succeeded in escaping by returning to his body.[58] In another instance of attack he "began to pray....I asked God to help me. I prayed in the name of Jesus Christ....I tried a few saints....The result? My tormentors laughed loudly and worked me over more enthusiastically." Monroe began to get angry and pushed back, but focussed mostly on getting back to his body, which he finally succeeded in doing.[59]

In this escape, he is like Muldoon but differs from Whiteman, whose possessing entity remained attached to him even after he regained his body (page 58). Unlike Fox and Whiteman, who were committed to nonviolent responses, Monroe in this instance did not hesitate to accept an ethic of fighting in self-defense. In the lack of response to his prayer, Monroe's experience differs from most reported NDEs.

Barbara Rommer notes that, of the group of hellish experiences in her study, over thirteen percent began as peaceful states before revealing devilish imagery, an unnerving development.

2. Sexually Charged Gang Violence

A very disturbing example of an NDE involving sexually charged gang violence is the 1974 case of Patricia, a desperate battered wife who tried to call for help by shooting herself in the neck, but did more damage than she intended.

Like Rosemary baby?

I went into a coma....In my NDE I found myself sitting in a chair...immobilized....There were grotesque little creatures...ugly and hideous (but no horns). I couldn't speak but only move my eyes. They were shooting holes in me, about the size of a quarter, anywhere in my body. I was totally conscious all this time....They did repulsive things—put bile in the holes, put in excrement or vomit....The holes weren't painful but extremely repulsive—I could taste it....It seemed to go on forever, but lasted for maybe twenty minutes at a time. It was as though they were preparing me, positioning me for something worse. They finally went away, but behind me I could hear raspy, heavy breathing, and smell a horrible stench worse than anything imaginable. But I couldn't even throw up, I was rigid. The heavy creature was getting closer, just beyond my right shoulder, just out of view....I was overwhelmingly terrified....At just the very instant before it appeared I screamed mentally "O my God, please help me!" The very next instant I opened my eyes and was alive and conscious...in the hospital....I cried for joy—I knew God was there, and that everything was fine.

Certain that God knew she had not intended suicide, Patricia was perplexed that she should have had such a hellish experience. However, she believes that if she had not recovered she would have gone on to the tunnel and the light after her cry to God. "The whole thing would have issued in something good."[60]

A similar case involving foulness and a magnetic evil power is the 1970 NCDE of Gary Wells. At this time Wells was distressed over an impending divorce, and alone at his job during the graveyard shift. It began with his asking "Is there a God? If you do exist, please let me know...." All at once he felt a strong sense of a benevolent presence, heard a command to be holy, and was hit by a severe migraine. When the headache approached the limit of endurance, Wells suddenly found himself

standing in a blackness...so thick it was almost like a physical substance. There was a dank, unearthly smell, and voices—two guys ridiculing each other...; it was phony, foul language. There were more voices inside the blackness....I felt a power like a vacuum pulling me into it further. As I moved toward the source, my speed increased proportionately....I was shocked, scared to death. I heard a yell, "O God, help me!" in my own voice, but I didn't consciously say this.

Then Wells found himself "back to normal," very grateful to be out of the darkness, and convinced of the reality of God. He felt slowly filled with the Holy Spirit, a tingling, euphoric feeling, "fresh, clean, pure."[61]

George Ritchie's guided tour of the worlds of the dead included a visit to a dimension where suicides who had destroyed themselves out of rage against others were confined until they should learn that hatred is not the way. (Note that Angie Fenimore's experience [page 64] confirms this picture.) Next, from the vantage point of a high porch in front of a large building, Ritchie was horrified to see beings filled with fury arguing about religion or politics, or trying to kill one another, or sexually abusing others. Ritchie could feel that this situation was causing heartbreaking grief to the Christ, who did not condemn the beings but only wanted their release. Ritchie also perceived bright presences, angels trying to persuade them to change their way of thinking, but the furious beings did not see them.[62] This violence is paralleled by the horrifying sights seen in the walls of the tunnel by NDEr Edward Smith: "Piles and piles of...anguished human beings and creatures whose bodies and souls fused with humans....Bodies were being torn apart, fought over, chewed on, raped, crushed, regurgitated, eaten again and again....The humans...were always alive...." (Smith's experience climaxed in loving union with the light.)[63]

Ritchie's vision of self-damned spirits was quite alien to anything in his religious background. He wrote in response to my questions that he "had no experience or encounter with astral beings before my experience" and that he knew nothing of earthbound beings—"only my grandfather's ghost stories." He had been taught in church that the dead slept until the Last Trump.[64] As we shall see, however, self-damned states very similar to what he saw appear in religious traditions far removed from his own.

Sexually charged gang violence appears in the very extensive and significant painful NDE of Howard Storm, then a professor of art from North Kentucky University. This case is as crucially important as Ritchie's. Storm was in Paris leading an art tour when suddenly he suffered the intense pain of a perforated duodenum, which causes stomach acids to leak into the abdominal cavity. He needed an operation desperately, but because it was a weekend it was uncertain whether a surgeon would be available.

What about invisible who just feel worthless?

Hospitalized, Storm lingered in increasing agony for ten hours before being told that the doctor had gone home. At this point he gave up on life, fully expecting extinction. But what happened was that, after first drifting into darkness, he found himself standing beside the bed looking at his inert body, feeling completely physical with senses very keen. His stomach still hurt (compare the "haunting" story of Muldoon), but not nearly as severely as before. When he spoke to his wife she did not respond.[65]

Confused, angry, and fearful that he had gone crazy, Storm began to hear voices outside the room, calling "Howard." "They were pleasant voices, male and female.... 'Come on out here.... We can get you fixed up....' " They evaded his questions.[66]

Storm was desperate for help and felt it was futile to stay where he was, ignored by his wife and hospital roommate. "I stepped, with a good deal of anxiety, out into the hall. The area seemed to be bright but very hazy...." The people were in the distance, and as he moved closer to them they withdrew further into the fog, luring him onward. Occasionally he was able to look back and see the hospital room, oddly from a perspective above his body on the bed. They walked seemingly forever; there was a sense of timelessness. The fog thickened, it grew darker, the number of the people seemed to increase, and they came closer.

> The more questioning and suspicious I was, the more antagonistic and rude and authoritarian they became. They began to make jokes about my bare rear end which wasn't covered by my hospital dicky....All my communication with them took place verbally...they didn't appear to know what I was thinking, and I didn't know what they were thinking....An enormous sense of dread was building within me. This experience was sickeningly real.[67]

Finally, finding himself in complete darkness, Storm accused the people of being liars and refused to go any further. They began to snarl insults and shove him about; he fought back.

> A wild orgy of frenzied taunting, screaming and hitting ensued....As I swung and kicked at them, they bit and tore

> at me. All the while it was obvious that they were having great fun....They began to physically humiliate me in the most degrading ways....Then...they began to tear off pieces of my flesh. To my horror I realized I was being taken apart and eaten alive, slowly, so their entertainment would last as long as possible...much that occurred was simply too gruesome...to recall.[68]

> In the darkness I had extensive physical contact with them. When they swarmed over me, their bodies felt exactly as human bodies do....I noticed that they seemed to feel no pain. Other than that they appeared to possess no special...superhuman abilities...in our intimate physical contact I never felt any clothing whatsoever.[69]

Finally, Storm recalls, he became too torn up and weak to resist, and most of the beings gave up in disappointment. At some point after this he heard his own voice, which oddly seemed to come from his chest. It said "Pray." This struck him as foolish, but at the voice's further urging he tried to put together bits of the Twenty-Third Psalm and the Lord's Prayer and the Pledge of Allegiance and

> ...whatever churchly sounding phrases...came to mind. To my incredible surprise the beings...were horrified....They screamed at me....But at the same time they started backing away. I could hear their voices in the darkness...getting more and more distant.[70]

Lying hopeless and dismembered on the ground, Storm felt such intense desolation that he "even hoped that one or two of the beings would come back." Then he heard in his head a fragment from a children's hymn he had sung long ago: *Jesus loves me—*" This awakened his hope in the reality of love, and with what strength he had left he called out to Jesus to save him. At once he saw a tiny star overhead in the darkness which brightened as it came hurtling downward toward him.

Emanating from the light was more intensity and beauty than I had ever seen before....It was a living entity....In a very vivid and beautiful experience I slowly rose up with no effort into the light, and the pieces of my body somehow assembled. Looking at myself, I could see that all my wounds had disappeared, and I had become whole and well.[71]

From this point on Storm's experience became a radiant one, involving vast knowledge and unconditional love. The angel (as Storm interpreted him) raised him upward, and they were joined by other beings of wonderful colors. Ashamed of his atheistic past, Storm even told his rescuer to "Put me back," but was assured he was in the right place. They approached the "great luminous center," God, and he felt himself "beyond any thoughts" as he was held in the light. After a very long and transforming interaction, they told him he had to go back. Extremely reluctant, he finally agreed to do so.[72]

Storm's experience is one of the very few demonic-type cases that involves not only rescue but resolution into an extensive radiant experience. His period of desolation in the darkness may well be an experience of the Void as well.

Commentary on Violent Entities

The needy and hostile beings described above have some resemblances to the "hallucinatory" voices reported by many schizophrenics, interviewed by Wilson Van Dusen when he was a clinical psychologist at Mendocino State Hospital, California. Van Dusen found a large degree of similarity between the voices that these unfortunates heard. Many voices were hostile: shouting, insulting, threatening. They suggested lewd acts and then abused the patient for considering them, made empty promises, falsely claimed psychic powers, threatened murder.

They never have a personal identity, though they accept most names or identities given them....Their voice quality can change or shift, leaving the patient quite confused as to who might be speaking....All of the lower orders are irreligious or antireligious....In a few instances they referred to themselves as from hell.[73]

It should be noted that Van Dusen reports that about one-fifth of the hallucinatory figures are quite different from this; they possess great spiritual wisdom that they offer the patient, and are respectful of his or her individuality.[74] They seem similar to spiritual guides in certain NDEs.

In making this comparison I am not implying that NDErs are psychotic, which is obviously false, but rather suggesting that schizophrenics may be uncontrollably victimized by energies or beings like those that threaten NDErs. I am suggesting that these entities in fact have a certain degree of independent existence, if not necessarily distinct identity. Several themes recur in the behavior of the entities in these cases: hostility to religion, attachment to the living, aggressiveness, deceit, and sexual abuse. In most cases they throng together, seeming to support the principle of "like attracts like." All these entities are needy, obsessed, exploitative, and out of control.

There are also differences. Monroe's and Van Dusen's beings were able to change their form or voice at will, whereas Storm's entities seemed, from his out-of-body perspective, very human and physical. Ritchie's scene was one in which all thoughts were public, whereas Storm and his tormenters lacked such telepathy (which made it possible for the tormentors to entice him with false promises). Muldoon, Monroe, and Storm while out-of-body were able to suffer physical-seeming pain from the attacks they received, whereas Patricia did not feel pain from the assaults but nausea and terror.

Hellfire Cases

There are some cases in which menacing entities and hellfire both appear, but one or the other usually predominates. One is the case from the Evergreen Study in which the experiencer was ushered into hell by mistake. There were several stereotypical elements: fire, myriads of hateful, screaming, naked people asking for water, and a horned devil and his cohorts overseeing the whole operation. The experience lasted about four hours, the NDEr being sent back because "you're not mean enough." (This NDE was the second of three that this person had, the first and third being "positive" experiences.)[75] Unfortunately, the authors give little detail, and one cannot tell the relationship between the devils and the fire, or whether the suffering denizens of hell were actually in the fire. The stress on heat and thirst suggests that the fire was the focus of the scene.

The NCDE of Norman Van Rooy in 1955 or 1956 involves both entities and a "fiery glow." Van Rooy tells that as a child of four or five, one evening when he was in bed but still awake he heard his name called telepathically and heard a humming or throbbing sound like an electrical transformer coming from the wall. The sound seemed to Van Rooy to have "a malevolent intelligent magnetism that was almost hypnotic." To his horror "the wall opened up in several places near the floor and out of each opening came a creature...shaped like the bottom sides of goat's hooves....Between the cloven hooves from where their voices came[,] a nexus of overwhelming magnetic malevolent intelligence pulsated with a fiery glow. They seemed to know me and were trying to pull me down with them using mental force." The whole scene vanished when Van Rooy's mother entered in response to his calls for help. The experience happened again after she left, and again the next night, each time vanishing when his mother came in.[76] After these three times it never happened again.

Analyzing the experiences, Van Rooy traces the goat-hoof shape of the beings to his earlier life as a small child of missionary parents in India where he had played with the hoofs of slaughtered goats. (He might possibly also have heard from his parents the biblical parable of "the sheep and the goats," in which hard-hearted people, likened to goats, are sent to the "eternal fire prepared for the devil and his angels."[77]) However, Van Rooy does not claim the experiences are only this earlier image reappearing; they contained a level of horror that he cannot really interpret, nor can he see that they have served any good purpose in his life.[78]

Van Rooy's experiences provide a casebook example of Rudolf Otto's analysis of the negative side of the *mysterium tremendum et fascinans*, the Something encountered in a basic religious experience. The experience may be either frightening or blissful, but in either case there is an enormous sense of flesh-creeping uncanniness, overpoweringness, and huge energy.[79] The several goat-hoof beings do not seem to be separate entities but manifestations of a single terrifying, consuming intelligence expressed by the fiery glow and the humming noise.

Another childhood case, involving a textbook hell, was the NDE of "Kay" who succumbed to pneumonia at age three. She found herself in a deep cave with fires and tall stairways on which wretched, moaning people were descending. Aware from her Sunday School teaching that this must be hell, she looked about for the devil but did not see him. There was "a feeling of evil and misery...a horrible place...."[80]

Needless to say, the problem of meaning created by the occurrence of such nightmarish visions to a small child is not a light one.

A hellfire case with more impersonal *mysterium tremendum* qualities appears in *Beyond Death's Door* by Maurice Rawlings. A lumber worker named Thomas Welch fell from a high trestle over a dam and seems to have been immersed in water for forty-five minutes before he was found. Rawlings quotes Welch's booklet, "Oregon's Amazing Miracle":

> The next thing I knew I was standing near a shoreline of a great ocean of fire...turbulent, rolling mass...[a]s far as my eyes could see....There was nobody in it....I saw other people [including]...a boy I had gone to school with who had died from cancer....They, too,...seemed to be perplexed...as though they could not believe what they saw....The scene was so awesome that words simply fail....There is no way to escape...except by Divine intervention.

Welch goes on to tell that he saw a man with a strong, compassionate face whom he knew to be Christ passing in front of him. He wished silently that this Christ would turn to him, and it happened. Within minutes, Welch found himself back in his body. During the next several days in the hospital, Welch felt in constant communication with the Holy Spirit, and dedicated his life to God.[81] On the fourth day he had a sudden, extraordinary healing of his severe injuries.[82]

Another hellfire case cited in *Beyond Death's Door*, from a pamphlet by evangelist Kenneth Hagin, tells of an NDE in 1933 in which Hagin left his body and descended into darkness and increasing heat:

> Finally, way down below me, I could see lights flickering on the walls of the caverns of the damned. They were caused by the fires of hell. The giant orb of flame, white crested, pulled me...drew me like a magnet draws metal unto itself. I did not want to go!...but just as metal jumps to the magnet, my spirit was drawn....I could not take my eyes off

> it....Upon reaching the bottom of the pit, I had become
> conscious of some kind of spirit-being by my side. I hadn't
> looked at him because I could not take my gaze off the fires
> of hell, but when I paused, that creature laid his hand on
> my arm...to escort me in.

Hagin goes on to tell that a giant voice from above, speaking in some unknown tongue, caused the whole scene to shake and the creature to lose its grip; Hagin was pulled upward back into the world.[83]

The entity in this case seems to have had no real function; the NDEr does not even spare him a glance, as the fire is already drawing him irresistibly. It is interesting that the flame is a unity, an orb that has a powerful quality of *fascinans* as well as of *tremendum*, making for a remarkable resemblance in the case to typical radiant NDEs. Except for the facts that the movement is downward and the magnet is an orb not primarily of light but of flame, the case might be an "inverted" one.

Rawlings' reliability has been seriously questioned, but checking with the original booklet by Welch, I found his citation accurate. What creates problems for many readers is that Rawlings interprets his cases to fit his fundamentalist Christian doctrine that hell is the lot of all who have not committed their lives to Christ (more of this in Chapter Twelve). He proposes that all non-born-again NDErs who have radiant experiences are deluded by Satan. He offers no evidence of evil effects in their lives nor does he deal with actual evidence of transforming effects. This failing suggests that he trims the material to fit his doctrines. He is, however, honest enough in *Beyond Death's Door* to include the case of a multiple NDEr, a committed Christian, who had first a hellish NDE, then two radiant ones, with no sign of a conversion between. Rawlings confesses his perplexity.[84] For this reason, and the reliability of his account of the Welch case, I have decided to accept his first book as probably reliable.

In the following case, a very powerful inverted NDE (recast in the third person by the investigator), both dimensions of the *mysterium tremendum et fascinans* appear. The experience was triggered by electroshock therapy for suicidal depression, therapy which the experiencer approached with terror and rage against the medical personnel. Although anesthetized and paralyzed, she remained acutely conscious during the preparation, certain she was going to die. When the electricity hit, "Billions upon billions of neurons ignited simultaneously, and a thousand suns exploded inside her head. For a few excruciating seconds, the conflagration raged as the electric current flashed across her brain lobes, and in that timeless moment of ego immolation, she had been...'to hell and back.' " She then "found herself rushing down a long, spiraling tunnel toward...a brilliant, dazzling pinpoint of light." She felt at once both intense desire and terrible dread. "[A]nxiety and ecstasy were exactly the same, 'not opposites at all—just mirror images of each other.' " The movement down the tunnel was interrupted by several vivid scenes from her past life, each of which she relived in full detail. (Among these scenes was one from an unrecognized cocktail party in an unfamiliar home; it was to be fulfilled, in exact detail but "in reverse," two years later.) "Drawn, 'as if by an inconceivably powerful electromagnet,' into that blinding radiance, her terror mounted," but she also felt a compelling desire to let go and enter. At last she willed to do so, expecting death, loss of her mind, immolation, and hell. What she experienced was "absolute ecstasy" and oneness with the light. When she awoke her depression had vanished, never to return.[85]

This is one of the few painful cases in which the experiencer is not rescued from hell but, having accepted it, goes through hellfire into the light.

Anomalous Cases
The painful cases cited so far can be seen as fitting more or less well into various patterns. It should be noted, however, that some painful NDEs and NCDEs are hard to categorize. I will give a few examples of these largely anomalous experiences.

On June 11, 1928, Oliver Fox had a perplexing and nightmarish NCDE. Having decided to make an astral visit to a certain Tibetan temple he had heard of from his spirit guide, he went out-of-body to find himself falling interminably down a dark shaft. He controlled his fear, finally coming to rest in darkness. As his awareness of his situation slowly intensified, he found his eyes had been mutilated by hot irons, but he could see a blur of moving colors which he thought might be the robes of people. He was naked and bound to an upright X-shaped framework, blood trickling down from many wounds, the multiple burns and gashes becoming more acutely painful by the second. A menacing voice by his ear told him to "*Say* thou art Theseus!" Barely controlling his panic, with a great effort Fox managed to speak, insisting on his own identity. What followed was a huge explosion, a chaos of blinding light, deafening noise, and a whirling tempest. Instantaneously, he was back in his own body.[86]

This is a case of torment by entities, but the feel of it is quite different from any of those cited above. The experiencer does not meet up with beings who attack him but finds himself coming to consciousness in an ongoing action; the escape is also different from most. This horrifying scene is a crucifixion, a fact that Fox misses because the X-shaped cross (associated with St. Andrew) is much less known than the post-and-crosspiece familiar to Christian history as the form by which Roman authorities enforced their rule upon the conquered.[87] There is no hint in the experience as to who the accused Theseus was; Fox believed that the scene might have been part of a former incarnation of his own.[88] The tormenter appears to have been speaking in English, but that would not necessarily count against the scene's historical accuracy, since it would essentially be a mental reconstruction of a vivid memory.

Margot Grey presents an anomalous case in which an attempted suicide found herself lying on a marble table in a cold, dim room. She felt the room to be a chapel, a kind of hospital. She felt desolate, afraid, guilty. Abruptly she became aware of a dazzling light from a beautiful gold lantern on a stand at her feet. A sympathetic young man with dark eyes urged her to "Be calm and have faith." Voices issued from an austere room above where dark-hooded figures were arguing over her fate: some defending, but more accusing. Then she heard the whole crowd come hurrying down a spiral staircase into her room, seeming about to attack her. Terrified, she appealed to "the being of light" and found that the dark figures were stopped by the light "a few centimetres from me. They withdrew and I knew I was absolved."[89]

Grey remarks that this case is atypical in two respects: It has both "positive" and "negative" elements, and it involves judgment by others more than by oneself.[20] The setting is cold and dim, but is felt to be a place of worship and healing. The beings do not seem to be needy or sadistic, but see themselves as ministers of justice or righteous vengeance. Furthermore, the comforting being might be called a guide, but he is not a welcomer; the light from the lamp is not like the wonderful light in radiant NDEs.

A further example of anomalous NDEs is the well-known case of A. J. Ayer who, in June 1988, while hospitalized for pneumonia, choked on a piece of salmon and was without heartbeat for four minutes. Upon his return to consciousness he told his attendants "You are all mad." Later he said to a friend, "Did you know that I was dead? The first time that I tried to cross the river I was frustrated, but my second attempt succeeded....My thoughts became persons."[91] Later he had no memory of these comments, but he did recall that he "was confronted by a red light, exceedingly bright, and also very painful even when I turned away from it....[T]his light was responsible for the government of the universe." Its ministers included beings responsible for space, and others responsible for time. Something was wrong with space, and Ayer felt obligated to set it right; he also wanted to get rid of the red light, which he assumed would then switch itself off. Unable to contact the entities in charge of space, he remembered Einstein's general theory of relativity and tried to contact those in charge of time. But they seemed unable to hear or understand him, so he "walked up and down, waving my watch, in the hope of drawing their attention...to the time which it measured." He became increasingly desperate, until the experience suddenly ended.[92]

This experience does partially fit the Moody-paradigm, because it has a boundary (the river, which Ayer interpreted as an image influenced by his knowledge of the Styx in Greek mythology), a light, and important beings. However, instead of being turned back at the boundary like Moody's experiencers, Ayer crosses it and yet returns. The beings are not welcomers or guides but unresponsive functionaries. Ayer's light is atypical in that it is very painful, yet apparently not fiery. Nor does it seem to have had a *mysterium tremendum* feel about it, for despite the light's responsibility for the government of the universe, Ayer also thinks it is only an indicator of something wrong, and that by righting the wrong he can get it to shut itself off. (It will be well to recall this case with its painful red light when we reach the discussion of the *Bardo Thodol* in Chapter Six.)

In contrast to painful scenes where the experiencer finds a comforting presence who aids her to escape, the case of "Vera" presents the disturbing scenario of a paradisal scene where a malevolent being is encountered. Vera was badly injured in an auto accident. After rising upward and going through a tunnel, she found herself in a bright, vivid place with many white pebbles (like a certain play area of her childhood), a blue sky, and green trees. She felt peaceful and calm. In the distance she could see what she thought was a church, though it had no steeple. She approached it, entered through large churchlike doors, and went down a red-carpeted aisle to the front. Each pew was filled with black-hooded people whose faces were not visible but whose hoods were lined with red. The altar held six silver goblets and a big silver jug. As she stood by the altar, a door opened to the right, and the Devil emerged. He told her to pick up a goblet; he picked up the jug and began to pour its contents—fire—into her goblet. Screaming, she dropped the goblet and ran out through the church doors, through a fence whose gate opened before her, then through another fence with iron bars that opened. The atmosphere was getting warmer and brighter. She awoke in the hospital.[93]

Vera interprets the scene with the Devil as God's judgment on her life: "the good and bad in her life...were of equal weight, and...she was being asked to suffer a drink from the goblet of fire in order to make the balance favorable. By refusing to comply with the devil's demand she was fated to suffer by way of compensation the physical disabilities that resulted from her car accident."[94] To her the "eucharist" was not a parody but a divinely given opportunity for purgation.

Frequency of Painful NDEs

How should painful cases be defined, and what is the proportion of such cases to radiant ones? There is no consensus among researchers. Maurice Rawlings, who must receive credit for calling attention to painful cases, identifies them as experiences of hell. He does not define hell precisely, but describes it as the "unquenchable fire," "the outer darkness," "a separation 'from the presence of the Lord.'" He also affirms the presence of demons in some hellish cases.

Rawlings claims that painful cases are much more frequent than other studies report. The first NDE he encountered—that of a patient in cardiac arrest—was largely a hellish one, but later the NDEr could remember only a pleasant paradisal scene. Rawlings theorizes that this blocking out of painful elements is common after NDEs and that, unless the stories are recorded very soon, investigators will tend to find only pleasant experiences. He has collected a number of hellish cases, but he has not done a systematic study; he claims only "large amounts of...negative material."[95]

Charles Garfield in a short essay published in 1979 summarizes the findings of his close, supportive contact with dying persons over a three-year period. Of 215 cancer patients, twenty-two percent told of states of altered consciousness. They fell into four groups:

> 1. One group experienced a powerful white light and celestial music...as well as an encounter...with a religious figure or deceased relative. The patients described these as "incredibly real, peaceful, and beautiful."
> 2. A second group experienced demonic figures, nightmarish images of great lucidity.
> 3. A third reported dreamlike images, sometimes "blissful," sometimes "terrifying," or alternating.
> 4. The final group experienced the Void or a tunnel or both. That is, the patients reported drifting endlessly in outer space or being encapsulated in a limited environment....A common theme...was the contrast between maximal freedom and maximal constraint with, in some cases, fluctuation from one to the other.[96]

Seeking to find out whether the findings of Moody and Elisabeth Kübler-Ross would be confirmed, Garfield interviewed in depth thirty-six persons who came close to death during heart attacks. Garfield comments that "no significant changes in content were expressed by any of [these] patients in three interviews conducted at weekly intervals following the event,"[97] which seems to discount Rawlings' theory of immediate repression. In summary, Garfield found almost as many reported "negative" visions as blissful ones.

In the Evergreen Study of 1981, investigators discovered some experiences they termed "negative," as well as the single "hellish" case cited above (page 84). The authors define a negative experience as "one that contains extreme fear, panic, or anger. It may also contain visions of demonic creatures that threaten or taunt the subject. In the hellish experience the subject witnesses the proverbial fiery pit and sees 'the devil himself.'"[98] The negative experiences were dual in nature, usually resolving into positive feelings of peace, although some had a negative episode at the end of a positive experience.[99] (Recall the case of Jer, page 8.) The negative cases totaled eleven out of fifty-five encounters with death, "with the remaining eighty percent either a positive experience or no experience at all."[100] The single hellish experience would amount to less than two percent of the *total* death-encounters, but we are not told what percentage of these fifty-five encounters involved NDEs, only that the percentage was "much higher" than Kenneth Ring's findings.[101]

George Gallup's 1982 study reveals a similar pattern: of those who had had a close brush with death, one percent told of having experienced hell or torment.[102] However, Gallup believes the one percent figure is misleading, for his study found quite a few (he does not say how many) other vaguely distressing experiences, including shadowy figures and floating in nothingness.[103] Gallup's questionnaire was unfortunately vague.

In Margot Grey's 1985 study of forty-one experiencers (thirty-two English, nine North American), the "negative" or "hellish" experiences were one-eighth of the total. As we saw, Grey is clear about what she means by these terms: a negative experience "is usually characterised by a feeling of extreme fear or panic...emotional and mental anguish....People report being lost and helpless and there is often an intense feeling of loneliness...desolation...."[104] Hellish experiences are defined as having all these elements, but greatly intensified. A sense of being dragged down by an evil force is frequent; demonic creatures are sometimes encountered, as are the wailing of tormented beings, the sounds of maddened beasts, or the traditional fire and devil.[105]

In the course of her researches since her own experience, P. M. H. Atwater has assembled a large file of NDE cases; she reports that of these, 105 out of more than seven hundred, a little over fourteen percent, are painful, a figure close to Margot Grey's.[106] Atwater defines an "unpleasant and/or hell-like experience" as follows:

> *Encounter with a threatening void or stark limbo or hellish purgatory, or scenes of a startling and unexpected indifference, even "hauntings" from one's own past. Usually experienced by those who seem to have deeply suppressed or repressed guilts, fears, and angers, and/or those who expect some kind of punishment or discomfort after death.*[107]

Barbara Rommer reports that of her 300 NDErs, nearly eighteen percent had painful, or "Less Than Positive" (LTP) experiences. She defines an LTP as "one which the experiencer interprets in part or whole to be frightening, because it elicits feelings of terror, despair, guilt and/or overwhelming aloneness."[108]

It can be seen that there is wide disagreement about the percentage of painful NDEs to total NDEs, ranging from findings of one percent to almost fifty percent, with four researchers finding between twelve and twenty percent. Causes of the disagreement may be sampling problems, selective repression of memories on the part of those with mixed experiences, unwillingness of survivors to talk about painful experiences, and/or reluctance of researchers in early studies to ask. At this point the matter must be left open.

Why Are Some NDEs Painful?

Another urgent issue, reflected in Atwater's definition and in some of the foregoing cases, is whether there are particular NDE circumstances or personality traits in the NDEr that help to explain why it developed into a painful experience. Because the issue naturally fosters anxiety, it is important to be cautious in answering this question; one size may not fit all. Pamela Kircher suggests that Void experiences may come to those who chose to be deeply isolated, keeping others at a distance by addiction, fearfulness, workaholism, anger, controllingness, rigidity, or a materialistic lifestyle. The Void is already operating in their lives, and only opens out further in an NDE or at death. This may well be the explanation for the cases she has encountered, but is not helpful in regard to experiencers such as Peggy Holladay who were already on a spiritual journey.

Margot Grey suggests that the explanation for painful NDEs may be that "negative emotions have become trapped in the psyche and released during the near-death experience."[109] Atwater, as we have seen, concurs: She sees repressed anxiety, guilt, and fear, or expectation of unpleasantness after death, as seeming to characterize those who have painful NDEs. She finds that heaven-like NDEs, on the other hand, are usually experienced by those who need reassurance that they are loved, that life matters, and that every effort has a purpose.[110] (Atwater does not claim that these characteristic patterns apply to all cases, simply that they predominate in her own sample.) The distinction, while helpful in regard to the factor of expectation of unpleasantness after death, is not otherwise clearcut (as Atwater herself acknowledges);[111] its capacity to predict which kind of experience a given person will have is limited. People who need reassurance of their worth and of life's meaning tend to be anxious people; in fact so many people show signs of suffering from submerged anxiety, guilt and/or fears, that one would expect a larger percentage of painful cases than are presently reported.

Rommer's explanation is similar to Atwater's: some people, given the message that they ought to be perfect, suffer from guilt and conflict. Some were raised with ideas of divine wrath and hellfire, which they project during the experience; some are caught up in self-pity. "Less than positive" experiences serve to awaken them, help them evaluate their lives, and bring about constructive change.[112] Rommer cites Nancy Evans Bush: "What we repress and refuse to acknowledge can control us. One of the cosmic laws is that one must do their shadow work....The dark experiences are an invitation, not an answer, to...find out who we really are...."[113] Rommer also observes that in her group, most of those who had inverted experiences had had a strong need to be in control.

These explanations reflect the good news that many who have painful NDEs do in fact respond to them as to a much-needed wake-up call. But since radiant experiences also trigger spiritual awakenings, we have not yet pinpointed the reasons why some are painful. Besides, some persons have had painful and radiant experiences in quick succession with no noticeable change of heart between them, and occasionally experiences will begin with peace and happiness then become painful, or vice versa.

Of the experienced out-of-body travelers I have cited, Monroe and Muldoon do not see their painful experiences as due to anxiety or guilt; rather they believe that on these occasions they had, for reasons not always known, simply ventured into realms where unhealthy entities congregated, a risk the frequent flier in other worlds must face. Whiteman, Yram, and Fox do see some of their painful encounters as triggered by their spiritual states.

The concept "like attracts like" suggests one possible explanation that deserves exploration, namely that anger just before or at the time of going out-of-body may attract angry entities. Muldoon suggests that his violent encounter with the newly-deceased abusive husband F. D. is such an instance (page 77); "Dee," an OBEr studied by Arvin Gibson, believes that the evil entity who pursued her during her OBE was attracted by her consuming hatred for her husband and living situation.[114] Howard Storm's persecuting entities may have been attracted by his fear that he was going crazy, fear that fed his rage at his wife's unresponsiveness to him (page 81).

While there may be important truth in this explanation, it cannot be reliably used to predict what class of experience one will have, as evidenced by Atwater's case of Alice Morrison-Mays. This NDEr, when out-of-body, went into a rage at the medical attendants surrounding her body, yet quickly moved into a blissful radiant experience.[115]

The same is true of atheism and belief that there is no survival of death. While strongly-held views on this issue may have influenced A. J. Ayer's NDE (page 89), causing the light he perceived to be painful, one can also find cases of other NDErs who were quite confirmed in their atheism before their experiences, but during it found themselves talking to Jesus or joyously entering the light.[116] Admittedly, atheists differ in the wholeheartedness of their commitment.

Scott Rogo offers several possible explanations for hellish NDEs. Some might be artifacts, "hallucinations produced by the witnesses' minds as a reaction to the violent physical ordeals...which are part...of normal resuscitation techniques."[117] Others might be dreams resulting from anesthetics or drug overdose.[118] Unfortunately, neither of these possibilities explains why an NDEr might at one time respond to these stresses with painful visions, but another time become peaceful or joyous.

In sum, at present we cannot name personality characteristics or NDE circumstances that reliably predict whether an NDE overall will be joyful or painful. There are a good many cases in which initial fear resolves into peace when the NDEr or OBEr accepts the situation, but, disturbingly and inexplicably, the opposite sometimes happens. With many more cases, and careful inquiries such as Atwater and Rommer are conducting into what the experiences mean to the NDErs, we may hope for more insight.

Painful Empathic Life Overviews

There is, however, another kind of sometimes painful NDE that is clearly and exactly linked to the experiencer's personal life: the expanded life review, or Empathic Life Overview (ELO). In ELOs, experiencers not only relive the events in their pasts but undergo an expansion of past consciousness to include others affected by their lives.

An early case (probably occurring during the 1920s) appears in the 1942 book *Release* by Starr Daily (pseudonym), a prison inmate who had a multi-stage NDE (or several NDEs). Trying to get himself committed to the prison hospital, he swallowed large amounts of strong soap and became dangerously ill:

> I sank into a swoon-like condition. From physical pain I passed into a state of...terror. I dreamed while I seemed wide awake. It was like a scroll or motion picture film....And the only pictures on it were the...people I had injured [directly or indirectly]. The minute history of my long criminal career was thus relived by me, plus all the small injuries I had inflicted unconsciously...every pang of suffering I had caused others was now felt by me...."[119]*

This vision was repeated no fewer than twelve times in the following weeks. In contrast to the series of pictures of individuals in Daily's experience, the empathic life overview of P. M. H. Atwater was felt as a total and literal reenactment, involving her whole surrounding environment.:

> For me, it was a total reliving of *every* thought..., *every* word..., and *every* deed...; *plus* the effect of each thought, word, and deed on everyone...who had ever come within my...sphere of influence...(including unknown passersby in the street); *plus* the effect...on weather, plants, animals, soil....No slip of the tongue or slur was missed....If there is such a thing as hell, as far as I am concerned this was hell....
>
> ...The old saying, "No man is an island," took on graphic proportions. There wasn't any heavenly St. Peter in charge. It was me judging me, and my judgment was most severe.[120]

The ELO gives the message that no boundaries isolate human beings in a special moral category from the rest of the world; all things are part of a "vast sea" in which they share in one another's energies.

---

*These empathic visions were not the turning-point of Daily's life; the crucial experience took place several weeks later when, during extreme stress from cold and hunger in solitary confinement, Daily had a vision of Christ. He then saw again all the persons he had injured, and gave them divine love.[121] (It may be noted that George Ritchie and Starr Daily became friends, and that Ritchie vouches for the transformation of Daily's life.)[122]

Perhaps the most vivid description of an ELO is that of Tom Sawyer (mentioned in Chapter Three) from Rochester, New York, who had an NDE in 1978 when the pickup truck he was repairing fell on him, suffocating him. He tells of experiencing a panorama of his entire life; he describes in detail a violent incident when he was nineteen and had an argument with a pedestrian who had nearly walked into Sawyer's pickup. Sawyer hit him thirty-two times. In the life overview, Sawyer not only re-experienced his own feelings of indignation but looked at his own flushed face out of the man's eyes, and felt the pain and humiliation of every one of those blows. More, Sawyer knew the man's age, knew the house where he lived, and knew he was drunk because he was in grief at the death of his wife. He knew the stool where the man had sat in a bar and the path he had taken to the scene of the altercation. He experienced intimate personal details of the man's life.[123] Sawyer also describes profound interaction with plant life on other occasions; he felt the response of a tree he had once loved. The same was true of animal life, he reports, even to tiny insects.[124] All things affect all other things. "As this takes place, you have total knowledge...you are your own spiritual teacher."[125]

The potential for pain as well as for joy in such interaction may be virtually unlimited. Tom Sawyer's life overview suggests that not only do empathic experiencers literally feel the impact of their own thoughts and deeds, but may even feel the *prior* experiences of those they interact with as they find that they are profoundly united to, or even one with, their neighbors.

Betty Eadie's empathic life overview speaks not only of feeling her impact on others but of the next stage, the effects these others have on still others (seen in the case of Starr Daily as well). "I was shown the 'ripple effect'....I saw how I had often wronged people and how they had often turned to others and committed a similar wrong. This chain continued from victim to victim, like a circle of dominoes....[M]y pain multiplied and became unbearable." She goes on to speak of Christ's compassion to her in her severe self-judgment; he showed her that the ripple effect also worked in situations of goodwill, spreading goodness.[126]

As we have noted, David Lorimer links such ELOs to experiences of telepathy, special atmospheres attached to places or objects, and to mystics' sense of participation in all things. He sees all these phenomena as evidence of a universal "empathic resonance," the basis of an "ethic of interconnectedness"[127] (above, page 54).

Aftereffects of Painful NDEs

Barbara Rommer reports that nearly all her experiencers "come back from the other side affirming that the main reason we are here is to learn and to practice unconditional love,"[128] having increased reverence for life,[129] and believing more strongly in God. "The bottom line with all of these experiences is love."[130] In her study, the percentages of certain life-affirming changes are not the same for NDErs and Less-than-Positive (LTP) experiencers; for example, decreased fear of death is about seventy-eight percent of NDErs versus about sixty-three percent of LTPrs).[131] However, she reports that all LTP experiences she studied are transformative.

P. M. H. Atwater gives a somewhat different picture. She reports that slightly over fifty percent of painful NDEs issue in changes of the same kind as occur with radiant NDEs: capacity for detached love, tendency to live in the present, enhanced psychic abilities, change in personality style, reduction of anxieties, difficulties in communication, and view of earth life as the temporary embodiment of an immortal child of God. However, "the others exhibited traits that ranged from the numbness you find with people who are in a state of shock to avoidance and denial, confusion, and/or occasional bouts with fatigue and depression."[132] The individual's way of viewing the experience is an important factor; Atwater found that "[m]en were less willing than women to view an unpleasant and/or hell-like scenario in a positive fashion and take steps to make constructive changes in their lives because of it." One reason for the difference between these researchers' findings may be that Rommer and a number of her experiencers are in a support group.

Two examples (independent of Rommer's and Atwater's studies): for years Nancy Evans Bush's response to her "yin/yang" experience was deep anxiety, which she suppressed. Matters changed when she encountered NDE studies and the Christian mystical tradition. She has come to see painful NDEs such as her own meaningless-void experience as "black holes" through which one may travel to reach a new universe.[133] Patricia, in spite of being physically paralyzed after awakening from her nightmarish NDE of sexually charged assault (page 78), took a strongly positive stance, laboring to regain physical movement and accepting the partial disabilities that remained. She affirms life, affirms many paths to God, and looks forward to the afterlife.[134]

Summary

It is clear that the picture of "the NDE" of peace or radiance is challenged by these comparatively few reports of painful NDEs and OBEs, which present the disturbing possibility of a painful life after death. Furthermore, except for Empathic Life Overviews, there seems no way to predict reliably why a given person may have a painful instead of a peaceful or radiant NDE. This does not mean, however, that chance necessarily has the last word. We shall explore this issue more in the concluding chapters.

Five

A CHALLENGE TO TRANSCENDENCE: THIS-WORLDLY INTERPRETATIONS

W E WILL NOW LOOK AT SEVERAL THIS-WORLDLY interpretations of the NDE. While most of these theories were intended to undercut the idea of survival of death, some of them can be seen as complementary to survivalist ones.

Reductionistic Interpretations

The Claimed Incoherence of Survival

One objection rules out NDE accounts as evidence for survival on the grounds that to experience death and return is a contradiction in terms. It is frequently said that the fact that NDErs return to consciousness shows that they had not actually died, for death is by definition permanent: "no traveller returns." It follows that we can learn nothing from NDEs about any existence after death. Some critics hold that all ideas and images derive from physical existence: "The state of death is impossible to conceptualize. Therefore, since being dead cannot even be imagined, a void evolve[s] that must be filled with superstitions, fantasies, and religious and poetic creations."[1] Christopher Cherry points out that David Hume had anticipated this position: "By what arguments or analysis can we prove any state of existence which no one ever saw, *and which no way resembles any that ever was seen?*"[2]

This argument actually offers two objections: (a) By definition, death is permanent. Therefore, no one can return from actual death and tell the living about it. (b) It is impossible to describe the state of death in meaningful concepts, because we have no information or experience to make them meaningful.

Now, one may choose to define death as permanent, meaning that the body does not revive. In that case, NDErs do not return from a state of death. But it is a mistake to conclude that no one whose body has failed to revive can return in any sense at all—such as through reincarnation, mediumistic trance, or an apparition. Such a conclusion means that *in the definition of death as permanent, one has smuggled in the idea that death is total extinction of consciousness.* It is not legitimate simply to define death as extinction, for this is what our inquiry is all about. As Cherry says, when the question "Are Near-Death Experiences really suggestive of life after death?" is answered in the negative because "no traveller returns," one is merely begging the question.[3] Carl Becker offers the same insight.[4] Most writers who use this death-by-definition argument are assuming a materialist view of body and mind. But as we will see, there are other body-mind views that deserve consideration. The argument falls, and the question is left open.

Therefore, it is very possible that NDErs, although by this definition they have not died, might in their near approach to death have experienced something of what the dying undergo. It is also possible that, just as NDEs vary due to individual and cultural influence, the experiences of the dying (and the deceased?) vary likewise.

The alternative explanations for NDEs are: (a) NDErs' accounts are merely "religious and poetic creations" based on earth experience; (b) they describe actual afterdeath states; or (c) they combine elements from both.

Psychological Interpretations

Another reductionistic objection to NDEs as foreshadowings of afterdeath states claims that the various elements of NDEs can be adequately explained as psychological defense strategies against the threat of extinction. One of these, the theory of depersonalization, comes from psychologist Russell Noyes and colleagues, who have been engaged in NDE research from the early 1970s onward. In one study Noyes and Roy Kletti collected 114 accounts, mostly of survivors of accidents. They analyzed the eighty-five completed questionnaires for frequency of various factors. Of those who believed themselves about to die, the frequency ranged from eighty percent experiencing altered passage of time, to twenty-five percent perceiving voices, music, or sounds.[5]

Although the most frequent factor in their cases was the perceived slowing of outer time with speedup of thoughts, what seemed most significant to Noyes and Kletti were the experiencers' sense of detachment, feeling of unreality, and lack of emotion. The authors concluded that depersonalization was the most prominent factor (among accident victims), and that it was very similar to depersonalization among psychiatric patients.[6] To depersonalized patients the world appears foreign and dreamlike; objects sometimes seem diminished in size and flat; mental imagery is pale and colorless or nonexistent; the patients cannot feel pain or pleasure, love or hate. They feel strangers to themselves. "Systematic investigation of subjective responses to life-threatening danger has confirmed the development of depersonalization, hyperalertness, and mystical consciousness."[7] Noyes and Kletti see NDE depersonalization as an adaptation to the pain and suffering of dying, enabling experiencers either to save themselves or deal with the brutal truth of extinction.[8]

The authors acknowledge that there are differences between survivors' experiences and those of pathologically depersonalized persons. Near-death survivors generally report heightened rather than dulled perceptions, as well as vivid mental images. Further, whereas the depersonalized are distressed by their emotional blunting, survivors are gratified to find themselves calm in otherwise terrifying situations.[9] In a later essay Noyes acknowledges that the depersonalization cluster cannot account for all NDEs; this cluster is the opposite of the hyperalertness and mystical consciousness clusters.[10] However, he and his colleagues do not maintain that these differences undermine their interpretation but rather "may add to our understanding of this curious disorder."[11]

But critics have objected that experiences of joy and mystical union, of coming "home," *do* undermine the theory, for depersonalization among psychiatric patients involves feelings of confusion over the reality and identity of the self,[12] and causes distress. In addition, critics have challenged features of Noyes and Kletti's questionnaires. For example, experiences of another world were classed as a sense of unreality,[13] which imposes the researchers' reductionistic interpretations on the data. The same is true of their reductionistic treatment of mystical and cosmic consciousness.[14] Other critics point out that depersonalization characteristically involves a split between an observing and a functioning self, a split not found in out-of-body experiences (at least it is rare in NDEs).[15]

Another challenge to Noyes' theory is its neglect of paranormal features in NDEs, such as the recently-deceased welcomers in Peak-in-Darien cases,[16] and veridical observations like Maria's report of the tennis shoe on the ledge.

It should be acknowledged, however, that in a later essay Noyes describes and comments favorably on the changes that NDEs can bring about in the lives of experiencers, such as reducing the fear of death, increased a sense of the meaningfulness of life, and resolving psychological crises. This essay gives the message that the NDE is a potentially valuable experience rather than a "curious disorder."[17] However, to my knowledge Noyes and his colleagues have not given up their theory of depersonalization as a device to deal with the prospect of extinction.

Another problem is that painful NDEs (little discussed at the time Noyes' theory was presented) are hardly wish-fulfilling fantasies to quell the terrors of extinction. Defenders of the theory might reply that painful NDEs are also psychological productions, expressions of suppressed guilt or rage rather than attempts at self-reassurance. This may in fact be true for some who have NDEs, but others such as Ritchie were mere onlookers (pages 57, 80). It might be added that the "everlasting void" experiences could not be called self-punishment, since both punishment and reward have lost all meaning.

Bruce Greyson suggests that several of the main elements of NDEs may be devices serving an ego threatened by death. When the NDEr gives up worldly attachments, he or she may regress to uterine feelings of peace and cosmic unity before ego boundaries were formed. The personality changes following the NDE would then result from the increased openness of childhood. The OBE, rather than being an accurate memory, may in some cases be a later elaboration by one who cannot tolerate being out-of-control. The Being of Light may benefit the OBEr psychologically by manifesting unconscious parts of the self; the life overview may benefit the self by giving distance from imminent death.[18] Greyson does not present these ideas as incompatible with genuine paranormal phenomena in NDEs,[19] or the idea of NDEs as glimpses of a transcendent realm.

Greyson's suggestions have merits. It is true that transformed NDErs sometimes demonstrate childlike traits, with ability to live in the moment. It is also true, as we have seen, that despite the justly celebrated life-transformations, there are some NDErs who use their experiences egotistically. However, the attempt to explain apparently transcendent features in terms of the ego serving its needs *during* the experience (without denying the possibility of the paranormal and the transcendent) faces difficulties. Greyson suggests that the Being of Light is a beneficial manifestation of unconscious parts of the self, which may well be true. But he also seems to put this manifestation at the service of the ego. However, according to NDErs, the transcendent self is serene precisely because the endangered body and insecure ego are eclipsed. It is hard to see how the ego can be abdicating control at the same time that it is shoring up its insecurity.

Another psychological interpretation explains the tunnel-and-light as a re-experience of birth. Carl Sagan expands upon Stanislav Grof's studies with psychedelic drugs in which four phases of psychedelic experience closely parallel the process of birth. Sagan proposes that in the womb everyone experiences the bliss of union with one's universe, goes through a tunnel toward a light during birth, and soon thereafter sees fuzzy-haloed godlike beings who have enormous power, namely the medical personnel. The phenomena of NDEs are thus only the result of an emergence into consciousness of these powerful forgotten memories.[20]

Carl Becker demolishes Sagan's central point by pointing out that the child in the birth canal does not actually move a long distance (its length is about four inches); the crown of the baby's head, not the face, is foremost; and the head, with eyes closed, is pressed tightly against the lips of the uterus, blocking out all light. It has also been argued that newborns have poor eyesight.[21] (In fact, as we shall see in Chapter Ten, some of them appear to see a great deal very clearly, sometimes from outside the body, but this view would hardly support Sagan's position.)

Sagan's "nothing-but" explanation of NDEs is out of keeping with the tone of the work of Grof, who does not reduce psychedelic experiences to birth memories, but holds that the reliving of the birth experience gives access to alternate realities.[22] However, the analogy between birth and NDEs should not be dismissed. We will see later on that Grof's studies of the birth pattern of psychedelic experience can be helpful in interpreting painful NDEs.

Ronald Siegel proposes that specific images, particularly of deceased welcomers and religious figures, are "retrieved memory images (or fantasy images) that were alive and well when originally stored."[23] Citing Hughlings Jackson and L. J. West's "perceptual-release" theory, Siegel points out that, ordinarily, many normal memories are suppressed as our consciousness is occupied with what we perceive with our senses. If this sensory flow is decreased or impaired, past perceptions will be released as fantasies, dreams, or hallucinations. This process can be compared to a man in a firelit room looking out the window at the sunset. As darkness falls the outdoor scene gradually fades, while the reflections on the window of the firelit interior, appearing to be outside, take their place.[24] Susan Blackmore also cites Jackson's work, comparing the situation of the sensorially deprived dying person to that of two miners who were trapped in total darkness for six days, during which time they saw lights, doorways, marble stairs, radiant figures, and a beautiful garden.[25] Moody suggests that isolation may be the major factor in some NDEs, adding that it does not explain away NDE visions any more than does the approach of death, but that both may be ways of entering new realms of consciousness.[26]

Since NDEs are often tailored to the individual, it seems quite likely that perceptual release is involved in NDE images. But to claim that NDEs are nothing but perceptual release will not do; clearly it cannot explain clairvoyant perceptions of this-worldly scenes or Peak-in-Darien welcomers, nor does it explain factors foreign to the experiencer's culture. Besides, some NDErs have had otherworldly visions without sensory deprivation; one of Moody's NDErs saw herself in a ship heading toward a shore thronged with welcomers, while still seeing the hospital maternity room.[27]

The perceptual-release theory also fails to explain Ring and Cooper's accounts of visual-type NDEs or OBEs in persons blind since birth. While the portions of their brains that deal with sight may not be themselves damaged, such persons had never had visual-type images, even in dreams; there could have been none stored up to be released.

These objections to reductionistic theories do not mean that the visionary scenes and figures in NDEs are necessarily what they literally appear to be. The point is simply that NDE visions cannot be reduced to subconscious projection, to "superstitions, fantasies, and religious and poetic creations."

Chemical and Neurological Interpretations

Some reductionistic thinkers see psychoactive drugs as a decisive factor in forming NDE images; Siegel, for example, claims that drugs cause the visions through their effects on the neurons and other structures of the body. "The bright light is characteristic of many types of mental imagery and is the result of stimulation of the central nervous system that mimics the effects of light on the retina."[28] Patterns seen in psychedelic trips, like the light and tunnel of NDEs, "are partially produced by entoptic phenomena (structures within the eye) and electrical activity in the visual system."[29]

As an example of a neurological explanation, Susan Blackmore suggests that the tunnel effect is produced when lack of oxygen (in NDEs) or psychedelics causes a disinhibition, a breakdown in the pattern of control of firing, in many neurons in that part of the brain that processes visual information. Disinhibition causes the cells to fire randomly. "[F]ar more cells are devoted to the centre of the visual field than to the edges....if all the cells start firing randomly, then there will be more in the middle, gradually fading toward the outside." This would look like a tunnel. The reason the experiencer seems to be moving forward through the tunnel is that the visual system is biased towards movements in an outward direction. Another possible explanation for the apparent forward movement is that if the "neural noise" caused by the random firing gradually increased, the light at the center would seem to get larger and brighter, thus seeming closer, until the experiencer seems to have entered the light.[30] (Blackmore acknowledges that oxygen starvation is not necessarily the only cause of an NDE.[31])

Elsewhere, Blackmore mentions variants in tunnel imagery—bricks, cobblestones, leaves, bands of gray, and luminous vapor—but does not offer a connection between her neurological explanation and the variant imagery. Some images, such as Elizabeth D'Espérance's dark path pitted with deep holes and overhung with huge rocks (pages 62–63), are even harder to fit into the theory. Presumably these variants are created by the NDEr on the basis of personal experience, but we are not told how they relate to the neurological events.

The tunnel does not seem to be found in all cultures, as one would expect if it were due to human anatomy. Blackmore reports that her pilot study by mail of NDEs in India found that thirty-eight percent reported tunnels or dark places, but because her sample was so small, this translates into three NDErs, only one of whom described a tunnel, and that in response to Blackmore's followup questionnaire. Furthermore, all her respondents were English-speaking, clearly influenced by Western culture.[32] Satwant Pasricha and Ian Stevenson in their studies in north and south India investigated forty-five NDE cases, but found no tunnels. They (with coauthors Allan Kellehear and Emily Cook) make the point that tunnels are common technological forms in certain societies, but might not appear in low-tech cultures influenced by primal religions.[33]

Daniel Carr proposes that the neurotransmitter chemicals released in the brain as a result of stress, particularly the enkephalins, beta-endorphin and the hormone ACTH, affect the limbic lobe of the brain and lead to several features of NDEs: memory recall, depersonalization, intense emotions, and hallucinations. In many brain areas, enkephalins suppress the firing of neurons, but in the hippocampus (crucial for the "laying down" of memories), they inhibit an inhibition. Therefore, they become the body's own psychedelics.[34]

Carr's essay has been much quoted by reductionists, but he is not himself a reductionist. He holds that these opioids of the body are not necessarily the only or even primary factors in creating NDE phenomena, since they do not explain the ESP that sometimes occurs, nor are they relevant to the philosophic or religious meaning of death.[35]

Melvin Morse also stresses the importance of neurological factors, citing Wilder Penfield's work. As with Penfield's brain surgery patients, who described feeling out-of-body and vividly reliving past scenes when he electronically stimulated areas of their brains, Morse suggests that the out-of-body and life overviews of NDEs are triggered when neuron connections in the brain's temporal lobe are activated by seratonin (released by stress), and/or by excess carbon dioxide and insufficient oxygen.[36] Morse does acknowledge that this explanation does not fit all cases.[37] In fact, far from reducing NDEs to neurological events, Morse suggests in his popular writing that the Sylvian fissure in the temporal lobe is the "seat of the soul," the area of contact with the Divine.[38]

We might notice also that the empathic sharing of others' experience in some NDE life overviews is not mentioned by Penfield's patients, nor are there "flashforwards" of events in the future. Since there is a good deal of evidence that vivid reliving of past scenes is correlated to temporal lobe activity, it is quite likely that the temporal lobes have a part in at least some NDEs. But the ESP in some life overviews, and the flatliner case of Reynolds, should give us second thoughts before we reduce NDEs to temporal lobe activity.

It is important to distinguish between the valid insights this-worldly explanations offer and the "nothing-but" reductionism of some of the authors' materialist worldviews. Doing so makes it possible for those who take survival seriously to judge each explanation on its own merits without feeling a need to demolish it. For example, there is no doubt that there are similarities between psychedelic experiences and NDEs. Since brain chemistry is involved in the effects of psychedelics, it seems likely that it has a part, at least at times, in the making of NDEs. But this is not to say that it tells the whole story.

It is when critics insist on the "nothing-but" that they neglect the paranormal elements and/or do violence to the numinous tone of some NDE accounts. For example, Siegel's claim that the NDEr's perception of the light is due to the "stimulation of the central nervous system that mimics the effects of light on the retina" is very inadequate in accounting for the feelings of bliss in the light. The claim also fails to deal with the cases in which bedside attendants see the light. Blackmore's assertion that enkephalins and endorphins explain the bliss of the mystical union[39] fails to account for the sense of a living presence enfolding one in unutterable love.

However, a claim that such neurotransmitters have a part in NDErs' initial feelings of peace and euphoria might be correct. Even in granting so much, however, one must be cautious, for an injection of endorphins apparently produces drowsiness, not the rapid, clear thinking NDErs often claim.[40]

Implied Metaphysical Issues

We have seen that there are issues of worldview implied in such explanations, issues which most reductionistic interpreters do not really deal with. They assume a monistic (one-world) materialist worldview, and thus they consider that physical, psychological, and sociological factors in NDEs are enough to explain them. Most of these critics ignore reports of paranormal elements and the history of survival research (see Chapter Eleven). Siegel, who does mention them, dismisses over a hundred years of survival research in two or three pages, even resorting to ridicule.[41]

Susan Blackmore shows more philosophical sophistication than many other critics. She holds to a materialistic monism: there is only one world, one kind of reality, because two completely different kinds of being cannot interact. Thus she rejects the dualism of mind and matter in which a soul might be separable from the body. Furthermore, she points out, the Principle of Parsimony requires that scientific explanations should not call for more entities than are needed.[42]

Blackmore's materialistic view is not typical, being influenced by Buddhist spirituality. But she does not consider other monistic worldviews, such as pantheism (all things are aspects of God) or panpsychism (everything has some degree of awareness). In such views, body and mind can be two things (duality) closely linked, without being two essentially different *kinds* of things (dualism). The issue of whether consciousness can exist separate from the body—that is, whether a soul is an "entity" that is "needed" to explain NDE phenomena— should not be determined by what any worldview declares to be impossible but by the evidence.

Flat EEGs as Evidence

There are many NDE accounts in which the body is pronounced dead, yet the NDEr finds her consciousness hovering above the scene, often thinking more rapidly and clearly than ever, seemingly independent of the brain. Afterwards, of course, the body revives, suggesting to some that during the period of apparent separation, the brain was still at work.

Is there any documented evidence that this seeming independence is what it appears to be? Various thinkers have suggested that the issue could be settled by a "flatliner" case, an EEG reading showing no brain activity during an OBE. (Moody, however, from the outset expressed doubt that a flat EEG would settle anything.[43])

Rumors of supposedly impressive flatliner cases circulated for years, but documented accounts were elusive until Michael Sabom in his Atlanta Study reported the case of Pam Reynolds. In August 1991 Reynolds underwent a daring form of brain surgery to remove a giant aneurysm from the base of her skull. Her skull was opened, her blood was circulated through a heart-lung machine and cooled, and her heart was stopped. "As Pam's heart arrested, her brain waves flattened into complete electrocerebral silence."[44] Twenty minutes later, even the brain stem (whose auditory nerve center was monitored by molded speakers in her ears) had ceased all activities: "Total brain shutdown."[45] Then the head of the operating table was tilted up, the blood was drained out of her body, causing the aneurism sac to collapse and enabling the surgeon to tie it and cut it off. Shortly after warmed blood began to be reinfused into her body, the electrogram (monitoring the brain stem) and the EEG screen showed that brain activity had resumed.[46] Her EEG had been flat for at least half an hour.

Reynolds lost consciousness when anesthetized, but became aware of leaving her body at the time the surgeon began cutting open her skull with a bone saw, whose noise she heard despite the blocking of her ears. In her account she tells of observing equipment and surgical personnel from close above with very focussed and clear vision, including the small bone saw and its case, which she described with reasonable accuracy. She heard a conversation about the cardiovascular surgeon's difficulty in finding a large enough femoral vein (confirmed in the records). The potential objection that the NDE took place before or after the flat line was being recorded[47] was countered in Reynolds' case, because without a perceptible break in consciousness she began an extensive, transcendent NDE including tunnel, light, and welcomers. She returned through the tunnel and gathered courage to jump into her body "like diving into a pool of ice water....When I came back, they were playing [rock music]."[48] The rock was played as the surgeon's younger assistants did the closing surgical duties. While one cannot rule out a period of complete unconsciousness after return and before awakening in the body, Reynolds' narrative overwhelmingly suggests that her experience encompassed the time when her brain was totally shut down.

Reynolds' intense spiritual consciousness during a period when her brain was completely nonfunctioning indicates strongly that, although consciousness is closely correlated to brain function, it does not originate from the brain any more than a TV program originates from the television set.

Objections to Evidential Cases

Unlike most critics, Susan Blackmore does examine the evidence for paranormal perception during the out-of-body phase of NDEs. She comments on Kimberly Clark [Sharp]'s account of Maria's tennis shoe and Sabom's cardiac patient who after his NDE was able to give fine details on the dial of the defibrillator (page 46). She dismisses both, suggesting that it had not been established that such a defibrillator was in fact used, or that the man may have learned details about the defibrillator later and unconsciously incorporated them into his memory.[49] (She does not comment on another case of Sabom's, involving a heart patient's report of being out-of-body and seeing in the hall his wife, son, and daughter whom he could not have seen normally. His wife corroborated their positions.)[50] The tennis shoe story also fails to impress her. Blackmore reports that she wrote to Clark Sharp (who was ill at the time, as she acknowledges) but received no replies.[51] "I have been unable to get any further information."[52] She, therefore, concludes that because the need to prove that what is seen is real "is so strong there is always the suspicion that the claims may be exaggerated or even invented."[53]* She does not deal with any distortions that may result from a strong desire to prove such an experience *unreal*.

Blackmore's suggestion that the case was invented by Clark Sharp is disturbing. Clark Sharp is a person of responsible position who has been in the public eye for some years, and the burden of proof would surely lie with anyone who asserted or suggested that she is lying. But Blackmore offers no evidence about Clark Sharp's character to support this innuendo of dishonesty. Such a response to a difficult case suggests that in a pinch Blackmore could find a way to evade any inconvenient piece of evidence. In fact, in an earlier work she suggests that she might be willing to use this argument if necessary.[56]

Blackmore also allows that visual perceptions in NDErs born blind would tell against her theories, citing several claimed cases available only in summary. Since no carefully-studied and verified case was available at the time of her writing, she concludes that the "lore" of the blind NDEr who could see during the experience is no more than lore.[57] Yet Vicki Umipeg's case is no rumor but a detailed first-person report; it emphatically asserts that she was blinded at birth and had never had visual-type images before her NDEs, but that during her NDEs, especially the otherworldly portions, she had abundant, clear and powerful images. Whether or not every detail of her account of the visions is accurate, this extraordinary central claim is unlikely to be a matter of unconscious embroidery.

It seems evident from Blackmore's repeated requests for "further information" that she provides an example of what Jule Eisenbud calls the "ever-receding horizon"[58]—better and stronger evidence is always asked for, but when the better and stronger case or experiment is offered, it is not accepted, and still stronger evidence is demanded. It seems likely that no evidence, however strong, will ever be accepted.

---

*In an attempt to give an ordinary explanation to this case, in 1994 two students, Hayden Ebbern and Sean Mulligan, checked out the Harborview Medical Center where the tennis

In summary, we may say that although this-worldly interpretations give valuable insight, they are not adequate explanations for all NDEs, and that paranormal activity, at least, is sometimes involved. Such NDEs do show that consciousness transcends the body's limitations.

There are also signs that certain NDEs transcend even cultural limitations, reflecting afterlife ideas incompatible with the NDEr's worldview (recall Ritchie's visions of spirits that are addicted or angry). Might such experiences give us transcultural pictures of what the afterlife really is? Before considering that question, it is important to look more closely at the issue of cultural influence and at the motifs that certain Western NDEs have in common with ancient religious traditions. Therefore, Part II will examine some afterdeath themes in certain Western and non-Western religions.

---

shoe event occurred. They found that when one stood at a certain distance from the entrance (necessary in their case because of a construction fence blocking closer access) it was easily possible to see a shoe they had placed on a third-floor window-ledge beside the entrance. They also found that it was easy to see the shoe from various points inside the room. They therefore concluded that Maria either saw the shoe in the ordinary way after her admission but before her heart attack, or heard other hospital personnel discussing it and unconsciously worked it into her account of her OBE.[54] However, their reconstruction is strained. To begin with, the shoe was not on the ledge of Maria's room near the entrance, but in an entirely different part of the hospital (the north wing), making it highly unlikely that she, a heart patient between cardiac arrests, would have been able to move about and enter another room to see it. Clark Sharp informed me that the ledges on the north wing, where she found the shoe, were differently located in relation to the windows than were the ledges on the entrance side where the students experimented, and that one could indeed not see the shoe either from below or from inside the room without pressing against the window as she had. Thus the possibility of a conversation about the shoe on the part of hospital attendants was virtually nil. (She also informed me that she had recently come back into contact with two of the persons who were present when the shoe was presented to Maria, and expected to get statements from them.)[55]

PART II

NDEs AND AFTERLIFE THEME
IN RELIGION: PARALLELS

Preface to Part II ⌐

WHY LOOK AT WORLD RELIGIONS?

LTHOUGH THE PICTURE PRESENTED BY NDES IS FAR
more complex than it first seemed, the familiar recurrent themes,
which are not found in ordinary dreams and hallucinations—the
OBE, the dark tunnel, the light, the welcomers, the radiant world, the
return—remain a challenge. Many of these features come as a great surprise
to the experiencers, upsetting their worldviews. It is not surprising that
many people are still convinced that "the NDE" is what awaits most if not
all of us at death.

What possible sources might there be for these recurrent features? It is
well known in religious studies that religious experiences are influenced by
the views of the experiencer's group and culture. For example, Western
NDEs who see Jesus are usually Christians; there are exceptions, but since
even nonreligious Westerners are familiar with the figure of Jesus, Christian
cultural influence could still be at work in these cases. In order to gauge

how extensive religiocultural influence might be, we need to look at afterlife themes in the religious background of contemporary experiences.

We also need a wider context within which to evaluate the themes. Some thinkers have found this context in world religions,* where they find obscure texts with descriptions of the afterlife that include some of the same motifs as Western NDEs, confirming for them that NDEs give us pictures of what really happens after death.

In this section we will also look at a few samples of religious views of the afterlife that almost surely did *not* influence contemporary Westerners in any ordinary way. The appearance of familiar NDE themes in the afterlife views of an alien culture would not necessarily prove that these elements are part of a real afterlife, although they might give some support to such a picture. But we must be alert to contradictions and incompatibilities between ancient and contemporary versions of a given theme. We must also consider the possibility that common motifs stem not from experiences of a real afterlife but from psychological bases in human nature.

---

*I use the term "religion" in Joachim Wach's sense of a spiritual tradition that has its own characteristic social grouping, practices, and spiritual ideas.[1] Some members of the groups described here may understand religion in a narrower sense.

Six

SOME AFTERLIFE VIEWS IN RELIGIONS OF THE WEST

T HERE HAVE BEEN VARIOUS RELIGIOUS MOVEMENTS IN THE
West with particular concern for the afterlife, but none, perhaps,
whose views show greater overlap with the phenomena of NDEs
than Spiritualism, Theosophy and Christianity. Several of the experiencers
discussed above held to the views of Spiritualism and Theosophy, or
entertained New Age ideas influenced by them, while others knew very little
about these movements. Many NDErs held Christian views; indeed,
Christianity has influenced almost every adult and school-age child in our
culture. How far can the impressive recurring images in NDEs be traced to
such background ideas?

Spiritualism

Spiritualism in some form is found in many traditional societies. Here I will
concentrate on the movement that arose in the United States in 1848,
spread internationally, retrenched, and continues today.

The central idea is, of course, that human beings are more than our
physical bodies, that we survive our deaths, and that communication
between the living and the dead can and does take place. The nature of this
afterlife depends on the character of the person, according to Emanuel
Swedenborg, whose writings influenced the movement. Spirits whose
minds center upon love and goodness are drawn to others of the same
nature; those who are selfish and cruel are likewise attracted to one
another.[1] This principle, mentioned in Part I, has been called the law that
"like attracts like."

Spiritualists hold that all human beings have a spiritual body, which
leaves the physical one during sleep and out-of body experiences, but
remains connected to it by an elastic cord. At death the cord breaks. Persons

who have been strongly attached to material things and have ignored or rejected spiritual realities are likely to be unaware that they have died, for their spirit body seems quite substantial to them. They may remain "earthbound," haunting the places and/or clinging to the living persons with whom they were emotionally involved, sometimes trying to make contact. Other types of earthbound personalities are some who died by violence, and find themselves compulsively re-enacting the traumas of their deaths. Spiritualists may gather in "rescue circles" to communicate with earthbound souls, explain to them their true situation, and encourage them to go on to higher things.[2] Depraved souls tend to gravitate to one another and exist in a domain of fog or darkness (some may be earthbound as well), where their evil natures become their own punishment. According to Spiritualism, persons seeking to communicate with deceased relatives must be on guard against depraved spirits, for they are deceitful and will attempt to impersonate the loved ones. Furthermore, unhealthy spirits can attach themselves to living persons (even strangers) who are psychically open, influencing or even possessing them, sometimes resulting in sudden addictions or outbursts of violence. These realms of misery, ignorance, and darkness are not necessarily permanent: all their denizens are free to change their ways and leave, and certain highly evolved spirits are always available to offer help.[3]

The earthbound and the depraved souls exist in the lowest two of a series of planes above the surface of the earth, a conception that first appears (in modern times) in the trance dictations of Andrew Jackson Davis.[4] The deceased who choose to open themselves to goodness and spiritual truth move upward to the "Summerland," a paradise created by the thoughts of those living there. They create beauty, guide and rear the souls of deceased children, seek knowledge, and support one another. These positively oriented beings will move upward through further planes as they evolve. However, it is also thought that certain evolved spirits remain in contact with (though not clinging to) the living, as spirit guides. Evolving spirits eventually leave earth behind and are united with the Divine.[5] It has been pointed out that these pervasive ideas of spiritual growth reflect nineteenth-century concerns with "progress" and evolution.

A minority of spiritualists in the United States, England, and elsewhere also affirm reincarnation. Belief in reincarnation is the norm in the spiritualism of France and Latin America, which was influenced by the writings of Allan Kardec (Hippolyte L.D. Rivail, 1804–1869), a French investigator. Trance communications, some of them evidential, in these cultures often relate present personality traits to former incarnations.

Theosophy

The worldview of Theosophy takes its rise from the writings of the Russian noblewoman Helena Petrovna Blavatsky (1831–1891), who traveled and read widely, absorbing ideas from Buddhism, Hindu Vedanta, Gnosticism, Neoplatonism, Kabbalism,[6] and Spiritualism. In New York in 1875, she and attorney Henry Steele Olcott (1832–1907) founded the Theosophical Society, a few years later moving their headquarters to India. Influential later thinkers were social activist Annie Besant (1847–1933) and clergyman C. W. Leadbeater (1854?–1934).[7] After 1891 the movement fractured.

Theosophy is not a monolithic system, but certain beliefs about the afterlife, strongly influenced by Vedanta, are held in common by most Theosophists. In the beginning, the core of the person, called the Pilgrim, separates itself from the Divine and lives for many eons on different planes gathering experience, finally returning to the Divine. The physical world, where the Pilgrim incarnates repeatedly, is only one of these planes. The physical body or "sheath" is connected to four others: the etheric body or energy field, the astral body or emotional self, the mental body, and the buddhic or intuitive body. The core of the Pilgrim is the Being-Awareness-Bliss that is the Divine within us, our point of union with the All.[8]

Shortly before death the events of one's physical life pass before one's consciousness. At the moment of death, the spiritual self (the nonphysical bodies and the divine core) separates from the physical, and the silver cord or line of force that linked it to the physical then breaks. The etheric sheath soon dissolves, but the astral form and the "higher" components continue. As in Spiritualist belief, the soul will gravitate either to one of the dark Lower Astral planes or the Summerland-like Upper Astral. But eventually the emotions of all those on the astral planes will work themselves out and the entity will fall into a sleep called the "second death." The astral body will be shed and dissolve and the entity will go on to an even wider life, a heaven called Devachan. Here, after a long period of detached contemplation and creativity, the Pilgrim is ready for another incarnation with further learning.[9]

There are exceptions to this general pattern. Occasionally the discarded astral body may fail to dissolve, instead maintaining a dim life as an "astral shell," which may attach itself to a medium or other congenial living host, purporting to be the full surviving spirit.[10] Also, some entities, after brief lives or violent deaths, may not go through this entire cycle but reincarnate quickly, still involved in memories and concerns from their former lives.[11]

Besides astral shells, Theosophists hold that there are nonconscious images called the "akashic records" created by all earthly activity; clairvoyants may see them as detailed visions of past events. Another kind of nonconscious image are "thought-forms," emotionally-charged, dynamic, colored patterns or figures created by a mind, which are able to affect other minds or reflect back upon their creators.[12]

Interface of Spiritualist and Theosophical Beliefs with NDEs

It is evident that several concepts of Spiritualism and Theosophy appear in OBEs and NDEs: the life overview, the paradise influenced by minds, spirit guardians, the "astral body," the silver cord, the addicted spirits moving among or attaching themselves to the living, "like attracting like," the dark planes with shadowy or depraved beings. In the case of Theosophists practicing OBEs, and Near-Death Experiencers familiar with New Age ideas, prior influence seems likely. This is not to say that these concepts may not in fact be true, only that their presence in several cases is not evidence of any kind of afterlife. However, these concepts also appear in the experiences of persons unfamiliar with movements such as Spiritualism and Theosophy, a challenging situation that will be discussed in Chapter Seven.

Christianity

In view of the major shaping influences Christianity has had in Western culture, it is important to sketch those Christian beliefs about an afterlife that are similar to NDE motifs.

Christianity was born from Judaism at a time when Judaism, having long suffered under the cruel heel of great empires, was being influenced by other-worldly apocalyptic expectations of the end of the age.[13] According to apocalypticism, a host of invisible beings both good and evil operate in the world, battling for control of individuals and nations. The powers of good will soon triumph, and those unjustly killed will be raised by God from the dead to enjoy the new age of God's rule. In some forms of apocalypticism, there is an expectation of universal resurrection, to be followed by a Great Judgment in which the wicked would be separated from the righteous and punished.[14]

Another theme, influenced by the Hellenistic mystery religions, Gnosticism, and later by Neoplatonism, focussed on a divine light or spark hidden within each person, derived from the divine Source from which all came. Salvation is the overcoming of ignorance and alienation until one fully realizes this inner divinity in reunion with the Divine.

The Gospels give us a picture of human life as influenced both by guardian angels and by unclean spirits who can possess individuals; Jesus' exorcisms are seen as a sign of God's victory over evil and of the incoming Kingdom.[15] One of the few references to the state of souls after death, the parable of the rich man and the beggar Lazarus, gives us the angels carrying Lazarus to Abraham's bosom while the rich man suffers thirst in a flaming hell.[16] This judgment is not purely impersonal but is in the hands of Abraham, who presides over both afterdeath realms.

Strongly dominating all other conceptions of the afterlife in the Gospels is the resurrection of Jesus. His resurrected body is described as concrete enough that he could eat and could be touched;[17] he is also described as rising up into heaven to reign with God until his imminent return to begin the new age.[18]

St. Paul combines these ideas of spiritual warfare and resurrection with devotion to Jesus as the heavenly Lord, to whom the Christian is united by the Spirit of God. At Jesus' return, deceased Christians will rise and together with the living will be drawn upward to meet him.[19] The book of Revelation greatly develops various of these themes, climaxing with a universal judgment. Books are opened containing a record of souls' deeds, and upon their contents an enthroned God makes his judicial decisions. The faithful will reign with God and Christ in a city with streets of gold and a paradisal garden, which is to come down from heaven. The wicked and the Devil will be cast into a lake of fire to suffer for their deeds.[20]

As time passed and expectation faded that Jesus would soon return, interest tended to shift to a judgment after individual death. The Virgin Mary and martyred saints were seen as assisting the faithful in life as well as helping them to reach heaven after death.[21]

The idea of purgatorial suffering for sin after death is hinted at during the early centuries of Christian history,[22] but is much more fully developed by the sixth century, as can be seen in some of the Near-Death cases collected by Pope Gregory the Great recounted in Carol Zaleski's *Otherworld Journeys*.[23] One finds guides, angels and demons, souls in purgatory or hells fiery or cold, journeys through darkness, flowering meadows, borderlines, music, supernal light, facing records of one's deeds in books, and transformed lives.

These cases obviously resemble contemporary cases, but they also differ. For example, common motifs are the bridge of testing, over which a good person may pass to paradise whereas a bad person will fall into an abyss, and the struggle between demonic and angelic figures over the fate of the newly deceased. Judgment may be based on objective evidence of deeds or the subjective decision of an authority figure, or both, but the subjective tends to predominate; the objective book or scale tends to be manipulated by the saints or demons as they battle for the soul.[24]

Overall, the medieval stories Zaleski cites are somber, with much purgation and punishment and relatively brief glimpses of heavenly bliss. The present-day situation seems to be the opposite; but, as we have seen, the frequency of painful cases is unknown.

Views of the afterlife were affected by the medieval development of devotionalism, in which intense love between the worshiper and the figure of Jesus or Mary became the center of the Christian spiritual life. (Comparable periods of devotionalism appear in the other world religions as well.) Devotionalist movements appear in the eighteenth, nineteenth, and twentieth centuries as well, all containing the theme that in the afterlife one might hope for the full fruition of this love. Thus devotionalism is part of the conception of religion inherited by contemporary persons, and doubtless has had some impact on NDEs.

The Black Death and other calamities in the late Middle Ages led to much fearful preoccupation with death, purgatory, and hell. The work of the saints and the prayers of the living to help the suffering "poor soul" into heaven became prominent in Christian thinking. Despite major twentieth-century changes in the Roman church, this framework of meaning is still powerful and lives in the prayer life of many Catholics today.

Because purgatory finds little support in the Bible, it was rejected by the Reformation churches, as was the role of saints in bringing the saved to heaven. Since angels and devils were biblical they were still acknowledged to some extent.

The anticipation of reunion in heaven with loved ones who have died is rare in Christian sources until early modern times, but became prominent in the eighteenth century. Especially influential in the United States were the visionary writings of Emanuel Swedenborg describing such reunions. Furthermore, the waves of Protestant revivals in the U.S., together with the relative isolation of frontier communities and the idealization of family life, encouraged the development of a folk Christianity (as well as Spiritualism) that stressed a concrete, realistic afterlife in which human ties still bind.[25] Although there has been considerable erosion of belief in life after death in modern times, several polls show that two-thirds of the people in the U.S. believe in life after death.[26]

Interface of Christian Beliefs With NDEs

When we compare traditional Christian ideas and themes with contemporary NDEs and deathbed visions, we see a good many parallels: angels as welcomers and escorts to the soul, demonic spirits, a paradisal garden, a celestial city, fiery hells, the soul's mystical union with the divine presence or Light, a Judgment upon recorded deeds, and a magnetic, loving Jesus. The more recent idea of loved ones as welcomers also appears.

But there are NDE themes that are largely or completely missing from orthodox Christian tradition. Examples are: tunnels and vortices; meeting companion animal souls; being totally accepted by the Divine whether or not one has had the right conversion experience, faith, or religious practice; the presence of Christ or angels in hell; release from hell; and the existence of earthbound spirits (though some Catholic folk ideas about the Poor Souls come close).[27] The early medieval ideas of the tug-of-war between angel and demon and the bridge of testing are rare in contemporary cases. One possible instance is Margot Grey's case of the would-be suicide who heard hooded beings arguing her fate.

When we look more closely at some of the resemblances, however, we find important differences of emphasis between the way Christian ideas appear in early medieval NDEs and in contemporary ones. For example, Carol Zaleski points out that angelic guides in medieval cases are authority figures, whereas in our more democratic society, guides are more likely to be on the same footing as the NDErs and leave it up to them whether or not to return to earth.[28] Similarly, in medieval cases, the judgment is imposed upon the NDEr by an authority figure holding a record, whereas in contemporary cases NDErs tend to encounter their past themselves and judge themselves accordingly.

In summary, the relationship of contemporary NDEs to the concepts of Spiritualism, Theosophy, and Christianity is ambiguous. Undeniably, there is influence from these traditions, as well as from certain pervasive cultural themes like democracy, upon experiencers who are familiar with them. But there are traditional ideas that take unusual forms in NDEs, and some NDE motifs that do not fit these traditions at all, as well as some obscure traditional motifs that appear in the experiences of NDErs who did not know about them.

Seven

SOME AFTERLIFE VIEWS IN NONWESTERN RELIGIONS

W E HAVE SKETCHED AFTERLIFE THEMES IN SOME Western religious movements and seen that they have influenced the NDEs of Westerners. It will be helpful now to look at some afterlife beliefs of a few Near-Eastern and East Asian religions, beliefs very unlikely to have been familiar to Western NDErs, to see what sort of parallels there might be. If major parallels exist, what explanations for them might there be?

Some Egyptian Afterlife Conceptions

Basic Motifs

In ancient Egypt, ideas of the afterlife evolved over millennia and varied considerably, but certain broad themes appear throughout. In texts inscribed on the pyramids between 2425 and 2300 BCE, the deceased pharaoh is the incarnate son of the deity Re, the sun, and is believed to return to his father after death, enjoying eternal beatitude as he crosses the heavens each day with his father. Already we see that light is very important. Themes of judgment also appear early; deeds done in the world are believed to have repercussions after death. The pharaoh, say the texts, will not be accused of having wronged other persons or wronged certain animals (as, by implication, some other deceased persons will). Other texts associate the deceased pharaoh with the deity Osiris, who, murdered by his brother Set and later restored to life, took his case against his brother to a tribunal of the gods; the tribunal vindicated Osiris and condemned Set. The deceased pharaoh thus claims to be justified before Maat (truth, justice). This identification with Osiris, as we shall see, is the first instance of an important theme of divine help and renewal.

Inscriptions in the tombs of wealthy private persons from the period 2200–2050 BCE develop further the theme of moral responsibility. One inscription emphasizes the deceased's positive deeds of charity—feeding the hungry, clothing the naked, ferrying the traveler—as well as his having avoided evil, because "I desired that it might be well with me in the Great God's presence." S. G. F. Brandon holds that "the god" or "the Great God" was undoubtedly Re, and that he functioned as a judge rewarding the righteous after death.[1] This implies a judicial judgment, partially subjective.

A work called *Instruction for King Meri-ka-re,* dating from approximately 2100, urges a life of compassion, asserting that "A man remains after death, and his deeds are placed beside him in heaps," as though they have a lasting existence in the next world. One who passes the test is transformed, virtually becoming a deity.[2] This judgment tends to be impersonal and objective, the deeds speaking for themselves, as with the typical present-day Life Overview.

The Book of Going Forth by Day

By the time of the New Kingdom (ca. 1580–1090 BCE), expectations for the afterlife had become very complex, and extensive instructions were thought to be needed. Illustrated papyrus rolls of a rather obscure text describing the next world in detailed, sometimes contradictory ways were placed in the tombs of those who could afford them. Once known as the *Egyptian Book of the Dead,* it is now more accurately called the *Book of Going Forth by Day.* (I shall refer to it as the *Going Forth.*) Because it shows parallels both to radiant and painful present-day NDEs, it is worthwhile to look at the book in some detail. What follows is based on the scroll found in the tomb of the scribe Ani, ca. 1250 BCE.

According to the *Going Forth,* the major forces to be reckoned with in the afterlife were as follows: original Chaos, represented by darkness and by Nun, the waters of the abyss below the earth; the procedure of the Weighing of the Heart, which determined whether the deceased were good or bad; the benevolent deity Osiris mentioned above who was once killed and dismembered by his brother Set but reassembled and revived by Isis, and came to preside with her over the Duath, the underworld; Re, the sun-god, who each day rose and crossed the heavenly vault in his boat, and each night crossed the underworld; and various beings with animal or human qualities, or both, who might either help or threaten to destroy the deceased person. The deceased hoped to pass these tests and dangers, to reach the paradisal Field of Reeds or Field of Offerings, and finally to join the radiant Re in his daily journey (thus "going forth by day").[3]

There is no question but that Osiris and Re are very powerful, yet neither is omnipotent; they themselves had to overcome the threats posed by Nun or the destructive beings of the Duath.[4] Clearly there is a continuum rather than a sharp distinction between deities and the spirits of human beings. The deceased reveres Re and Osiris but does not hesitate to identify with them.[5]

After introductory hymns to Re and Osiris, Ani's scroll gives the critical scene of the Weighing of the Heart. The illustration shows the god Thoth presiding, while the jackal-headed Anubis steadies the scale. It has Ani's heart on the left pan and a feather, representing Maat or perfect justice, on the other. A fearsome composite beast named Ammit waits beside Thoth, ready to devour the deceased if he fails the test; Ani and his wife Tutu wait on the left for the outcome. The text first addresses the heart, beseeching it not to testify against Ani (suggesting that it might blurt out some repressed or forgotten sin). Then Thoth speaks, pronouncing that Ani has passed the test: His deeds are righteous, he has no sin. A council of the gods declares Ani vindicated or "true-of-speech;" he is to have a grant of land in the Field of Offerings.[6]

Much later on in the book Ani has to face a tribunal of forty-two deities, and he makes forty-two declarations of his innocence of misdeeds ranging from murder to talkativeness. The moral accounting implied by this catalog of declarations, as well as the depiction of Maat as a feather on one pan of the scale, is extremely severe. To make the event even more fearsome, nothing is said in the whole book about forgiveness. A guilty person facing death may hope, however: the magical power of the words and images connects him to the power of Osiris (magic itself being a gift of the gods). Like the pharaoh of earlier ages, the deceased identifies with Osiris' mythical situation of bringing to a tribunal his claims against those of his murderous brother. Like Osiris, "Osiris Ani" is vindicated."[7]

Thus Ani is depicted as a paragon of moral perfection who passes the test. But he must still face many threats from irrationally destructive beings and forces not so different from those in present-day painful NDEs. Ani will be helped by knowledge in the scroll that will enable him to answer their test questions correctly,[8] and by asserting his divine identity and power. Some of these entities seem merely to block his way to the world of the light of Re;[9] others are viciously hostile. For example, Ani is threatened by forces that would slaughter him with bloody knives like a sacrificial animal, but he is described as being protected by magical knots with pieces of hair in them.[10] Or he could face burning in a fiery lake, or floating forever as a Drowned One in a dark ocean (probably the abyss, Nun).[11] There are hostile clutching beings who seek to steal his heart (the center of both emotion and intellect),[12] or his head (which would logically result in drastic reduction of consciousness, probably amnesia). An important weapon of defense is knowledge of the names of threatening entities, which gives control over them. Another defense is the prayers and offerings made on his behalf by a priest before the funeral slab.[13]

Ani hopes to escape these threats, but even if he does not there are images suggesting that the processes of being consumed by the powers of the underworld may give new life through their own mysterious inner logic.[14] The best example appears at the end of the *Going Forth* when the deceased faces two goddesses—Hathor, whose head is emerging from the tomb-slope into the light, and a sharp-toothed pregnant goddess associated with childbirth. Both have the sun-disk on their heads, representing light. Both pictures and text imply that Ani is reborn from the darkness of the underworld into the light of Re.[15]

In New Kingdom copies of the *Going Forth*, the idea of judgment develops in a more realistic direction. Instead of a weighing of the heart against the feather of Maat, which demands perfection, the deceased's good and evil deeds are weighed against one another. Only if the evil deeds outweigh the good is the deceased fed to the monster Amait (Ammit).

The story of Senosiris, preserved in a manuscript of the second century CE (though probably older), shows how important moral issues had become.[16] In this tale, Senosiris is a child who takes his father (both living persons) on a journey into the underworld. There he learns that the fate of a wealthy man buried with great ceremony is in fact terrible punishment, while a poor man buried without ceremony or mourners is conducted to the presence of Osiris. Obviously some Egyptians had come to believe that resources valued in earlier times, especially the magically powerful scroll of the *Going Forth* available only to the wealthy, achieved nothing, and moral goodness was everything.[17]

Interface of the Going Forth *and NDEs*

Much of the book is incomprehensible to modern readers, and many passages seem to have no overlap with contemporary NDEs. Yet there are meaningful themes and images that do show resemblances to present-day experiences.

Both in the ancient text and in contemporary NDEs, a severe moral judgment of an impersonal kind takes place early in the afterlife. At certain points in the evolution of Egyptian beliefs, this judgment involved an actual encounter with one's past deeds, very similar to the contemporary Life Overview. The more symbolic conception of the weighing of the heart against the feather of perfect justice, and the detailed interrogation by the forty-two deities, are judicial rather than completely impersonal, but so all-searching that, as in some present-day experiences, "no slip of the tongue or slur was missed."[18]

In both ancient and contemporary situations, there is help from divine beings in this severe judgment. How the Egyptian's identification with Re or Osiris saves the dead person is never really clear; he does not call out to Osiris for rescue, but somehow unites himself to the magical power of Osiris' ordeal and vindication. In contemporary NDEs the wrongdoer is punished by the situation itself; the divine presence lovingly supports the experiencer as he faces and forgives himself.

Besides the ordeal of the judgment, for both ancient Egyptians and some present-day NDErs there are irrational, nonmoral evils to encounter. The Egyptians faced violent entities, a lake or tank of fire, perhaps being lost in chaos and darkness. As we have seen, all three of these themes appear in some form in modern NDEs. The Egyptians clearly believed that such experiences could happen to good people who did not deserve them, an idea that could benefit modern persons who assume that a painful afterlife is for great sinners, and thus find it hard to talk about their painful NDEs.

The Egyptians who valued the *Going Forth* had faith that there existed certain protections and rescues from these irrational threats. The particular forms these protections took seem alien to us, but the very fact of this faith, especially in caring divine beings, can speak to contemporary persons. Present-day NDErs who are threatened by demonic beings tend either to freeze in terror, call out for immediate help, or fight them (as did Howard Storm, page 82). The deceased person in the *Going Forth* does not respond in any of these ways; he is neither terrified and helpless nor pugnacious, but responds assertively with a certain courage and hopefulness. He believes not only in magical words and amulets, but that Osiris is present in the underworld, and that he himself is united to the power of the God's mythical adventure. Although traditional Christian conceptions of hell give no hope that angels or the risen Christ (whose death was similar to that of Osiris) might be there to rescue anyone, some NDErs have in fact been rescued thus. The hopeful worldview expressed in the *Going Forth* suggests ways to make sense of this modern situation.

Even the word-magic of the Egyptian underworld traveler can be meaningful for us; to say "I am Osiris Ani" or "I am the beloved son of Re" may link the journeyer with a powerful level of consciousness. Compare the young man who faced a tiger in his vision and found it shrinking into the size of a house cat (page 68). Similarly, when Oliver Fox was able to respond to a horrifying figure with compassion, it "changed into a thing of beauty" (page 69). That which is without is not separate from that which is within.

Blissful paradises are another important element that ancient Egyptians and contemporary NDErs have in common. In our radiant NDEs the experiencer usually finds herself passing very soon into paradise or heaven, whereas in the *Going Forth by Day,* one must first pass through painful ordeals and be reborn. This theme of initiatory suffering as a potential way to make sense of painful NDEs will be discussed in Chapter Fifteen.

The theme of light, especially the deceased person's being accepted by the light-presence, is a particularly important element found both in the views of ancient Egyptians and the experiences of present-day persons near death. In both, the light is personal and loves the deceased person. But there are also differences. The Egyptian light is always linked to the sun; it is not beyond time, as in many NDEs, but has some of its power from its daily circular journey around the earth,[19] repeatedly dying and rising to new life. Further, to join the Sun God in his boat is never presented as the mystical union with all finite beings that some NDErs report. Perhaps what is most crucial is that, in both cases, the deceased person may find union with the ultimate source of life.

Could the resemblances between Egyptian conceptions and contemporary NDEs be due at least in part to the ordinary spread of ideas via ancient Judaism and later Christianity? By the first century CE, there was much cultural exchange around the Mediterranean; the Egyptian story of Senosiris may be a source of the biblical parable of the rich man and

* The burning off of oil in Nigeria + other
places - some here in U.S. could be part of contemporary
lakes of fire

AFTERDEATH VIEWS IN NONWESTERN RELIGIONS   131

Lazarus, in which the self-indulgent, uncaring rich man is thrown into the flames of Hades after death, while the beggar Lazarus is comforted by Abraham.[20] If so, the lake or tank of fire in the *Going Forth* may also have influenced the image of the flaming lake in the book of Revelation and thus, indirectly, the fiery lakes of contemporary NDErs.

But what do we make of the resemblance between the Egyptian forms of impersonal judgment, especially the heaps of deeds and the weighing of deeds, and contemporary life overviews? Christian tradition does have the (partially impersonal) idea of the books of deeds being opened before the Throne, but the idea of God as judge has been central for so long that it is hard to imagine how contemporary NDErs, seeing replays of their lives "like a movie" and judging themselves, could have been influenced in this pattern by Christianity.

It seems more likely that they both come, independently, from a deep level of human consciousness. Is this because some kind of reckoning really takes place after death? Or might it be due to a universal need in the human psyche? Before answering these questions, it is important to look at the ideas of the afterlife in another ancient Near Eastern civilization.

Some Sumerian Afterlife Conceptions

For thousands of years, the ideas of Egyptians were quite different from those of several of their Near-Eastern neighbors. We will look at certain Sumerian ideas, which were much more typical of views in the ancient Near East.

The Land of No Return

In Sumerian thought, when humans have outlived their usefulness to the Gods and die, their spirits pass into the underground Land of No Return.[21] Their state there is unrelievedly grim. "This place of the dead was imagined as a city, enclosed by seven walls and gates, shrouded in darkness and inhabited by awful monsters: there the dead existed miserably."[22] They faced no moral judgment; good and evil fared alike. Racked with insatiable desires, they would clutch at any living person (or deity) who ventured down among them, trying to trap him or her.[23]

Inanna's Journey

According to a Sumerian epic, for unknown reasons Inanna, the bright goddess of love, descends into this underworld. Her situation is particularly dangerous because the underworld's queen is her widowed sister Ereshkigal, who suffers from extreme sexual frustration and physical pain and is totally unable to sympathize with the sufferings of others drawn into her realm.[24] Inanna, having had to give up her various jewels and garments at each of the dark city's seven gates, bows down naked before the jealous Ereshkigal. Ereshkigal's seven "judges" pronounce against her and the dark queen herself kills her sister with the "eye of death" and the "word of death."

There is no hope for Inanna in the underworld itself, but when she fails to return her servant appeals to the god Enki, who sends down two creatures with the "food of life" and "water of life" to sprinkle over her body. These creatures express sympathy with Ereshkigal in her wails of pain; surprised and appeased, she agrees to give up Inanna's body. They are able to revive Inanna with their powerful food and water. But no one who enters the dark city has ever left it before; Inanna is permitted to return to the world only if she finds someone else to take her place.[25]

She ascends to the earth plane, surrounded by demonic creatures who try to seize one or another of her associates to take her place. At first Inanna protests in each case, but she lets them take her (human) husband Dumuzi, a beautiful but immature figure who had lost interest in her earlier and ignored her recent plight. The demons attack him mercilessly and, after his several escapes, succeed in dragging him down to the Great Below. Eventually an agreement is reached in which he is allowed to come back to the world for six months of the year, while his loving sister Geshtinanna takes his place in the dark.[26]

Interface Between Sumerian Conceptions and NDEs

The view of the afterlife in the epic of Inanna is grim, with joys such as those of radiant NDEs unheard-of. Some of the features of painful NDEs appear: burning desires, pain, and vicious aggression rule in the form of Ereshkigal and her demonic servants. We also see darkness, dull and listless spirits, and meaninglessness. The story shows Inanna being reborn, but this depends on a god outside rather than on a Christ or Osiris present in the darkness, and happens only because Inanna returns to the physical world (as does Dumuzi). Probably the story's rebirths, especially Dumuzi's, represent the yearly renewal of life on earth; the human dead do not return.

This gloomy picture has parallels in the idea of Hades in heroic Greece and Sheol among the ancient Hebrews, and similar concepts among other peoples. Both John Hick and Michael Grosso point out that this ancient material undercuts the claim of contemporary anti-survivalists that life after death is wish-fulfillment.[27] Nor are these dark pictures likely to have arisen from negative wishes due to guilt, since the misery is not punishment for evil deeds but happens to good and bad alike.

In view of the resemblances to painful NDEs, we may speculate that such experiences among the ancients contributed to the formation of these grim views. If so, why radiant experiences did not also contribute remains a mystery.

Some Buddhist Afterlife Conceptions

My last example of a religion with afterdeath themes that may help to cast light on NDEs is Buddhism. Though the Buddha himself seems to have discouraged interest in life after death, and though Buddhism sees human consciousness as a process rather than an abiding entity, various Buddhist traditions do show considerable interest in the subject of personal survival.

The Six Lokas

From the folk religion of its background in ancient India, Buddhism absorbed ideas of spiritual beings and spiritual realms. With the passage of time these varying views became streamlined into the six *lokas* or realms of *kama,* craving, together forming the wheel of life to which living beings are bound. Ignorant that their precious selves are illusory, propelled by craving to actions that will lead to more pain and more craving, living beings circle around the wheel age after age until they finally learn how to find release into Nirvana, infinity.

Two of the six realms, those of the hells and of the ghosts, are wholly painful; one (the heavens) is purely pleasant, while the rest are a mixture of pleasure and pain. The realm of human life on earth is the most promising, for it is here that one makes crucial moral decisions and gains understanding,[28] and can be enabled to pass to Nirvana. In the other five realms the karmic consequences of these actions are experienced.[29] These ideas show important parallels with themes in contemporary Western NDEs.

The realm of the *asuras* or fighters is somewhat complex. In early texts they are deities, or later, anti-deities, and morally ambivalent.[30, 31] But eventually they were demoted to the status of demonic figures dwelling in the darkness of the underworld.[32] According to later Buddhist tradition, to these mythological figures were drawn the deceased, especially warriors, who in life were combative and violent. Lines from a Japanese No play describe them thus: "Fire leaps from their swords; / The sparks of their own anger fall upon them like rain."[33] Trapped by their own violence into constant warfare, they must suffer until their karma has exhausted itself.

In the realm of the ghosts—an intensely needy state—are reborn the greedy, the lustful, and the verbally violent.[34] "These beings haunt the earth's surface, continually tormented by insatiable hunger. They stand outside walls and gates, mutely pleading to be fed."[35] Often they are called "hungry ghosts" and are depicted as having large bellies and tiny mouths, unable by their very shape to gain what they so intensely crave.[36]

In China and Japan, bad luck and disasters of all sorts among the living are attributed to the hostility of these and other spirits. The living take pity on the hungry ghosts (and ward off their spite) by a festival lasting throughout the seventh month. During this time they are given offerings of food[37] as well as religious instruction, to ease their suffering and help them reincarnate in a higher realm.[38]

The lowest and most dreadful of the six realms is the Hells or Purgatories. This realm differ from Western concepts of hell in that when the inhabitants' karma is exhausted, they return to earth for another try. However, the idea of cleansing and cure implied by purgatory seems far removed from most accounts of the realm, for they present scenes of sadistic torture of the most nauseous sort, out of all proportion to the sins committed. For example, the Pali canon proclaims that the crime of defaming a saint leads to torture in the ninth hell, which lasts 160 times longer than the already eons-long tortures of the first hell.[39]

Chinese Hells

In China the hells are seen as a bureaucratic maze administered, appropriately, by the souls of Confucian bureaucrats.[40] According to a text dated circa 1935, after death souls needing correction soon arrive in the first of nine hells, a receiving station whose focus is a mirror in which all the person's sins are visible. A trial is held, and the verdict determines where the sinner goes. Punishments vary greatly, ranging from having to pore over books in near-darkness, to tortures such as having livers or eyes cut out, or being boiled in oil. These are for such real or supposed crimes as buying the daughters of the poor for sexual slavery and abuse, or adopting foreign religions (clearly Christianity is meant). There is particular emphasis on punishing women who fail to accept their properly submissive status in life according to Confucian morality. Sinners may have to suffer first in one sub-hell, then another. Finally, in the tenth hell, the souls' files are checked and their next incarnation determined.[41]

Violations of Buddhist morality also come in for punishment. The paintings and writings of Genshin, a Japanese evangelist of Pure Land Buddhism of the eleventh century, present such horrors as domains in which violent spirits torment one another by clawing and slashing, or persons who have killed and eaten animals are boiled in a vat.[42] In addition to the fiery hells, there are also some eight frigid hells.

The worst hell of all is called *Avici*,[43] a place of unrelieved fire of a heat to melt bones; it is reserved for those who have killed a parent or a disciple of the Buddha.[44] Of this more below.

Ti-Tsang to the Rescue

But these horrors do not have the last word. Not only do all stays in the hells come to an end, rescue before that time is possible by the heroic Ksitigarbha (Earth Womb), called Ti-Tsang in China. A text of the ninth century tells how, in an early incarnation as a woman, Ti-Tsang learned of her mother's fate in the Avici hell as a result of having slandered Buddhist precepts. The daughter vowed to rescue the damned and empty all the hells, even if it should take forever. She thus became a bodhisattva, one who refuses to enter the bliss of Nirvana until all sentient beings are saved. In later incarnations Ti-Tsang is male, and is often shown holding a flaming pearl with which he lights up the darkness of the hells. He can appear in many forms. He will rescue any in the hells who call on him; he is also there for those who do not call (perhaps because they are too occupied with abusing one another), sharing their sufferings until he persuades them to give up their obsessions and leave.[45] The name Earth Womb and the frequent appearance of the pearl, linked as it is with shells, the depths of the sea, and the moon, suggest that Ti-Tsang is essentially still female, giving rebirth out of the dark deeps.

Ti-Tsang is a very important figure in Chinese devotionalism, going back more than fifteen hundred years, but as we have seen there are depictions of the hells that show no sign of him/her. Perhaps because Ti-Tsang is one strand among others in popular religion, one cannot look for total consistency.

The Animal, Human, and Heaven Realms

From seven to nine o'clock on the wheel we find the realm of animals, which refers not to some spirit-locale but incarnate animals on earth. "[I]t is held that many human beings are reborn as animals in a form roughly equivalent to their ruling disposition as a human being. Thus a gluttonous person may well become a hog, a violent one a tiger, etc."[46] This belief that animals are the embodiments of human souls is part of the basis for Buddhist universal compassion. However, this ideal does not prevent widespread cruelty to animals in some Buddhist countries.[47]

Unlike the hells or the realm of the ghosts, the human realm is a mixture of good and bad, a place where souls whose karma is mixed will be reborn, in a setting largely favorable or otherwise depending on their past. Despite widespread suffering on earth, the human realm is a favorable place for rebirth, because here one can reflect, come to see the emptiness of all karma-burdened existence, and seek Enlightenment. Among the ghosts or the damned or the *asuras*, however, intense pain and craving are likely to block out such aspirations.[48]

The sixth realm is the various heavens, where those who have distinguished themselves by good deeds or depth of meditation are reborn. This realm has gorgeous palaces, paradises, and ethereal states of intense, all-pervading bliss. But as with the other five *lokas*, all stays here too have their end. The heavens are not an ideal place, because the inhabitants are too happy to reflect on the need for Enlightenment.[49] Further, they have no chance to exercise compassion and grow spiritually; they can only wait until their karma is exhausted[50] and return to human form on earth.

The Pure Land and NDEs

It is important not to confuse these lengthy but temporary heavens with the Western Paradise or Pure Land of Mahayana Buddhism. A myth tells that early in his journey toward Nirvana, a saint named Dharmakaya vowed not to achieve Enlightenment until he had created a beautiful land where those who have reflected on him, or even just appealed to him before death, could be reborn. He became the Buddha Amitabha (Amida), center of a major devotional movement. At death the devotee will see Amitabha and other bodhisattvas welcoming him;[51] then he will awaken in a golden lotus bud, which unfolds to reveal a lake with other lotus blossoms in which sit many Buddhas, all teaching about the need for Enlightenment. In their center is Amitabha. In a surrounding forest of jewelled trees, birds sing songs reminding one of the impermanence of all things. A wonderful light permeates everything. There need be no fear of falling back into the six *lokas*; here in a state of perfect happiness one can grow spiritually until one is ready for Enlightenment.[52]

Several cases of deathbed visions of Amida (Amitabha) and the Western Paradise have come down to us from the early centuries of the Pure Land movement in China. Early in the fifth century, some members of a well-known monastic devotional guild, the White Lotus Society, described their deathbed visions to fellow monks who recorded them carefully. An example is the case of Seng-Chi, who as he neared death handed a candle to his fellow students:

> Then he lay down for a moment, and in his dream he saw himself proceed through the void, [still] holding the candle, and he beheld the Buddha Amitabha, who took him up and placed him...on the palm of his hand, and [in this position] he went through the whole [universe] in all directions....Suddenly he woke up and told everything about his dream to those who nursed him....When he examined his own body, there were no [longer any signs of] disease and suffering whatsoever.
>
> The following night, he suddenly...stood up, his eyes [looking into] the void in anticipation, as if he was seeing something. A moment later he lay down again, with a joyful expression on his face [and shortly thereafter died].[53]

The Tibetan Book of the Dead

An important afterlife tradition in Buddhism is found in the *Bardo Thodol* or *Tibetan Book of the Dead*, a twelfth-century book of guidance for the dying and newly deceased. The book contains many features similar to contemporary NDEs, as well as significant differences. Its three parts are as follows:

1. The First Stage: The Clear Light and the Earth-Plane

The subject is told to expect a great light, "open and empty like space, luminous void, pure naked mind without centre or circumference,"[54] ultimate reality. The dying person is urged to recognize that his own mind is one with it, and to accept it; he will then attain liberation.[55] However, unless the subject has practiced a spiritual discipline, the Void/Light will pass quickly and he will probably fail to recognize it. His consciousness emerges from his body, he sees his relatives crying, and is uncertain whether he is living or dead. The text urges him to concentrate on the figure that was his meditational focus and avoid wandering thoughts.[56]

2. The Second Stage: Archetypal Figures

Now with a thunderous noise unfolds a series of visions of intense beauty, projections of the deceased's own buddha-nature, so bright they hurt his eyes. The first figure is the Sun Buddha in the center, whose body is pure white and who radiates the sharp blue light of inner wisdom. Due to negative karma, especially ignorance, the deceased is likely to shrink away from it and move instead toward a soft white light coming from one of the six *lokas* (the heavens). He is urged instead to unite with the painful blue light, which will result in his becoming a buddha in *Sambhogakaya,*[57] the archetypal realm.[58]

This pattern continues on succeeding days, as the deceased encounters one by one the serene Buddhas of the four directions, each in a glowing radiant color. The subject is urged to unite with the Buddhas, and warned against being drawn to a softer light of the same color, which will cause him to be reborn in one or another of the *lokas,* depending on his personal karma.[59]

The next stage seems the opposite: terrifying Buddhas appear, glaring in rage at the deceased. Their colors are dark rather than pure, they have multiple limbs, they make loud threatening noises, they are adorned with sharp instruments, severed heads, snakes and other horrors, and they drink blood from skulls. But they are only the five Buddhas in another form. Because the mind is nine times clearer in the Bardo than in the body, if one can overcome fear and unite with any of them one can find Enlightenment.[60]

3. The Third Stage: Judgment and Reincarnation

In the third stage the deceased finds himself on the earth-plane, seemingly in his familiar physical body; but if he was blind or deaf he is now well. He can move by thought right through obstructions, but he is invisible to family and friends, and longs painfully to be in touch with them. He is urged to ignore his new powers, to detach himself from his loved ones, and to call on the Lord of Compassion for help.[61]

The third stage is a time of distress for many because they are "blown by the moving wind of karma." They may be in a pervading gray haze; caught up in a great fiercely whirling tornado; lost in dense darkness; threatened by flesh-eating demons; terrified by pursuing armies, avalanche, storm, or fire. Others, who have good karma, will encounter images of bliss. In either case, the deceased is reminded that the images are projections representing karma; she is urged to detach herself from all she fears or desires, and to focus on her meditational figure.[62]

If the subject is unable to focus on a positive symbol, specific deeds from his past lives will arise in consciousness. His good angel will count out a white pebble for every good action, while his tempter will count out a black pebble for every evil action. The subject will be terrified and try to lie, but Yama, the Lord of the Dead, will see all his deeds in the mirror of karma. Then Yama will drag him away with a rope and cut him to pieces, over and over. He is reminded that despite this agony, his supposed physical body is really a projection from the Void, as is Yama. Giving up fear and recognizing the Clear Light/Void, even now he can be liberated.[63]

Pursued again by storms, darkness and hostile armies, the subject frantically seeks refuge in one of the six realms, whose variously colored dull lights he can see. Because consciousness is very open and flexible in the Intermediate State, even now he can find Enlightenment, if he affirms that the light of his destined realm (brighter to him than the other five) is one with the Lord of Compassion. If this fails, the subject sees his future parents in sexual embrace. He is urged to focus on a favorable place of rebirth, such as the Western Paradise, a family of faith, or a setting in which he will be able to grow up to benefit all living beings.[64]

Interface Between Buddhist Afterlife Views and NDEs

Obviously there are a good many parallels between the *Bardo Thodol's* descriptions of the Intermediate State and contemporary Western OBEs and NDEs. Moody draws attention to several of these in *Life After Life*, including out-of-body states, a void, loud noises, sharp and clear thought, inability to communicate with relatives, ability to go through walls and travel anywhere instantaneously, encountering other similar beings, and seeing a bright light.[65] Other common features are beautiful buildings, high winds and whirling vortices, the idea that the images seen are projections, the importance of controlling one's fear, influences from the thoughts and intentions of survivors. The idea that the terrifying Buddhas and the radiant ones are two forms of the same reality resemble Bush and Greyson's category of "inverted" NDEs, and Ring's interpretation of the attacks of demonic beings upon NDErs as potentially functioning to destroy the walls of the ego, which obstruct the divine light.[66] A particularly important parallel: the mirror of karma in which sins are visible and the black and white pebbles counted out for each deed, which resemble the Life Overview.

In the hell *loka,* the abuse by demons and the mutual abuse of the deceased, as well as (perhaps) the rage of the *asuras,* clearly resemble scenes witnessed or experienced by NDErs, especially Howard Storm (page 80), George Ritchie (on the dark plain, page 80), and Patricia (page 78). Ritchie's hell as a distinct realm among several particularly calls to mind the traditional Buddhist scheme (though his hell is apparently not subdivided). Although the preoccupation with sexual gratification or abuse that appears in several NDE and OBE visions is not prominent in the verbal accounts of the Buddhist hells, woodcuts and paintings do show scenes of sexual tortures.[67]

The luminous figure of Ti-Tsang, whose patience and compassion outweigh all the horrors of the hells, is unmistakably like active rescuing figures in NDEs, particularly Christ and angels. This is particularly remarkable since Christian hells traditionally rule out rescuers (except for a one-time visit by Christ between his death and resurrection). A Ti-Tsang devotee would have no doubt that compassionate NDE figures are Ti-Tsang in forms appropriate for benighted Westerners; and these figures may in fact be culturally differing forms of an underlying reality.

However, rescuers are not always consistently related to NDErs' states of mind. In Chinese conceptions, the hell inhabitants must ask for or at least accept Ti-Tsang's help. Consistent with this, Howard Storm (page 82) and Patricia (page 79) did call for and receive help, and Ritchie (page 80) saw compassionate waiting angels who were invisible to the closed-minded denizens of hell. But some NDErs escaped without knowing how or why, and in Cathy Baker's vision some desperate sufferers called out for help but apparently did not receive any from her female guide (page 67).

The *loka* of the ghosts also has resemblances to certain Western NDEs. (In fact many traditional cultures hold a belief in ghosts among the living.) It is near the surface of the earth or on it, and the ghosts seek to draw what they need from the living. Ritchie's ghosts in the tavern fit this conception very closely (page 57). But, for Monroe, ghosts exist in a rather formless environment (page 65).

The chief trait of the ghosts in both Western and Eastern views is their craving—addictions and starvation. In both cultures, the ghosts, though largely unseen, may harm the living by clinging to them and causing depression and disasters. Some of them are not merely pathetic but hostile, virtually demonic. In both Mahayana Buddhism and Western Spiritualism the living can potentially ease the ghosts' sufferings.

The Western (including Egyptian) and Buddhist paradises also show similarities. The supremely desirable presence of the deity or savior—Re, Amitabha, Christ, or other Being of Light—is perhaps the most prominent feature, as well as garden scenes, often with glorious colors, and wonderful light. (The popularity of Thomas Kinkade's paintings of luminous gardens and cottages, with a path leading toward the horizon, suggests that such a paradise is still a preoccupation in our culture.) Another common factor is social joys with other happy beings, both in accounts of Amitabha's Western Paradise and many contemporary Western NDEs.

Contrasts

The Buddhist hells are thought to be perfect karma, but some are incompatible both with karma and with the concept of the Empathic Life Overview. The agelong horrors of the hells are far from being exact consequences of brief deeds (some of them victimless) committed in the flesh. Furthermore, the tortures are sometimes inflicted by monstrous demons, whose sadism would be reinforced thereby; this is not impersonal justice but irrational evil like that in Egyptian and Sumerian views.

There are also significant contrasts among the different heavens. The speaker in the *Book of Going Forth by Day* praises Re and desires to reach his presence, but there is little sign of love for him. By contrast, Amitabha and Jesus are clearly described in our sources in the language of love. Devotional love for a deity or savior is essentially the product of vast ancient (and medieval) religious changes that replaced tribal religions with the world religions of salvation. The first clear signs of Pure Land devotion appeared in sutras compiled in India as early as the second century CE, apparently influenced by Indian devotionalism that had already flourished there for three hundred years,[68] and were early translated into Chinese.

Welcomers as guides, so prominent in contemporary Western accounts, do not appear in the *Bardo Thodol*: pre-deceased loved ones are presumed to have been either reincarnated or possibly enlightened, which is why the book's guidance is so important. The response to the light also differs. The vast majority of Western NDErs who have described the light need no urging to enter it, feel unutterable joy and peace, and experience intense disappointment at leaving it. The NDEr sometimes experiences all of reality in the light, something that suggests that it represents the fullness of being. The *Bardo Thodol*, however, does not mention love or joy in connection with the Clear Light, and it is assumed that the dying person will shrink from it; or, because of undisciplined thoughts, will have so brief a glimpse that he misses his chance. Furthermore, the Clear Light is identified with the Void. In a sense the Void is the source of all things, but perhaps the Clear Light seems to the average dying Tibetan like the Meaningless Void of contemporary painful NDEs.

Ambiguity of Afterdeath Themes in World Religions

This sketch of some Egyptian, Sumerian, and Buddhist afterdeath themes, when compared with present-day NDE features, shows a very complex and ambiguous situation. There are significant parallels that are very hard to explain by the ordinary spread of ideas, and which suggest that these themes transcend cultures. Could it be that they appear repeatedly because they reflect actual afterlife realities? But if we are tempted to explain them thus, we are brought up short by major incompatibilities. What other sources might there be for the parallels?

One Explanation: Field Memory

Could some of these parallels, as Greyson suggests, result from a common psychological mindset that is "universally available cross-culturally," involving, say, a pattern of regression to an unborn state in which all needs are met, followed by an archetypal birthing movement from darkness into light? [69] Remembering painful NDEs, might we include in such a common mindset universal fears—fears of destructive spiritual forces, fears of meeting the consequences of one's deeds?

About some of the parallels it is hard to say. Fears of spiritual forces may be universal, but conceptions of postmortem oceanic bliss and rebirth into light, as well as meeting the consequences of one's deeds, though they are found in ancient Egypt, apparently did not exist in the Sumeria of the epic of Inanna and some neighboring lands. Why might such ideas be widespread in the present, but oddly limited in far ancient times? Could it be that certain archetypal patterns are not universal but come into existence in time, develop and change?

One theory about how they might do so is Rupert Sheldrake's concept of morphic fields. [70] Seeking to cast light on the mysteries of the development of organisms when embryonic and at other stages, Sheldrake examines the view that the unfolding process is governed by the action of "morphogenetic fields," non-material regions of influence surrounding the organisms. Extending this theory, Sheldrake proposes that there are "morphic fields" surrounding everything that is an organized unit and has wholeness. This would include everything from atoms through animal species and animal individuals through human cultural patterns to galaxies. The morphic field can operate at a distance. It carries memory—conscious or unconscious[71]—since memory is not necessarily stored in the DNA or the brain, but rather the brain tunes in to the memory in the field.[72] The way a new spider develops in her egg, the "instinctive" way she later builds her web, are due to "morphic resonance" from the fields of thousands of previous spiders. Nature, in other words, does not obey laws but has habits. Habits can seem almost as strong as laws when millions of units follow them for a very long time—but they can change.

What happens to these morphic fields when a species becomes extinct or a human culture is destroyed? It is well known that sometimes features from long-vanished ancestors turn up in later bodies; for example, babies with tails, whales with legs. This fact of atavism leads Sheldrake to propose that morphic fields do not disappear when all the units they control are gone; rarely, they may be reactivated. He suggests that "atavism would also be expected in the social and cultural realms."[73]

This conception could help to explain how contemporary Westerners can have NDEs with features resembling archaic ideas. For example, present-day NDErs might for obscure reasons tune in to ancient Egyptian and Tibetan morphic fields containing the meeting with one's deeds and express them in new ways. The weakening of a morphic field for obscure reasons may explain why the "silver cord," frequently reported by OBErs a hundred years ago, is seldom reported by NDErs today.

Non-Conclusion

The issue of world religions and NDEs is complex and ambiguous. The fact that certain features in NDEs echo afterdeath ideas of long ago and far away is not necessarily evidence for an afterlife. At the same time, if there were other, stronger reasons for affirming an afterlife, these widespread features might take on new importance on a possible map of this realm. Therefore, the next section will deal with the question of the survival of death.

PART III

THE QUESTION OF SURVIVAL OF DEATH

Eight

THE POSSIBILITY OF SURVIVAL: BODY AND MIND

O NE REASON PEOPLE WITH VERY DIFFERENT POSITIONS about life after death have so much trouble communicating is that their different ways of thinking are not brought out into the open. Philosopher David Griffin has provided a helpful analysis of three thinking styles (although no one thinks purely in one style). The first is the *paradigmatic mind*, whose chief concern is whether or not survival is possible based upon a consistent paradigm or figure representing a worldview. Thus, if a person's worldview claims that the physical is all that exists and that life after death is thus impossible, this person may quickly conclude that there is no good evidence for survival of death. By contrast, the *data-led mind* is chiefly interested in examining the evidence; if it is good, survival must be possible, and one's worldview must be adjusted to fit it. The third type is the *wishful-and-fearful-thinking mind*, one inclined to decide the issue according to whether or not survival is a good thing. Thus if one believes that without survival all morality collapses, *or* if one holds that survival means that manipulative religious leaders and hellfire have the last word, a conclusion for or against survival may be reached without a careful look at the evidence.[1,2]

As a data-led thinker myself, I hold that paradigms and feelings must take second place to the evidence. Yet our need for a consistent worldview and for deep human values must not be ignored. In this chapter I will look at issues that have to do with consistency of worldview. The main concern of data-led minds, the evidence, will be dealt with in chapters Nine and Ten.

Nonsurvivalist Positions

Roots of Nonsurvivalist Positions

Educated people in our culture find it difficult to accept that there may be survival of death because of the common materialist view of the relationship between mind and body. Materialism has serious problems, whose roots lie in developments in religion, philosophy and science in the sixteenth and seventeenth centuries. Central is René Descartes' philosophical position that reality is divided into mind, which is conscious and self-moving, and matter, which is extended in space and inert. This dualism was taken up by religious scientists and philosophers who wanted to shore up belief in the existence of God and the authority of the Church against rising doubts. For example, they reasoned that if only mind is self-moving, and if physical things are inert and are now in motion, there must be a God who put them in motion.[3]

At this time, the immortality of the human mind or spirit was also under attack; some Renaissance thinkers pointed out although the human body is self-moving, it still dies, so the fact that the mind is self-moving does not prove it can survive death. The dualists, by insisting that matter (including the body) is inert and not self-moving, intended to safeguard the human soul as different in kind from matter and thus presumably immortal.[4]

However, these moves intended to safeguard the existence of God and the immortal soul have backfired in late modern times because of a problem inherent in strict dualism. If mind and matter are totally different, how can they relate at all? The result of this problem has been that for thinkers in the eighteenth and nineteenth centuries, mind tends to collapse into matter, while God increasingly drops out of most scientific and philosophical thought. For most contemporary philosophers, mind is only an offshoot of the brain, or is the same thing as the brain, or is even a fiction; thus the destruction of the body means the end of the person.[5] There are several kinds of mind-body positions tending toward materialism, and it is impossible to do them justice in a small space. I will sketch one confident materialist position together with another thinker's critique of such reductionist views.

Eliminative Materialism

Philosopher Paul Churchland is one of those who holds that mind is the same thing as brain (identity theory). He aims for a clear description of the relation of mind and body by promising eventually to eliminate "folk psychology." Folk psychology is the common-sense position, held by nearly all people, that human selves have real beliefs, memories, and feelings such as desire, fear, hatred; and that these cause people to do particular things. This informal system, which grows out of experience, works quite well; it enables us to make fairly accurate predictions of others' behavior. But for the eliminative materialist, the language of science is the only acceptable way to describe these inner experiences, and Churchland believes that a physical theory of the brain explaining how it causes behavior will take the place of "folk psychology." Churchland acknowledges that we do not at present know enough about brain states to establish this, but "identity theory is committed to the idea that brain research will eventually reveal them."[6]

Churchland presents four arguments to support his form of materialism: 1) Each individual person is purely physical in origins and (apparently) in makeup. 2) Each *type* of animal appears to be only physical in nature, in its evolutionary beginnings. 3) All known mental phenomena are dependent on the brain and nervous system. 4) The neurosciences are succeeding more and more in explaining the behavior of many creatures in terms of their nervous systems.[7]

An often-heard criticism of identity theory has to do with the fact that, amid all the thousands of details we take in and can bring up from memory, we are able to choose a particular thing or set of things and focus on it to the exclusion of others. How is the brain, with its various centers and billions of neurons, able to do this? Churchland admits that the brain has the ability for "monitoring and controlling many aspects of its own operations." One way it does this is by a system of "descending control" mechanisms. To give a specific example in technical language, the visual cortex is perhaps able to influence "the lateral geniculate body of the thalamus, where the optic nerve terminates" to focus on certain features of a scene. He supposes that such decisions are made by the brain as a whole.[8]

Most people assume that the human self, the "I" with my continuous stream of thoughts and feelings, really exists. Churchland however, like some other philosophers, does not trust this self-perceived self. One reason for his distrust is that thanks to psychology it is known that a person can misunderstand his or her own sensations and feelings; further, it can be shown that one has split-second perceptions that never reach the conscious "I." There is a great deal going on in the brain, and the stream of thought of the "I" is not an accurate reflection of it. Churchland does not hold that the self—the "I"—is a fiction, but simply a physical organism that evolved to be uncommonly self-reliant, able to learn, and creative.[9]

Perhaps the main criticism made of identity theory is that when we look into our minds we find thoughts, feelings, and sensations, but not the workings of nerves and brain centers. Churchland replies that our senses are not keen enough to detect the electromagnetic and other properties of our nervous systems. When we describe what it feels like to see red or feel the pain of a cut, we may not "mean" such-and-such brain states, but this fact only tells us that our language is inadequate. Churchland expects that with increasing scientific knowledge we will be able to train our perceptions until by looking inward we will be able to understand a great deal of our intricate neurological workings.

Since we have space only for a quick sketch of Churchland's position, it would not be fair to critique what he says point by point. What interests us in his position is its relationship to survival of death, which Churchland of course excludes when he declares that all mental activity depends on the brain and nervous system. It is legitimate for us to point out that in order to make this generalization, Churchland rules out the possibility of any evidence that suggests otherwise. Some of the material we have already looked at—out-of-body perceptions of details the NDEr could not have known, Peak-in-Darien visions of welcomers, and especially the flatliner case of Pam Reynolds—challenge Churchland's assertion. Churchland shows no interest in this kind of evidence; he mentions parapsychology, but only to give it a hasty and contemptuous dismissal.[10] Thus he cannot fairly claim the last word on the subject.

Churchland's position shows virtually boundless faith in the future of the methods of science. Although he rejects the *language* of consciousness, interestingly he has remarkable confidence in the potential *power* of what most people would call consciousness, particularly the introspection of one's own thoughts and feelings. There is, in fact, some evidence that introspection may have powers of this kind; but so far it is not scientific training but the NDE and other mystical-type states that (apparently) make such acts possible. For example, P. M. H. Atwater, whose NDEs were described in Part One, tells that after her third NDE she was able to perceive and converse with her cells, to set up a partnership of healing with them.[11] Clearly she regarded them as having a form of consciousness. This is hardly what Churchland has in mind, but it can give us pause before we dismiss him too quickly.

A Critique of Reductionism

Thomas Nagel's analysis of the mind-body relationship offers a drastic critique of Churchland's kind of position. Philosophy, says Nagel, tends to be "infected by scientism," meaning that it puts one (limited) type of understanding in charge of what may be said about the world.[12] Materialistic mind-body philosophies seek to be objective, but in the process something is left out, namely experience and subjectivity: what red looks like, what scrambled eggs taste like.[13] Observations of behavior and explanations of brain states and are not adequate to deal with consciousness,[14] because they could be applied to robot-like beings that had no experiences. Says Nagel, "Every subjective phenomenon is essentially connected with a single point of view," which an objective physical theory will abandon.[15]

Not only are the points of view of individual human beings left out in the attempt to gain completely objective knowledge; there are also kinds of beings that have consciousness but whose interior life we are largely unable even to imagine. Nagel's essay "What is It Like to Be a Bat?" points out that while a bat clearly has consciousness, (his or her) subjective experience— perceiving things by sonar, catching insects in (her) mouth in flight, hanging upside down to sleep—is closed to us. The facts such as scientists might study about how (her) body operates physically are accessible from many points of view, but what it feels like to be a bat is knowable only from the bat's point of view.[16]

The fact that materialist theories have largely ignored these realities does not mean that materialism is false, says Nagel, but perhaps only that we cannot at present understand *how* it could be true. An assertion that mental states are physical states may seem clear, but we lack the concepts to make the assertion meaningful, and the analogies we depend on do not supply this.[17]

However, Nagel is not opposed to objectivity per se; in fact, he considers objectivity necessary to understand consciousness (as well as brains). He states that a consciousness may seem to itself independent of the body, as in a conviction of reincarnation, but we know from objective study that it is not.[18] A consciousness may also feel that it knows itself completely, but this, he holds, is also misleading.[19]

What am I? What is the hidden factor that can straddle the gap between neurons and consciousness? Nagel considers whether there may not in fact *be* any good candidate for what I am.[20] Could it be that "mental events are not properties...of anything, but simply occur, neither in a soul nor in the body..."? This view seems unintelligible to Nagel: "*Something* must be there in advance, with the potential of being affected with [thoughts and feelings]....Experiences can't be created out of nothing." This something might even be some kind of world soul.[21]

Although pessimistic that the search will be successful, Nagel is willing to try. He suggests the dual-aspect theory (that mind and body are two aspects of the same reality) and makes clear that at best this theory indicates "where the truth might be located, not what it is." Processes in the mind and properties of the brain may be "essential components of a more fundamental essence...."[22] We have no conception of this third term, the "intermediate link," which is neither mental nor physical.[23]

Nagel acknowledges that, like the other theories he critiques, his is not really intelligible. To say that the brain has nonphysical properties does not increase our understanding.[24] "How can experience inhere in something with physical parts?"[25] For mind to emerge from completely inert matter seems unintelligible.[26]

As we have seen, Nagel denies, almost in passing, that survival of death is possible. He does not examine the evidence. However, his style is not dogmatic; he has a sense that our minds are not equal to the great philosophical problems.[27] That he would make an extensive attempt to identify with the consciousness of an animal, and half-seriously refer to world-souls as a possibility,[28] suggests that other, stranger orders of consciousness might at least not be ruled out in advance.

In Nagel's critique a voice of common sense is heard, pointing out that something essential has been ignored in materialist accounts. His is not the only voice; other philosophers acknowledge that consciousness cannot be reduced to physical processes. It is becoming increasingly clear that much of twentieth-century thought on mind and body is inadequate.[29] This point has been made by dualists repeatedly, as well as by thinkers of minority persuasions who have scarcely been heard. To examples of these positions, which allow for survival, I will now turn.

Body-Mind Positions Allowing for Survival

Dualism

Dualism affirms that mind and matter are both real, and *different in kind*. An example of a dualist position is the joint work of philosopher Karl Popper and neurologist John Eccles. Their book *The Self and Its Brain* is particularly useful in light of identity-theory work such as Churchland's, because as data-led thinkers they have much to say about neurological findings that are hard to square with such positions.

Materialists share the conviction that the physical world is a closed system: only a physical thing can affect another physical thing. Popper disagrees at the outset; he affirms that the physical world, which he calls World One, is open to World Two, the mental world, with things in each able to influence the other. (He also affirms a World Three of human creations such as myths and theories.)[30] Common sense supports him; everyone knows of many ways in which physical happenings that influence our bodies affect our minds, and that our minds make decisions that affect our bodies as well as, through them, other things in the physical world.

Popper agrees with most thinkers in our culture that the self develops out of the many perceptions and memories of human experience in the physical world (an idea that will be challenged in Chapter Eight); but he takes issue with materialists in his conviction that the self is focussed in an "entity" that directs attention and makes decisions—a kind of pilot of the ship, who continues roughly from birth to death (despite interruptions by sleep).[31] This decision-making entity evolved as a result of facing unusual biological problems that could not be solved in the unconscious way that had prevailed before.[32] What ?

Eccles, in his discussion of the difficult issue of the interaction of mind and brain, emphasizes the fact that the mind's ability to focus on certain matters in a meaningful way requires an explanation:

> the self-conscious mind is actively engaged in *reading out* from the multitude of active centres...the liaison areas of the dominant cerebral hemisphere. The self-conscious mind *selects* from these centres according to attention, and

from moment to moment *integrates* its selection to give
unity even to the most transient experiences.[33]

The brain itself, with its vast number of processes going on at once, cannot
do this (as Churchland had to conclude it could).

Even more dramatically, there are significant ways, Eccles points out, in
which these choices of attention actually change the brain—e.g., the way
that the synapses between certain neurons apparently develop and
proliferate with active use and atrophy with disuse.[34] Choose to think long
and hard in certain ways about certain things and you strengthen the
relevant parts of your brain. Eccles sees no way that the brain could do such
things to itself.

While materialistic thinkers usually claim that their views are consistent
with human freedom and the reality of right and wrong, the claims
sometimes seem questionable, at least. Popper and Eccles' position,
however, leaves no doubt that the human self is morally responsible for its
decisions. The same is true of personal identity; the self as they conceive it
is unquestionably real, continues over time, and is not reducible to any
lesser processes.

The picture they draw has other strengths, which we will see in the
discussion below of the evidence for the power of mind over body, as well
as for psi (or paranormal activity) and the physical phenomena of
mysticism. Popper and Eccles' view is compatible with survival. In short,
their outlook is a large-minded, profoundly humane one that has no need
for blinkers against inconvenient evidence.

However, the basic difficulty of their view is obvious: it cannot resolve
the old problem that things completely unlike cannot relate. How could a
self completely different from matter appear in the course of evolution?
How can a wish relate to a billiard ball, a ghost to a machine? "I believe in
the ghost in the machine," says Popper half-jokingly. He prefers the image
of the pilot of the ship,[35] but he does not really try to solve the problem in
literal language. Eccles does try. He suggests that certain neurons in the
brain are "critically poised" and require that the mind spend only a minute
amount of energy to affect them. But this attempted solution does not deal
with the basic problem that the likes remain unlikes, however refined. If
both mind and brain have (or are) the same *kind* of energy, they would not

after all be completely unlike, and the problem might be solvable. But such a position would not be (ontological) dualism.

Dualism can cover much more ground than materialist positions, but both are stopped by a Gordian knot: mind and matter, in the very different ways that we experience them, do not fit together. John Searle holds that the problem stems from the fact that materialists have taken over the categories of Descartes' dualism, in which that which is physical cannot be mental and vice versa. "[T]here is something wrong with the terms of the debate,"[36] he points out; they must be reconceived. Nagel has also called for radical rethinking of the problem.[37]

I now turn to a position that does face this challenge, conceiving the mind-body issue in terms radically different from mainline views.

Aurobindo's Panpsychism

A quite different body-mind position in which survival and other claims of NDErs can be seen as meaningful is the panpsychism ("everything is alive") of Indian philosopher Aurobindo Ghose. His thought was influenced by his studies in Western biological science and a profound mystical experience he had around 1911. Sri Aurobindo began with the worldview of Hindu Vedanta, in which the world flows or unfolds out of the Divine. He interpreted this process in terms of evolution, which he sees as the means by which Absolute Spirit, Being-Consciousness-Bliss, manifests itself. Human body and mind are both forms of this manifestation.

For Aurobindo the body-mind relation does not pose the problem it does for the Western philosophers mentioned above. For him, evolution is not a course of development of nonliving matter in which consciousness inexplicably appears; *consciousness is primary*. "Spirit being the fundamental truth of existence, life can be only its manifestation....The forms of life as they appear to us are...its disguises...."[38] Aurobindo sees this manifestation and disguise as a process of the (partial) descent of the Divine into conditions of limited physical existence—that is, involution—eventually to return to the Divine fullness via biological and spiritual evolution.

According to Aurobindo, between the Spirit as self-possessed, infinite consciousness, and the Spirit as a flux of many finite things, there is an intermediate principle, Supermind: all-knowing, the Creatrix.[39] (The Creatrix is similar to divine Sophia in ancient Hebrew thought.) Out of the Creatrix comes our finite mind; this takes place as infinite consciousness, focussing on particulars, eclipsing all the rest that it knows. The result is divided consciousness.[40]

Prior to that, says Aurobindo, having descended to its lowest point to manifest as matter and energy, consciousness is partially lost to itself in sleep.[41] Evolution is the ages-long process of awakening. On the animal or vital level (in which human bodies participate), there is a partial awakening; in the human mind we have a further level of awakening, for mind is capable of reflection, conscious invention, religious and ethical feeling, and thought.[42]

Aurobindo holds that there are two elements in the spiritual side of a human being. The first element is the Purusha or spiritual Person, one in nature and being with the divine Spirit (Being-Consciousness-Bliss) who has willed the involution and evolution process and presides over it. Aurobindo calls this Person or Self the "concealed Witness and Control, the hidden Guide...the inner voice of the mystic."[43] The other element is the ego or personality, the individual not yet aware of the full depths of consciousness within.[44]

The relation of these two aspects of consciousness to the body is complex. Aurobindo definitely sees body and mind as two that interact; he speaks of the Self as assuming the body,[45] the body as encasing the mind.[46] But he denies that the body is a mere garment; it inherits the vital stage of evolution with its plant and animal hungers.[47] Thus the body may be said to have its own kind of aliveness, and its interaction with the personality is complex, involving a certain amount of conflict. The personality sometimes abdicates control and leadership of the body level, sometimes attempts it and fails, and sometimes achieves it.[48] (Though Aurobindo does not deal with the neurological and psychological studies available in his time, his basic conception of the mind-body relation would have no difficulty fitting itself to facts such as those cited by Eccles.)

In Aurobindo's view, one cannot say that a soul descends ready-made from heaven into an otherwise inert human body, for there is no body that is not in itself the form of soul, even at the level of matter and of life.[49] He believes rather that many embodiments are necessary because the human possibilities of the soul cannot all be worked out in a single life; and also because the last word is not the existence of finite mind but *the full flowering of the divine Spirit in the embodied human being.*[50, 51]

Aurobindo acknowledges that human beings and discarnate spirits can hinder the evolutionary return to the Divine fullness. This gives a place to freedom, though it is a restricted one; one cannot permanently block the process. Freedom for Aurobindo means chiefly the overcoming of the limitations imposed by ignorance and hunger, as one achieves unity with the divine Person within and harmony with other persons and the physical world. This state is the Life Divine.[52]

The pattern of descent and ascent, which I will call the U-shaped feature, will appear again in chapters Twelve and Fourteen.

Commentary

There are several features of Aurobindo's position particularly congenial to radiant NDEs. Both have profound concern with mystical oneness; the Guide or Being of Light in many NDEs closely resembles Aurobindo's divine Person within each human being. The unutterable joy in the light, and certain NDErs' conviction of knowing all things in the light, are compatible with the Divine as Being-Awareness-Bliss and Supermind. The conviction of several NDErs that the light is "home," that their earthly life had been a period of strange forgetfulness, fits the U-shaped Descent and Ascent framework, with involution as the falling asleep of Divine Consciousness. The later transformation experienced by some NDErs is like the Life Divine in the body, as Aurobindo sees it. There are also features of his thought compatible with hellish NDEs; for example, evil spiritual beings have a real existence. For these reasons, I find it the most usable of the various kinds of body-mind views, and have given it at greater length. However, in keeping with his view of freedom as limited, Aurobindo's Vedantan understanding of evil as stemming from *Lila,* divine play, seems to take evil less than fully seriously.

Aurobindo's is not the only panpsychist position in which the body-mind problem is resolved. Another can be found in the process philosophical movement originating from the work of Alfred North Whitehead, but we lack space to say more than a few words about it. Process thought takes its rise from developments in modern science, especially physics and biology. Einstein's well-known equation $E = mc^2$ suggests that matter and energy may be fundamentally the same, "that matter is 'frozen energy.'" If so, then everything that actually exists may be the same in kind.

Writing in this tradition, David Griffin calls his position panexperientialism ("everything has experience"). Everything has inwardness; all things have, or rather are, experiences. True, they differ greatly in complexity. Atoms, molecules, and cells, which can be thought of as individuals, can perceive, enjoy, and choose on very rudimentary levels. (Not everything is an individual; a rock or a sculpture, for example, is an aggregate of molecules, and lacking in unity. As units such things do not have experiences.) Human and animal minds, being far more complex than molecules, have a much greater capacity for harmony and enjoyment; but they are of the same *kind* as individuals on the microscopic level.

It is evident that according to panexperientialism there is no difficulty in interaction of body and mind; though numerically two, they are the same in kind.[53] (Clearly, numerical *duality* differs from the ontological *dualism* such as that of of Popper and Eccles.) The mind perceives the bodily members sympathetically in a nonsensory manner; as philosopher Charles Hartshorne eloquently puts it, "Hurt certain of my cells and you hurt me...My cells are [my] friends...."[54] Likewise, the mind can directly influence the cells of the body, which is the same thing as the cells perceiving the mind. The mind might influence the body in more extraordinary ways, as we shall see below; the mind might also survive the body's death.

The Transmission Theory

If we suppose some form of panexperientialism or panpsychism to be true, what relationship might there be between mind and brain if mind is an equal or even a senior partner in the interaction between them? A senior-partner view, the transmission theory, appears in the writings of philosophers F. C. S. Schiller, William James, and Henri Bergson. They propose that it is not the case that brain is primary and consciousness secondary, but the other way around. According to Schiller, mind in itself has much greater scope and power than does body, but its scope is restricted by embodiment. Citing "the extraordinary memories of the drowning and dying generally," he suggests that *what needs accounting for is not memory, but forgetfulness.* Our memory may well be total, but the brain usually prevents us from recalling most of it.[55]

Schiller calls himself a "troglodyte" or cave-dweller, referring to Plato's myth of humans as prisoners chained in a cave, ignorant of the world of daylight, able to see only shadows on a wall and thinking them to be real. Thus Schiller suggests that the true, wider world of mind is linked with superhuman consciousness. Bergson offers a similar view, also supporting it by referring to the vast life-memories of the dying.

William James, a friend of both Bergson and Schiller, suggests that "when we think of the law that thought is a function of the brain, we are not required to think of productive function only; *we are entitled also to consider...transmissive function.*"[56] He cites Shelley's lines: "Life, like a dome of many-colored glass, / Stains the white radiance of eternity." James compares the dome to the whole of the physical world. It may be opaque for the most part to the full blaze of the sun, but at certain times and places it becomes translucent. Our brains would be such places. The rays shining through, finite consciousness, will be highly individualized, will be affected by the state of the body, and at death will seem (to others) to disappear. "But the sphere of being that supplied the consciousness would still be intact; and in that more real world...the consciousness might...continue still."[57]

The expanded consciousness that many mystics and returning NDErs describe can be better explained by the transmission theory than by reductionistic theories. Chiefly for this reason I will assume that some form of the transmission theory is true.

Body and Mind in Out-of-Body Experiences

What is going on when NDErs experience themselves as hovering up near the ceiling? Has the mind actually left the body? At least three answers have been given.

In the extrasomatic theory (using Griffin's terms), the psyche in some form actually leaves the physical body and remains outside it for a period. To those who have OBEs, this view is common sense; supporting them is the fact that the returned OBEr sometimes knows things she could not have learned normally.

In the introsomatic theory, the mind cannot leave the body (perhaps because mind and body are one and the same), and the sense of being outside it is an illusion that can be explained in neurological or psychological terms (as in Chapter Five). Most reductionists who hold to this theory simply ignore the evidence for NDErs' paranormal knowledge; some thinkers explain it as due to clairvoyance or telepathy. In the extrasomatic view survival is possible, or even likely, whereas for most who hold to the introsomatic theory, death means extinction.[58]

We have seen that reductionist body-mind theories have serious problems. If clairvoyance and telepathy are added to the introsomatic theory, however, the theory will go much further. But telepathy and clairvoyance cannot explain why NDErs blind from birth are able to cast their ESP in the form of clear images after a lifetime of visual blankness. It also cannot explain the spiritual transformation and the gifts, such as ability to heal others and to influence electronic equipment, that develop in some NDErs. The more extraordinary the potential powers that must be attributed to the mind to explain these developments, the less reason there would seem to be to insist that mind is so dependent upon the body as to be inseparable from it. The extrasomatic theory fits the data more naturally.

However, William James' borrowed image of the stained-glass dome through which the eternal light shines, and Schiller's reference to the cave-dweller who has seen the full blaze of the sun, both suggest a third theory: that consciousness is not "in" the body but always transcends it, and that the brain ordinarily serves to filter and focus consciousness. This is the *transsomatic* theory.[59] Developing this theory, Harvey Irwin, Michael Grosso, and others suggest that to be "out" of the body might mean a shift of conscious attention from bodily orientation toward the deeper or higher levels of consciousness.[60] This might be experienced as a change of location, as expansion, or both. Transsomatic consciousness may have great creative power; it might unite with that of others, or even be linked with the infinite.

A good deal of the evidence for OBEs and NDEs is consistent with this theory: the paranormal knowledge of certain OBErs and NDErs, the culturally influenced features in their experiences, the variations in how they perceive themselves—some finding themselves in a duplicate body, some as a cloud or point. The many reports of mystical reunion with the Divine or with the whole of reality, and detailed Life Overview experiences seem especially to support it. Painful experiences in which the self feels hemmed in do not necessarily undermine the theory, but may indicate that the body is not the only factor that restricts and focuses consciousness.

Provisionally accepting the transsomatic theory, we can define death as follows: it is the process (prolonged or short) in which consciousness is released from its restrictive focus in the body, and the body begins to break down. In a Near-Death Experience, while the body is still capable of being revived, the process would be halted part way (or after release), and consciousness would (largely) resume its focus.

Conclusions

All the thinkers cited in this chapter seek to understand the relation of body and mind in the light of some of the findings of science. However, the materialist and dualist positions are hampered by beliefs that are not scientific findings but philosophical assumptions inherited from the past; therefore, it is important to expand the range of options by including panpsychist-type views. I do not claim that either the Whiteheadian or the Aurobindian positions are without problems, only that survival cannot be dismissed as impossible, incoherent, or even improbable without a serious look at them.

Nine

THE POSSIBILITY OF SURVIVAL: EMPIRICAL ARGUMENTS

T HE HUMAN SCIENCES, SUPPORTED BY COMMONSENSE observations, have produced a great deal of evidence that human consciousness is influenced by the body in radical ways. Reductionists often cite this evidence to support their position that survival is either impossible or very improbable. Any responsible treatment of the subject must include at least a brief look at this material.

Arguments Against Survival

Influence of Body Over Mind

The evidence can be broken down as follows: chemical alterations of consciousness, alterations of consciousness by injury or other bodily invasion, and alterations of consciousness due to illness.

1. Chemical Alterations of Consciousness

It is well known that consciousness is altered by ordinary changes in body chemistry. Children who come to school hungry have difficulty concentrating; the person who is tense or depressed often feels more relaxed and cheerful after physical exercise.

Well-known examples of chemical substances that alter consciousness are: caffeine, which has an energizing effect, and nicotine, which has a calming effect; alcohol and hard drugs such as cocaine, which tend to lead to euphoria and reduced inhibitions; a number of food additives and refined sugar, which can lead to wild, hyperactive behavior in certain children. Psychedelic drugs such as LSD and mescaline have elements in common with certain NDEs; they can trigger experiences that seem indistinguishable from spontaneous religious experiences.[1] (See Chapter Fourteen.) Other effects are less known: neurologist Oliver Sacks has shown that an overdose of aspirin in certain aged persons triggers hallucinatory memories of songs heard in early life,[2] and that L-Dopa taken by postencephalitic patients arouses them from their trances to a hyperexcited state with detailed memories of events long past.[3]

2. Alterations of Consciousness by Invasion or Injury

Some examples of alterations of consciousness by invasion or injury are as follows: the severing of the corpus callosum between the two lobes of the brain can lead to a form of splitting of consciousness; various skills (such as ability to read or to write) can be lost following removal of parts of the left brain; particular past scenes are relived when certain parts of the cerebral cortex are stimulated with electrodes, as Wilder Penfield discovered;[4] uncharacteristic tendencies to violent behavior can follow brain injury; and certain psychotic symptoms can be relieved after electroshock.[5] An even more remarkable example: the composer Dmitri Shostakovich claimed that he had a fragment of an exploded shell lodged in his brain; when he tilted his head in a certain way, the fragment would move against his temporal lobe and the melodies would start.[6]

3. Alterations of Consciousness Due to Illness

Illness affects consciousness is various ways. Immediately before a seizure, some epileptics can perceive visionary music or images, or have mystical-type experiences. Creativity has been linked to mental illness: people of artistic achievement have a higher hospitalization rate for mental illness than the average.[7] Oliver Sacks has noted both sparkling creativity and a tendency to violence in connection with Tourette's syndrome, a highly "wired" state with repetitive, compulsive actions. These can be controlled with the drug Haldol, but then the creativity also vanishes.[8] It is well known that the memory loss in Alzheimer's disease and senile degeneration is linked with major neurological breakdown due to illness.

Two examples particularly relevant to the issue of painful NDEs concern illnesses leading to radical changes in one's sense of meaning. The title case in Sacks' *The Man who Mistook His Wife for a Hat* concerns a musician and painter who suffered from a tumor on his right brain. Increasingly he lost the ability to perceive wholes such as persons or scenes, seeing only a loose collection of individual features; his paintings became more and more abstract. He could not tell a human being from an inanimate object such as a grandfather clock; he could not recognize his own photo. He actually reached for his wife's head and tried to lift it off, thinking it was his hat.[9]

The other illness is schizophrenia. Various forms of schizophrenia appear to have different physiological correlates, but certain symptoms are more or less constant: tormenting hallucinatory voices, a sense of participation in other worlds,[10] a sense of cosmic meaningfulness in everyday things, delusory ideas about one's body, a conviction that one's own and others' thoughts flow together. In some cases, megavitamins, drugs such as Haldol, or even kidney dialysis diminish the symptoms.

One can see that the vivid reliving of memories resulting from aspirin poisoning and electrode stimulation somewhat resemble the life review; that the loss of meaning correlated with a right-brain tumor is similar to the breakdown of meaning in certain Meaningless Void NDEs; and that the tormenting voices of schizophrenia have much in common with the demonic "welcomers" of hellish NDEs, as suggested in Chapter Four. Such resemblances have been used to support reductionistic interpretations of NDEs, but there are alternatives.

Cultural Differences in Interpretation of Evidence for Survival

One argument against survival is the fact that certain kinds of phenomena that are offered to support survival in one culture can be interpreted in another with no reference to survival. For example, E. R. Dodds points out that whereas the possessing entities in mediumistic trances in the nineteenth and twentieth centuries were understood to be spirits of the dead, in the sixteenth and seventeenth centuries witches interpreted their possessing entities to be demons.[11] Dodds also notes that the trances (some of them evidential) of the psychic sensitives studied by French investigator Eugene Osty do not presuppose survival.[12]

I gave a similar example in the material on world religions above. The spirits of deceased relatives as loving welcomers to the realms of light abound in contemporary Western NDEs and deathbed visions, some of them even being evidential. But the *Bardo Thodol* assumes a rapid-reincarnation view that would make welcoming relatives extremely rare. Both views affirm survival, but the particular conceptions of survival seem incompatible.

It may be noted that this cross-cultural argument does not in itself rule out survival, but only argues against certain types of evidence for it.[13]

Arguments for the Probability of Survival

The examples given above of body's influence on mind must be balanced by evidence for the mind's effects on the body. Some of this evidence not only challenges materialist mind-body views, but suggests that the mind is the sort of reality that could survive apart from its base in the body.

Influence of Mind Over Body

1. Psychosomatic Effects in Normal Consciousness

The evidence for psychosomatic effects in normal consciousness is massive. It is well known that the placebo effect demonstrates that faith in the effectiveness of the placebo leads to physical changes in the body. Hope and faith also seem to help prevent illness. Holocaust survivor Viktor Frankl observed that prisoners in the camps with something to live for tended to resist disease, while those who collapsed into despair soon grew ill and died.[14]

Similarly, while stress is well-known to trigger illness, in *Who Gets Sick: Thinking and Health,* Blair Justice cites many studies showing that the coping style one chooses is perhaps even more important. Those who judge a stressful situation optimistically, act to try to change it, and use exercise, relaxation training, or the like to safeguard themselves have a lower disease rate. Justice sees the optimistic judgment as the most important factor. For example, among those diagnosed with cancer, those who view themselves positively have higher immune-system NK cell activity than those who feel helpless and hopeless.[15] This point is similar to Eccles' findings that choices of attention can actually alter brain cells.

2. Psychosomatic Effects in Altered States of Consciousness

Psychosomatic effects in altered states of consciousness are sometimes very dramatic. It is known that persons capable of deep hypnotic trance can show extraordinary bodily strength, make themselves anesthetized to pain, as well as raise warts or welts and make them disappear. Less known are the phenomena of certain mystics and other deeply religious people: stigmata, the ability to live for long periods on no or virtually no food, levitation, and the like.[16] For example, the levitations of Teresa of Avila were described in her own journals and supported by several eyewitnesses.[17]

Perhaps the best-known psychosomatic effect in altered states is unorthodox healing, often linked with religious faith. Some of these are dramatic, involving abrupt recovery from longterm, organic disorders. I heard a firsthand account of a recovery from multiple sclerosis from a Roman Catholic whom I will call Marian Kent, a devotee of the Virgin of Medjugorje. In the summer of 1986, without actually going to the shrine, she went into an altered state which included a life review. The next morning she experienced her paralyzed toes moving for the first time in eight years, and her twisted atrophied legs returning to normal size and shape. She removed the braces that had been necessary for walking, and was able to climb stairs, run, and dance. She tells that the transformation was attested to by her physicians, one of whom insisted that the well woman before him was Marian Kent's (nonexistent) twin.[18]

Healings in connection with religious shrines and apparitions are of course not new. The medical board at the shrine of Lourdes accepts as cures only those cases in which the illness (certified by prior medical records) was organic, the healing was instantaneous and complete, no medication could have accounted for it, and there was no regression within four to six years afterwards. As of 1968, sixty-two cases had met these stringent requirements.[19]

Psychosomatic action is also found in pathological cases. An example is that of Anna Ecklund, a young Roman Catholic woman living in Iowa in the teens and twenties of the present century, who believed herself possessed by a devil. She showed gross body distortions, sudden dramatic weight changes, levitations (at one point she rose upward and clung to the wall above the door), and mysterious stenches during a successful exorcism performed in 1928 by Capuchin monk Theophilus Reisinger.[20] Still another class of pathological examples is found in the study of multiple personality; for example, one personality may show wounds from past torture, while another does not; one has an allergy and another does not, and the like.[21]

These examples show mind as having initiative and power in relation to body, though they do not necessarily point toward survival. It is clear that the relation of body and mind is extremely complex, with each having powerful potential to shape the experience of the other, either for harm or for health. The general impression given is that mind has greater power than body, but the issue cannot be settled by a few examples. The evidence for psychical phenomena (psi) gives a clearer answer.

Psi

The study of psi was launched in the second half of the nineteenth century by a group of open-minded scholars and scientists: philosophers Henry Sidgwick and William James, classics scholar F. W. H. Myers, mathematician Eleanor Balfour Sidgwick, research psychologist Edmund Gurney, physicists William Crookes and William Barrett, and others. They established the (English) Society for Psychical Research (SPR) and the American Society for Psychical Research (ASPR) to investigate in a scientific manner claims of extraordinary human powers that were inexplicable by recognized theories. The phenomena included automatic writing, apparent telepathy and clairvoyance, and evidence for survival of death. In the analysis of philosopher C. D. Broad, these phenomena appear to violate the "basic limiting principles" of the modern worldview. Two of these principles are: mind cannot gain knowledge directly from another mind, but only indirectly, through the senses; mind can directly affect only its own body, and can affect the rest of the world only indirectly through its body.[22] But the phenomena seem to show that mind can interact directly with other minds or physical events at a distance from the body. Psi may be broken down into "receptive psi" and "expressive psi."

Receptive Psi

Receptive psi includes telepathy, clairvoyance or remote viewing, precognition, and retrocognition (paranormally gained knowledge of the past). The following is a spontaneous case that could be interpreted either as telepathy or precognition. The principal witness, Walter Franklin Prince, was a person of strong integrity, a psychologist and parapsychologist who kept careful records and sought corroboration. On the night of November 27, 1917, Prince had a nightmare in which a woman of about thirty-five, blonde, slender, and pretty, was to be executed. She declared she was willing to die if he would only hold her hand. She sat down (or at least lowered herself) calmly, the lights went out, and he felt her hand grip his as the deed was done. With his hand he felt her head, now loose from the body, the hair wet with blood. His other hand was caught in her teeth, and he felt her teeth open and close several times. He was horrified at the idea of the severed yet living head. Vivid and powerful, the dream haunted him for several days, and he told it the following day both to his wife, Lelia Prince, and the secretary at the American Society for Psychical Research, Gertrude Tubby.[23]

On the afternoon of November 29, Thanksgiving Day, Prince read in the newspaper *The Evening Telegram* that a woman named Sarah Hand had committed suicide the night of November 28 (the night after the dream) by placing her neck on a rail at the Hollis, Long Island railroad station (about six miles from Prince's home). She had left a letter in her handbag explaining that her head would live on after being severed from her body. After reading the article, Prince wrote out his dream on November 30 and asked his wife and Miss Tubby to write out their recollections of his accounts to them. Their narratives (Miss Tubby's dated November 30, Mrs. Prince's December 2) give the chief events of the dream, though each added one incorrect detail.[24]

On January 10, 1918, Prince interviewed Mrs. Hand's widowed husband and saw a picture of her. She was thirty-one, dark-blonde, slender, and pretty, but her face did not resemble that of the figure in his dream. He learned that Mrs. Hand had spoken several times about her idea that her head would live on and speak after being cut off. At the time of her death she was on a holiday leave from a mental hospital.[25]

Prince points out the matches between his dream and the event: the general description and age of the woman, her name and the emphasis on hands in the dream, the darkness, her lowering herself, death by decapitation, her consent to it, the idea of the head's still being alive and its mouth moving after being severed from the body. Either telepathy or precognition, he concludes, could be the explanation.[26]

This dream was one of four vivid, unforgettable dreams Prince had, one sublime and the other three horrifying, three of which matched impressively with events at a distance of which Prince had no normal knowledge. In view of the several correlating details, chance coincidence seems an unlikely explanation. Considering Prince's character, sophistication, and self-discipline, as well as the two confirming accounts, claims of fraud or major mistakes of memory are far-fetched. The evidence is strong that Prince participated in Mrs. Hand's state of mind before or during her suicide, at a distance from his own body.

Expressive Psi

Expressive psi means that mind affects the physical world at a distance from its body directly, without using its body as means.[27] It includes poltergeist phenomena, the bending of spoons without touching them, psychic photography, the healing of others by prayer or laying-on-of hands, and the like.[28]

An unusually well-attested spontaneous case is the Miami poltergeist of 1967. Workers at a novelty company called Tropication Arts were experiencing unusual movement of objects with much breakage; several times objects were seen to sail off shelves when no one was near. Events were investigated by Susy Smith, a responsible writer of books on psychic subjects for the general public, and parapsychologists William Roll and Gaither Pratt. Roll was present for ten days, and Pratt for three days, while the phenomena were at their height.[29] In all, 225 poltergeist events were witnessed and recorded, including a fifteen-pound box moving horizontally twenty-four feet. In a single day (when Roll was absent) there were fifty-two incidents.[30]

It soon became evident that the phenomena centered around a nineteen-year-old Cuban refugee named Julio Vasquez, a shipping clerk. This is not to say that he was a prankster; nine times the investigators were looking directly at him when an object fell, and could see no way he could have moved it normally. Julio suffered from much anger and frustration both at home and on the job; at one point he told Roll that when an object fell it made him feel good. When Vasquez left the job on February 2, all paranormal activity at the firm ceased abruptly. When Roll and Pratt took him to be tested at the parapsychology laboratory in Durham, North Carolina, several inexplicable incidents took place, including the falling and shattering of a vase while Vasquez was being directly observed.[31]

Poltergeist activity is nearly always unconscious in intent; in many cases it centers around an unhappy person, usually an adolescent, who seems to vent her or his boxed-up frustrations by flinging objects about paranormally. In contrast, psychic photography, metal-bending, and unorthodox healing of others usually involve conscious intent.

The Miami case is a particularly strong one in view of the many movements of objects observed and recorded by several sophisticated witnesses. As with the dream of W. F. Prince, ordinary explanations for this case must be very strained.

Were these two cases the only ones, however well attested to by credible people they may be, for most people they would not be enough to establish the reality of psi. But during the more than one hundred years of the history of parapsychology, a large number of persons of education, intelligence, discipline, and integrity have reported many examples of phenomena of these and similar kinds, and have found them convincing. Not only spontaneous cases but a good many careful studies of gifted persons able to produce psi semi-regularly—including Eileen Garrett, Leonora Piper, and Gladys Osborne Leonard—have been published (see Chapter Nine). In addition, contrary to the idea that parapsychology has no repeatable laboratory experiments, the social-science technique of meta-analysis shows statistical repeatability, particularly with the "Ganzfeld" (sensory deprivation) clairvoyance experiments.[32, 33, 34] Interested persons unfamiliar with the field may wish to sample the journals and proceedings of the societies for psychical research.

This brief discussion can do no more than serve as a pointer to the abundant evidence for the reality of psi. Taken together, that evidence greatly strengthens the case for the seniority of mind over body, suggesting that mind, either in receiving or expressing, is not limited to using the body as means.

Mind as Initially Transcending Body

There is another class of evidence that mind transcends body: apparent memories (after this, I will drop the "apparent") of the womb and of birth. In some cases these memories present a picture of a mature consciousness capable of deciding to incarnate; some include details verified by medical records and the memories of the parents and of attendants at the birth.

The sources of these memories are small children between about two and four years of age and in ordinary consciousness, as well as older persons undergoing therapy in normal or altered states. P. M. H. Atwater reports that half of the child experiencers she interviewed can remember their births, and a third have prenatal memories. In some cases these memories appear spontaneously, to the surprise of the person, who perhaps did not believe such things were possible. In some instances they are painful, casting light on psychological problems and resulting in noticeable improvement for the person.

Consciousness researcher Jenny Wade sees prenatal memories as of two overlapping kinds: in one the fetus develops a kind of animal consciousness, whose memories are lost to consciousness as a result of birth. In the other, a mature consciousness is linked to the fetus or newborn, is able to move in and out, observe surroundings, and tune in telepathically to the thoughts of others.[35] The majority of 750 subjects of researcher Helen Wambach's hypnotic regression experiments reported both kinds, identifying strongly with the mature consciousness. Most of Wambach's subjects claimed to have existed before conception, entering the fetus at some point between the beginning of the third trimester and a day or two after birth.[36] Hypnotherapist Michael Gabriel's clients also reported a reflective consciousness able to move in and out, though his subjects were in some cases unable to distinguish between the mother's feelings and their own at early stages.[37]

Here is an example of a child's report, from researcher David Chamberlain: a three-and-a-half-year-old boy named Jason spontaneously told his mother that he remembered being born. He had heard her crying and was trying hard to get out.

> It was "tight," he felt "wet," and felt something around his neck and throat. In addition something hurt his head and he remembered his face had been "scratched up."

Jason's mother said she had "never talked to him about the birth," but the facts were correct. The umbilical cord was wrapped around his neck, he was monitored via an electrode on his scalp, and was pulled out by forceps. The photo taken by the hospital shows scratches on his face.[38]

Memories may include the circumstances of conception, parents' reactions to their first news of the pregnancy, and attempted abortions. Some of these are confirmed by the parents. Chamberlain hypnotically regressed ten mother-child pairs to elicit their birth memories. The children, who had no conscious memories of birth, produced remarkably detailed accounts, including instruments used and position at birth, that were in major agreement with their mothers' accounts and birth records. There were only nine serious contradictions, as opposed to 137 agreements. The following is an example of knowledge that could not have been gained from inside the womb: a woman named Debbie recalled from her gestation her pregnant mother sitting on a couch knitting; she wore a dark green plaid dress. Her father entered and asked why she was knitting something for a *girl*. Asked about this incident, Debbie's mother in astonishment confirmed that just such an event had happened late in the fourth month of her pregnancy, including even the wearing of the plaid dress, which she had given away right after her pregnancy.[39]

There is no obvious way Debbie could have seen her mother's dress or understood her father's comment. It might be claimed that Debbie's mother had told her of the incident and that both had forgotten it. But there are also cases of embarrassing memories—irregular circumstances of conception, or attempted abortions—that mothers would have been very reluctant to tell. To find normal explanations for unusual details in prebirth and birth accounts, one might resort to fraud or very lucky guesses, but the more cases are recorded, the less convincing such explanations would be.

Sometimes the memories include a mixture of interior and exterior perspectives, puzzling to the narrator.[40] According to some accounts, when not actually in the womb, the consciousness is free-floating in the vicinity of the mother, observing the scene in a generally detached way but often reluctant to incarnate. Some persons tell of having intended to incarnate previously, but changing their minds, resulting in a miscarriage.[41] It might be added that these memories are consistent with memories of former lives, and in fact several researchers have found them together. About the evidence for reincarnation, more in Chapter Nine.

William Wordsworth's well-known lines—

> Our birth is but a sleep and a forgetting:
> The Soul that rises with us, our life's Star,
> Hath had elsewhere its setting,
> And cometh from afar....[42]

are partially supported by these puzzling accounts. And as his title "Ode: Intimations of Immortality From Recollections of Early Childhood" implies, Wordsworth also believed that memories of having transcended the body at the beginning of life support the likelihood that one will also transcend it at the end.

In summary, we find much empirical evidence both that consciousness is influenced by the body and the body by consciousness; but indications are that consciousness is the senior partner.

Ten

DOCUMENTED EVIDENCE
FOR SURVIVAL

T HE CASE FOR SURVIVAL DOES NOT DEPEND ON NDES; THE records of psychical research include many studies of apparent communication with the deceased. They may be divided as follows: (1) Mediumship (including "star" mediums, the cross correspondences, and drop-in cases); (2) Apparitions of the deceased; (3) Apparent spirit influence in daily life (possession, overshadowing, and inspiration); and (4) Reincarnation-type cases.

Mediumship

"Star" Mediums

The pioneers of psychical research mentioned in Chapter Eight had particular interest in the possibility of survival of death. Cautious and disciplined thinkers, after only a few years of careful research most of them became convinced that certain mediums were receiving information, supposedly from deceased persons communicating, that could not be explained by normal means. However, the researchers did not think survival had been proved because they also had considerable evidence for telepathy and clairvoyance among the living. If a medium's information could be confirmed as veridical (true) by letters or diaries, or knowledgeable friends or relatives, it could have been gleaned from those sources by telepathy or clairvoyance. The researchers, therefore, looked for further ways to probe the identity of communicators.

A "star" medium whom William James and other members of the American Society for Psychical Research (ASPR) studied exhaustively for many years was the gifted Leonora Piper of Boston (1857–1950). Like many other trance mediums, Mrs. Piper had a master of ceremonies or "control" who relayed the messages of her other communicators. Her first major control, Phinuit, claimed to be the spirit of a French physician, but he knew little about medicine and there were no records of him at his supposed alma mater. However, Phinuit produced a good deal of information Mrs. Piper could not have known normally.

An example of the paranormal knowledge Phinuit showed is the "Uncle Jerry" case. In 1889 Mrs. Piper was invited to visit the family of physicist Oliver Lodge in England, where she knew no one. Lodge wrote to his uncle Robert living in London to ask for some object that had belonged to Robert's deceased twin brother Jerry. The object Robert sent, a gold watch, was given to Mrs. Piper in trance. Phinuit reported that it had belonged to an "Uncle Jerry" who had a brother Robert, and declared that Jerry was present. "Uncle Jerry" described events from his early years: swimming in a flooded creek; killing a cat in Smith's field; owning a small rifle and a long skin like a snake-skin.[1]

These things were news to Lodge, who wrote to Robert seeking verification. Robert was able to verify two of them: he remembered the creek-swimming episode, though he had only watched, and the snakeskin. But he denied killing the cat, and had no memory of Smith's field. Robert inquired of a third brother, Frank, living in Cornwall. Frank did remember Smith's field, and remembered that the cat had been killed by another brother. He remembered that he and Jerry had swum in the flooded creek. Frank could not remember the snakeskin. If Mrs. Piper obtained this information by telepathy from the living, it had to be pieced together from the minds of two persons, unknown to her, living separately.[2]

(Incidentally, Mrs. Piper did not have such spectacular success in every seance; she had "off days" when nothing worthwhile came through.)

A new development in Mrs. Piper's mediumship in 1892 took the search a major step further. A new control, "George Pelham," or G.P., appeared four or five weeks after the sudden death of attorney George Pellew. Pellew had had a single sitting with Mrs. Piper several years earlier, but aside from that she had not known him (though she may have seen his obituary). "George Pelham" not only knew much about the life of Pellew, he was able to recognize and name, among 150 persons who had sittings with Mrs. Piper, thirty who had been Pellew's former friends. He made no clearly false recognitions (though two were questionable), and failed in only three or four cases to recognize someone Pellew had known, one being a young woman who had been a child when Pellew knew her.[3,4] The control showed in numerous subtle ways traits of the historical Pellew: Investigator Richard Hodgson, who was previously skeptical about survival and who had known Pellew fairly well, was greatly impressed by "[t]he continual manifestation of this personality,...with its own reservoir of memories, with its swift appreciation of any reference to friends of G.P., with its "give-and-take" in little incidental conversations with myself...."[5] Pelham's interactions with the thirty recognized sitters fit Pellew's relationship with them.[6] The Pelham control also showed the conversational gifts and the point of view of Pellew over a five-year period, 1892–1897. This sustained performance shows a considerable advance over merely providing paranormal information about the deceased.

A recent study citing Eleanor Sidgwick and researcher Gerald Balfour points out that the author of report, Hodgson, failed to mention certain weaknesses in this material. For example, the thirty acquaintances of Pellew were not presented at random; Mrs. Piper knew beforehand that particular seances were set up specifically for certain of them, and some were known to Mrs. Piper socially.[7] However, this critical study does not claim that Pelham's recognition of all or even most of the thirty persons was contaminated. I conclude, therefore, that at least some of the recognitions still stand. (Other problems with Pelham will be discussed below.)

The ability to recognize a particular person involves more than is usually thought. Ian Stevenson, citing philosopher Michael Polanyi, points out that a recognition assumes a great deal of knowledge gained by interaction. This knowledge cannot be reduced to an informational description or a photograph.[8] While telepathy might have given Mrs. Piper information about all thirty of the people, it would not have been enough for the appropriate and subtle give-and-take that Pelham achieved. That required the unique point of view of Pellew, which Pelham showed,[9] an ability amounting to a skill. Omniscient telepathy and clairvoyance (superpsi) do not necessarily account for this ability. One form of superpsi that might, retroprehensive inclusion, will be discussed below.

Another "star" medium, the English Gladys Osborne Leonard (1882–1967), was studied for years by members of the SPR. As with Mrs. Piper, careful on-the-spot records were kept of many of her seances, and countless veridical messages were given. One remarkable phenomenon of

Mrs. Leonard's trances (not unique to her) was the Direct Voice. Mrs. Leonard's control Feda, a childish personality with a piping voice, usually seemed to be talking with someone directly in front of her. She would tell the sitters what the communicator said, sometimes complaining that she couldn't hear properly, sometimes mispronouncing a name. Most of the time the sitters heard only what Feda said through Mrs. Leonard's lips, but occasionally they heard a whisper from the apparently empty space a few feet in front of Mrs. Leonard. Researcher Drayton Thomas, who had over 500 sittings with Mrs. Leonard,[10] summarizes: "The Direct Voice supplies the required word...when Feda asks for it....It corrects Feda's mistakes....It may be unheard...mis-heard, or...only partly heard by Feda."[11] The effect was impressive and uncanny. The Direct Voice is hard to evaluate as evidence for survival, but suggests that mediumship involves more than dissociation, telepathy, and dramatization.

Cross Correspondences

Appearing in the early years of the twentieth century, the cross correspondences are a long series of interrelated automatic scripts from several mediums, including Mrs. Piper in the United States, classics scholars Mrs. Margaret Verrall and her daughter Helen Verrall, magistrate Winifred Coomb-Tennant ("Mrs. Willett"), all in England, and Alice Kipling Fleming ("Mrs. Holland") in India. The purported authors are deceased pioneers of the SPR, especially Myers, Sidgwick, Gurney, A. W. Verrall, and S. H. Butcher, all of whom would have been very familiar with the problems of establishing the identity of a communicator.

The writings (about three thousand scripts) are important because they not only reveal obscure knowledge of Greek and Latin classics, which Myers and the others had,[12] and many of their personality traits, but *initiative and purpose* appropriate to their interests. Some (not all) of the classics quoted were known to Margaret and Helen Verrall, but the other mediums did not know Greek or Latin. A given script by itself would give isolated words or phrases that made little sense. However, when put together with scripts from the others received at roughly the same time, it became evident that a literary puzzle had been planned by the communicators. Normal communication between the mediums was carefully controlled to prevent contamination. Some of the cases are quite impressive, but overall the material is hard to evaluate for one not expert in classical languages.

A detailed example of a non-classical cross correspondence is the "Palm Sunday" case, which continued for over fifteen years. It dealt with the poignant story of the secret love of Arthur Balfour, later prime minister of England, and Mary "May" Lyttelton, who died at age twenty-four on Palm Sunday in 1875, before Arthur had proposed marriage. Visiting the bereaved family, Arthur asked that his mother's emerald ring be buried with her. Mary's sister Lavinia Talbot showed him a lock of her beautiful golden brown hair, for which he had an engraved silver box made. Arthur Balfour never married; for many years he spent each Palm Sunday with Lavinia, reminiscing about Mary.

The story was known to very few, certainly not to the mediums. But beginning in 1901 a series of specially designated scripts referred to the Palm Maiden, the May Flower ("a slender girl with quantities of hair"), the Lady with the Candle (the last picture taken of Mary alive shows her holding a candle), the Faithful Knight, the Arthuriad, a palm tree (a reference to the Balfour coat of arms), cockleshells (a motif on the Lyttelton coat of arms), a silver box and a beautiful lock of hair, emeralds, Dante and Beatrice (his deceased beloved, whose eyes Dante called "emeralds"), the Blessed Damozel (a maiden in a poem by Dante Gabriel Rosetti, looking longingly down from heaven toward her lover on earth), and the signature Mary L.

Although the investigators perceived that there was some purpose linking these scripts, they could not guess what it was. Matters changed on Palm Sunday of 1912 when Mrs. Willett entered the case. At the request of her control "Gurney," the investigator Gerald Balfour, Arthur's brother, was present. "Gurney" now gave stronger clues to the solution, speaking of "the love that waits beyond death." In response to the appeals of the Mary-communicator, Arthur himself sat with Mrs. Willett in 1916, and he now explained the reference to the lock of hair in the silver box. Mrs. Willett described the Mary-communicator as radiating love and joy.[13] The story was finally written down and published in 1960 in the *Journal SPR* by Jean Balfour, Arthur's sister-in-law.

Several prominent psychical researchers, after careful study, became convinced that the scripts did come at least partially from the deceased. One such researcher was the rigorous-minded Eleanor Balfour Sidgwick, longterm investigator and later president of the SPR,[14] who herself never received any evidential information in seances.

But an alternative explanation made was that the supposed correspondences were the result of chance, or were due to the fact that the living persons who read them happened to share certain interests, and thus read into them what they chose to see. Another explanation was telepathy from the living, particularly from the unconscious mind of Margaret Verrall, who knew Greek and Latin; however, the scripts continued after she died in 1916.

This telepathy theory eventually developed into the super-ESP hypothesis. Its gist is that a psychically gifted person can reach out to tap any memory, any records, and, as the occasion requires, convincingly impersonate any deceased person. Some still invoke this hypothesis, but the chief objection to it is that there is no other evidence that anyone has access to unlimited paranormal powers.

Intending to test the chance and telepathy hypotheses, in 1927 investigator W. H. Salter arranged for dummy cross correspondences. He chose twelve phrases taken from various poets and sent them to fourteen persons serving as pseudo-mediums, asking them to write down two hundred to three hundred words and phrases suggested by the quotations, and return them in ten days. During these ten days, he tried to send them telepathic information by concentrating on two classical topics, one from Aeschylus and another from Homer. The material produced by this experiment, Salter reported, was quite different from the real cross correspondences; scarcely anything in the individual scripts showed contact with the target scenes he was thinking about, or with each other. The scripts also showed much more influence from the individual writers' lives than did the real cross-correspondence scripts.

Salter's experiment does not prove that telepathy *cannot* be the answer to these correspondences, but it does strongly suggest that, in the words of G. N. M. Tyrrell, "the hypothesis of telepathy and common association of ideas must not be rashly invoked as...satisfactory explanations of...the real scripts."[15]

Drop-In Communicators

"Drop-in" communicators are valuable as evidence for survival, because they too show *initiative and purpose*. They are so called because they drop in uninvited at a seance, apparently unknown to all present, giving information about themselves that can be later verified.

A challenging example is the case of Robert Passanah, from a home-circle seance in Zürich, Switzerland in 1962. As the sitters took notes, the medium, Mrs. Schutz, in trance reported the presence of "a little lad" who asked her to "Give my love to my mother." He said he had had appendicitis, together with an unusual illness with a lot of fever, and had died in the children's hospital. His name, he said, was Hans-Peter, but formerly he had had another name. His family name was Indian—Pasona or Basonna. His family had lived in the seventh district of the city. His father had something to do with tea professionally, and the family drank a lot of tea. He had dark hair and eyes; he had two brothers still living.[16]

Neither the medium nor the sitters recognized any of this information. The sitters checked the Zürich telephone book, found the name Passanah, and called the family. A son of the family verified that they did have a business of importing tea and drank a lot of it, had lived in the seventh district of the city, and had lost a son of the family who died of appendicitis in the children's hospital many years earlier. The parents of the deceased child were distressed by the call, so the inquirers pursued it no further.[17]

Learning of the case in 1964, Ian Stevenson took up the investigation; he interviewed the two surviving brothers, Richard and John Passanah, and consulted obituaries and hospital records. He found that the name was Portuguese rather than Indian, but that the family had indeed lived in British India, and in 1931 moved to Zürich, where they lived in the seventh district (later moving to the tenth district). The father imported products from India, including tea; the family did indeed drink a lot of tea.[18]

At age twenty months the youngest, Robert, became ill and spent thirteen days in the children's hospital with a high fever. He died there December 6, 1932. According to the autopsy he died of pneumonia, pleurisy, and empyema, but there had been no appendicitis. According to his brothers and to a photograph Stevenson saw, Robert had dark (or brown) hair and eyes.[19]

About the two items in which the communicated information was wrong, the illness and the given name, Stevenson notes that since the German word for appendicitis (Blindarmentzündung) resembles the word for pneumonia (Lungenentzündung), and since the medium spoke softly in trance, the sitters may have misheard her. There is no explanation for the communicator failing to give his first name, Robert, and saying he now had another name, Hans-Peter. Since Robert was a toddler when he died, it seems surprising that the communicator omitted his first name but gave details like living in the seventh district, which would have meant little to a small child.[20] (However, difficulty with names is common even among otherwise impressive trance communicators.)

In an attempt to find normal explanations for the appearance of this information, Stevenson decided it was unlikely that the medium and the Passanah family had any acquaintances in common. The Passanah parents were British and had difficulty understanding the Swiss-German dialect of the sitters (although Richard and John could understand it). The telephone book gave the father's name and occupation, but it did not indicate that the family had once lived in the seventh district, had had three sons, and that one with dark hair and eyes had died. Three obituaries of 1932 gave Robert's birth and death dates and the family's address (thus, by implication, the seventh district) but did not mention the father's occupation. The hospital records mention British India and the two brothers, but not occupation. Robert's gravestone mentions only his name and the dates of birth and death.

If the medium had learned all these details normally and then forgotten them, she would have to have brought them together from at least three sources. The same is true if she had received them by reaching out via telepathy and clairvoyance. Furthermore, what would have been the motivation for selecting these data about this unknown child from the billions of data about millions of former and present citizens of Zürich?[21] A surviving Robert Passanah, however, would have had a motivation. Fraud can always be claimed, but Stevenson found no sign of it either in the family or the members of the seance; furthermore, for two years, none of those involved made any attempt to publicize the case.

Stevenson notes the oddity that thirty years after Robert's death the communicator was perceived as a child ("little lad") but clearly not a toddler barely able to talk; it would seem he had grown since his death, although not very much! Stevenson suggests that the communicator was a "persona" constructed by the medium from information gained from a real discarnate personality and other sources.[22] (More on the persona theory near the end of this chapter.)

If survival is in fact the true explanation, and the motivation of Robert Passanah was to console and support his mother—for "losing a child is a life sentence"[23]—then his intention was not only defeated but with sad irony had the opposite effect, for the mother (and the father) did not accept the expression of love but became upset by a happening apparently incompatible with their worldview.

Like other drop-in cases, the Robert Passanah case is not easy to account for by normal explanations or even telepathy.

Apparitions

A type of spontaneous case that overlaps with NDEs and sometimes offers evidence for survival is apparitions. These may be classed as Crisis Apparitions, Haunting Apparitions, and Apparitions of the Living. Alan Gauld in *Mediumship and Survival* adds Collectively Perceived Apparitions and Apparitions of the Deceased.

Crisis Apparitions

The following case, recorded in the early years of psychical research, fits the last two categories, and perhaps also the first. On Christmas Eve of 1869 a Mrs P. was sitting propped up in bed when she saw standing at the foot of the bed a tall man in navy officer's dress. His face was in shadow, the only light in the room being from a lamp on a dresser against the far wall. Mrs. P. was astonished and anxious that the figure might mean bad news about her brother in the navy. Waking her husband, she asked, "Willie, who is this?" Mr. P. awoke, stared at the figure, and demanded to know what he was doing there. The figure only looked at him reproachfully and said "Willie, Willie!" Mr. P. then leaped out of bed. The figure moved away, throwing the room into shadow as he passed the lamp, and disappeared through the wall.

Mr. P. unlocked the door and went to search the house, fruitlessly. Upon returning, he explained to the wife that the apparition was his father (whom Mrs. P. had never met), deceased for fourteen years. A few weeks later she learned that her husband had been about to take some ill-advised financial steps that would have ruined them if the apparition had not intervened. The case, written down in 1885 by the wife, was confirmed by the husband and by a pair of friends to whom they had told it shortly after it occurred.[24]

This case is weakened by the long distance in time between 1869 and 1885. But the fact that there were four witnesses, and that plans were changed as a result of the event, means that it deserves to be taken seriously. The fact that it was Mrs. P. who first saw the figure means that it is not easy to dismiss it as a hallucination, either "subjective" (private) or telepathically created. She had not known her father-in-law had been in the navy, nor did she know of her husband's financial plans; thus she had no purpose or motivation in the matter.

Two parties might have had purpose and motivation. According to the super-ESP hypothesis, Mr. P. may have been anxious and have wondered unconsciously what his father would have said about his plans. His wife read his mind and constructed the apparition; when he awoke, he telepathically perceived her vision and constructed one on the same spot. Researcher Alan Gauld finds this explanation rather far-fetched and suggests that it is simpler to suppose that it was a discarnate being with particular knowledge and a purpose, who influenced both percipients.[25] I find this view to be the most plausible.

Haunting Apparitions

Haunting apparitions are not usually thought to give particularly strong evidence for survival, because in many cases haunting ghosts (even evidential ones) behave like sleepwalkers, repeatedly going through the same actions and often ignoring the living; they seem more like mere images. Others, however, seem more aware and may notice the living. But both resemble figures seen in painful NDEs: the low-energy gray beings, the addicted figures trying to interact with the living. There is also a resemblance to the repeated nightmare of the living Sylvan Muldoon "haunting" the spot where he had been nearly electrocuted (page 60), which suggests that "sleepwalking" ghosts might be deceased persons having repeated nightmares. Thus, if we can make a case that haunting ghosts are sometimes manifestations of "the unquiet dead," it would strengthen the case for NDEs as foreshadowings of some afterdeath conditions. (However, hauntings also present problems for such a case, which will be discussed below.)

A particularly strong and relevant case is that of the ghost seen in a house in Cheltenham, England. The investigator, a resident of the house and the chief person to see the apparition, was Rosina Despard, who later became a physician. Her cautious and disciplined account, "Record of a Haunted House," appeared in the *Proceedings* of the SPR in 1892.

She summarizes the short history of the house, focussing on the first family to reside there, Mr. S. [Henry Swinhoe] and his second wife I. S. [Imogen Swinhoe]. The marriage was an unhappy and violent one; in 1876 Imogen left Henry, and a few months later he died. She died in 1878. The

4

house was empty for several years despite the very low rent asked; there were rumors it was haunted by Imogen.[26]

The Despard family of seven had not heard the rumors when they rented the house in April 1882. One night in June of that year Rosina, then nineteen, first saw near the door of her room the apparition of a tall woman in widow's black garb, holding a handkerchief to her face. She made records of this and later perceptions of the figure, but said nothing to her family for two years. During that time several other persons—namely three family members, a servant, and a guest—also saw the figure; one thought she was a nun, another an intruder. In all about twenty people saw the figure and/or heard poltergeist noises, several of them independently of one another.[27]

The apparition tended to go through the same routine, following the same path through the house. Several times she (or it) would pass people on the stairs but appear not to see them. On July 21, 1884, Rosina saw the figure come into the drawing room where she was seated with her father and sisters (none of whom, to her astonishment, could see her) and stand in the bow window for half an hour ignoring them. Then the apparition walked out, Rosina following. On August 12, 1884, Rosina's sister Edith, while playing the piano, saw the figure behind her reaching as if to turn the page; Edith left the room and found Rosina, who returned to the room with her. Rosina could then see the figure, but Edith now could not.[28] That same day Rosina again saw the figure in the bow window behind the sofa in the drawing room, her father being present. He could see nothing, but when he went up to stand beside the place Rosina indicated, Rosina saw the figure walk around behind him and leave the room.[29] Rosina tried to talk with the ghost; on January 29, 1884, Rosina went up to her as she stood in the bow window: "I asked if I could help her. She moved, and I thought she was going to speak, but she only gave a slight gasp and moved toward the door."[30]

In May and June of that year Rosina several times late at night pasted fine threads across the stairs at various heights, securing them with pellets of marine glue so they could be knocked down at a touch. However, at least twice she saw the figure pass through the cords.[31] She tried several times to touch the figure, even attempting to "pounce upon it" suddenly, but did not succeed; the ghost always seemed to be *beyond* her and, if followed into a corner, simply disappeared.[32]

The apparition continued to appear until 1889. At first so clear she was sometimes mistaken for a living person, in the last appearances the figure became indistinct.[33] This summary of the first phase of the case gives only a fraction of its many and evidential details.

Remarkably, seventy and more years after the apparition faded from sight, what seems to be the same ghost has been seen several times in the neighborhood, in some cases by people who had never heard of the Despards' apparition. During the 1950s a postman emptying a postbox near the former Despard house suddenly felt strangely cold; glancing toward the gate of the house he saw a tall woman dressed in old-fashioned clothes. He turned to close the box, but upon looking up again toward the gate, found that the figure had disappeared.[34] The figure appeared also in October 1958 to a John Thorne, who lived in the upstairs apartment of a house across the street. He awoke in the night to see a woman in a long Victorian dress standing near his bed, apparently looking down at him. He was frightened and woke his wife Pauline, but she saw no figure. They told no one. In November 1961, Thorne's brother William and William's teenage son, who were spending the night, both saw a woman in a long dress holding a handkerchief to her face (like the postman, they felt uncommonly cold). She did not seem to see them. There were small discrepancies between the Thorne accounts on the one hand and Rosina Despard's report on the other, but the chief features tallied.

William Thorne first became aware of the history of the ghost from an article he read in 1963. The Thornes' stories were not recorded until they came to the attention of investigator Andrew MacKenzie in 1969, a rather long gap that perhaps explains the comparative lack of detail. MacKenzie suggests that William Thorne's memories of the event, particularly the handkerchief, might have been influenced by the article.[35]

The ghost was again seen in January 1970 by a local resident, Doreen Jackson, who was taking a driving lesson. As her car approached the gate of the onetime Despard house, she saw a tall woman in a long black dress, with her hand (holding nothing) to her face, stepping into the street. She seemed oblivious of the car. When Mrs. Jackson braked to avoid hitting the figure, the instructor, seeing nothing, scolded her. Mrs. Jackson had never heard of the haunting.[36] When recorded?

At dusk on a day in July of 1984 two persons taking a walk, Randolf Marsh (pseudonym) and Sheila Brown, saw a woman in a long dark dress on a footpath in the area behind the house that had been its garden, now occupied by bungalows. The figure was about seventy feet away (the length of one-and-a-half city lots). They could see that her hand was held to her face; at one point the figure stopped and appeared to look straight toward them, her face exposed. She was in view for about two minutes. Aware that the figure was an apparition, Mr. Marsh, wondering if the ghost saw the present-day scene or the past scene, waved to her for some time; the figure moved to the center of the path, still glancing at them. Ms. Brown could not make out her facial features, but both noticed that she seemed to glide rather than walk.[37]

Mr. Marsh saw the apparition again late on the night of August 29, 1985, gliding toward the overgrown driveway of an empty house in the neighborhood. Mr. Marsh later heard a report that Imogen Swinhoe's sister stayed for a time in this particular house.[38]

The case is important not only because of the many witnesses and Rosina Despard's careful record, but because the ghost seemed to vary in the degree of her awareness of movement around her. She nearly always held the handkerchief to her face, as though crying; in the first series of appearances she often acted repetitively, oblivious of the bustling household around her. Philosopher David Lorimer offers the suggestion that places and objects are associated with force-fields that can absorb thoughts and feelings of a conscious being (in this case, of Imogen Swinhoe during her residency there) so that a later personality (Rosina Despard), resonating to them, can perceive the feelings, with images.[39] The ghost would then be an emotionally charged image of past events.

However, we have seen that there were times when the figure did seem to be aware of the presence of others, as when she leaned over Edith at the piano, walked around Rosina's father, and looked at John Thorne and at Randolph Marsh and Sheila Brown. This suggests rather some kind of continuing consciousness, or at least semi-consciousness. Furthermore, Imogen Swinhoe was not a widow during her residency in the house (though she perhaps wished she were), so the figure was not like a moving picture.

Whatever degree of consciousness the apparition had, there are signs that Rosina and others who saw her contributed to the apparition. Rosina mentions feeling that she had "lost power to the figure."[40] The idea that the deceased draw energy out of the living in order to meet their own needs and to manifest as ghosts appears frequently in the writings and the trance utterances of Eileen Garrett and others.[41] Feelings of cold have also been interpreted as a symptom of this process. Such psychic vampirism is consistent with the needy, addicted nature of the earthbound spirits Ritchie (page 59) and Monroe (page 65) described; it fits the idea of "hungry ghosts." Similarly, G. N. M. Tyrrell understands a ghost to be an "idea-pattern" originating from the deceased and produced by the subconscious of the perceiver.[42]

Although haunting ghosts are similar to the gray and needy figures seen in NDEs, they are out of keeping with characteristics of many NDErs themselves: serenity, rapid and clear thought, bliss, openness to the light, freedom, flight into another world. If ghosts are manifestations of spirits of the deceased, why are they so different from many NDErs? Is it because, as popular tradition claims, before death these souls were addicted, debased, ignorant of survival, or caught in a trauma? Yet there are NDErs who before their experience were in one or another of these traps, yet had peaceful or even radiant NDEs. From another side, it is true that most persons with painful NDEs had restricted rather than expanded consciousness, but none of them behaved like haunting ghosts.

Frederic Myers, Tyrrell, H. H. Price and others have suggested that ghosts are dissociated fragments of fuller minds living or deceased.[43] This hypothesis can be squared with the restricted consciousness of those in painful NDEs. Both Gary Wells (page 79) and Howard Storm (page 81) heard their own dissociated voices speaking (although the voices did not show a trapped consciousness but a wiser and freer one). The scenario fits Sylvan Muldoon's repetitive nightmares (page 60) quite well. Perhaps the sleepwalking metaphor often used for ghosts is more than a metaphor.

Apparitions of the Living

A digression to look at apparitions of the living is helpful toward understanding apparitions of the dead, since living persons can report what was going on in their minds at the time. There are apparitions of the living in which the person has no idea that his or her image appeared to someone. But in some cases the person who is seen as an apparition intended to appear, but was not fully aware of having succeeded. An example is S. H. Beard, who several times was able to make an apparition of himself visible to members of the Verity family, longtime friends. The first time, in November 1881, he decided before going to bed that he would try the experiment, and concentrated very intensely on these friends. Eventually he went to sleep without any memory of having succeeded. However, two sisters, L. S. Verity and E. C. Verity, awoke in alarm (one screamed) to see his figure standing by their bed.[44]

In a later experiment, he began to concentrate in the evening, intending to appear to the Veritys at midnight. During this time but before midnight, his apparition was seen walking in a hall between rooms by a visiting sister. At midnight, one sister perceived his apparition come into the room where she lay awake, take her long hair into his hand, then take her hand and gaze into it as though reading her palm. Such touching is very rare in apparition cases; clearly this incident is quite different from a haunting case, and is more like the intentional nature of a crisis apparition.[45] In his account, Beard reports that during concentration he seemed to himself actually to be in the house. But as he gives no further details, he was probably unaware of the hair- and hand-holding incident. At best, then, Beard had only a partial awareness of what was going on.

A more self-aware case is that of Martha Johnson (pseudonym), who in a dream on January 26, 1957, decided that she had to talk to her mother, who in fact lived some nine hundred miles away, about a frustrating matter in her work. Johnson began walking, passed through a cloud-banked environment, then through, in her words, "a great blackness. Then all at once way down below me...I could see a small bright oasis of light...the [house]...where my Mother lives." Johnson passed through the walls that felt like cobwebs into her mother's kitchen. She leaned against a cupboard and watched her mother "bending over something white and doing something with her hands." The mother looked up and saw her. Johnson walked a few steps but then was pulled up into a dark mist. She awoke immediately, and noted the time as 2:10 am.[46]

Johnson's mother wrote her on January 29 saying that she had seen her daughter for a few seconds at that hour on the 26th while ironing in the kitchen (she had had insomnia). She remarked that her dogs had also seen the apparition and had gotten very excited. This strong evidential case shows that apparitions of the living can be conscious and can have purpose and initiative (even though Martha was unable to fulfill her purpose).

Can the same be true of apparitions of the dead? Seeking to find out, investigator Hornell Hart did two studies of apparitions in the 1950s. He gives twenty-five evidential cases like that of Martha Johnson in which one person consciously travels out-of-body to a specific place and is seen there as an apparition. Comparing them to apparitions of the dying and the dead,

Hart found that, overall, they had twenty-three characteristics in common. For example, the apparition looked vivid and real, related to the surroundings and to other people as a normal person would, spoke briefly, gave veridical information, was seen by more than one person present, and disappeared inexplicably. He concluded that apparitions of the living and those of the dead cannot otherwise be distinguished, and that, therefore, some "apparitions of the dead presumably carry with them the memories and purposes of the personalities which they represent, and...constitute evidence of survival...."[47] This conclusion is, of course, a matter of likelihood and not of proof.

Thus it may well be that some apparitions of the dead are as conscious as Martha Johnson's was, while others like S. H. Beard's are created by the intentions of the deceased but are largely dissociated from her or his consciousness. Still other apparitions may have virtually no consciousness at all—they may have been generated by the perceiver (like the inhabitants in P. M. H. Atwater's town) or by a third party. An example of the latter is psychologist M. Schatzman's client "Ruth," who was able to create visionary images of herself or others at will, images that were occasionally seen by others.[48] One must be careful, therefore, in interpreting apparitions of the dead.

Apparent Spirit Influence: Possession, Overshadowing, and Inspiration

Another class of evidence for survival, somewhat similar to mediumship, I will refer to as possession, overshadowing, and inspiration. Whereas mediums are usually in control of the circumstances in which the claimed spirits of the deceased communicate, cases of the possession and overshadowing types involve spontaneous and often unwelcome influence or takeover. The term "possession" will be used to refer to takeover by a claimed spirit, displacing the person's consciousness; "overshadowing" will refer to persistent influence, major or minor, from such a spirit (or source later interpreted as a spirit), interfering with the person's life as it seems to fuse with her or his consciousness but not displace it. When the possession or overshadowing shows creative gifts, becoming partly or wholly beneficial, I will refer to it as "inspiration."

Possession

The strongest case of the possession type in the literature is that of Uttara/Sharada, studied virtually independently by Ian Stevenson and V. V. Akolkar, whose reports strongly support one another. At the times they were published, the case was ongoing.

Uttara Huddar is a college lecturer living in Nagpur in west central India. During a period in her childhood Uttara suffered from an intense fear of snakes; she also had vivid dreams of a husband riding to her on a pony and caressing her. She shared with her father an interest in Bengali culture and enjoyed reading Bengali novels in translation. Her marital status was somewhat unconventional. Originally she had decided against marriage, but during her school years she changed her mind when she fell in love with a classmate. This relationship ended in painful disappointment and she devoted herself to a spiritual quest.

In 1973 Uttara was thirty-two years old and living in a hospital-ashram headed by a Dr. Joshi (pseudonym) to whom she felt a deep spiritual attraction. During this time she took training in meditation and began to enter extraordinary altered states in which she was unable to speak her native language, Marathi, and instead spoke Bengali, which she had never really studied. During these states she seemed to regard Dr. Joshi as her husband, which led to jealousy and an embarrassing scene. After being sent back to her parents' home she continued from time to time to enter these states, which varied in length from hours to weeks.

In these altered states, her personality was very different. Normally, Uttara was an educated, generally liberated woman who was single, plain-spoken, interested in mysticism but not in conventional religion. In her altered state, however, she called herself Sharada Chattopadhaya. She was demure and feminine, devoted to the Goddess Durga, warmly attached to a husband (who, however, battered her at times). She had a great deal of knowledge about early nineteenth-century Bengali life, and possessed Bengali tastes and skills. During one of these periods Sharada was ill with the symptoms of cobra-venom poisoning. She was perplexed about modern inventions such as automobiles and household appliances; she assumed that letters must be hand-carried. She reported that in the seventh month of a long-desired pregnancy she had been bitten by a cobra and had lost consciousness, but she had no awareness of having died or now being in a different body. She could not understand why she found herself in this strange place, and asked to be taken home by ox-cart to her husband and her village in Bengal (now Bangladesh).[49]

Investigators determined that Sharada spoke Bengali fluently and responsively, while obscure sources on life in East Bengal in the early nineteenth century supported her accounts. The Chattopadhaya (now called Chatterji) family still lived in the region, and the investigators confirmed Sharada's detailed descriptions of the area of her home. The family also consulted their family tree and found in the 1820s six of the names Sharada gave of male members of her immediate family; a deed of sale confirmed a seventh name. (There were no women's names recorded.) A present-day family member recalled having heard that a female family member in his great-grandmother's day had died of cobra bite.[50] (This is a very brief summary of an extraordinary and highly detailed case.)

Commentary

The Uttara/Sharada case has many strong evidential features. Of course, not all of Sharada's extensive knowledge of Bengali life needs a paranormal interpretation; some information could have come from Uttara's reading of Bengali novels in translation. However, Uttara's reading would not explain Sharada's knowledge of the seven names of the Chattopadhaya family, her knowledge, for example, that the Hansheshwari Temple could be seen from the Chattopadhaya house,[51] her ability to tell genuine Bengali sweets from imitations,[52] her severe illnesses with symptoms of venom poisoning,[53] and especially her fluency in the language. Eight Bengali-speaking persons talked with her, some for hours, and confirmed that she did indeed speak the language responsively (that is, she did not merely recite set passages).[54] Further, the Bengali she used had almost no English loan words, which is the way Bengali was before 1830 (in contrast to the present, in which approximately twenty percent are English loan words).[55]

The investigators looked into several possible explanations for the case. Could Uttara have learned Bengali in her childhood and forgotten it? After inquiring in detail into Uttara's childhood, Stevenson judged this explanation to be very unlikely. He also considered fraud very unconvincing, considering all the problems that Sharada's appearance created for the Huddar family: parents and daughter could not talk to each other and needed a translator; Uttara was suspended for a year from her teaching job, which created financial problems; therapists were needed, an expense; the aged mother's household workload was greatly increased because Sharada was so much at sea in the twentieth century; newspapers printed unfavorable stories.[56] Stevenson points out that the case may seem to resemble multiple personality disorder; alternate personalities differ greatly from each other, and some are mutually unaware.[57] However, multiple personality disorder is almost always triggered by severe stress and trauma in childhood, whereas Uttara's childhood was relatively normal and Sharada appeared in Uttara's adulthood, partly as a result of practice of meditation. It is also very rare for an alternate personality to have detailed knowledge of a foreign language and culture.

Stevenson considers possession and reincarnation as more convincing explanations, reincarnation being more likely (though he sees reincarnation and possession as on a continuum rather than being sharp alternatives). The following features, showing seeds of the Sharada phenomenon, recommend reincarnation: Uttara's early phobia for snakes, her dreams of the man on a horse or pony coming to her, and her later fondness for Bengali fiction and Bengali heroines (such phobias and enthusiasms are common among Stevenson's many reincarnation-type cases). Another factor is the appearance over time of increasing signs of a merger between Uttara and Sharada. Uttara began to show interest in devotional songs to Sharada's Goddess, Durga, and to worship her regularly; at the same time, Sharada's intonation and accent came to be closer to Uttara's, indicating that the two were beginning to fuse.[58] Akolkar makes the same point.[59]

Sharada's ability to speak Bengali is perhaps the most impressive feature of this case, and appears to be strong evidence for survival, either as possession or reincarnation. As we have seen, Stevenson holds that a skill such as ability to converse in an unlearned language cannot be explained by either normal means or by ESP, since a skill contains more than mere information. The learning of a skill often involves studying a model and absorbing facts, but necessarily requires practice. For this reason he holds that anyone who has the ability to speak a language must have learned the language himself some time previously. And if we can show there is no way the speaker learned the language earlier in this life, it must have been learned by some other personality that is either a previous incarnation or a discarnate spirit attached to him (or her).[60] This means, for all intents and purposes, that ability to speak an unlearned language of the past requires survival.

Not all scholars agree. David Griffin, building on process theory, suggests a form of super-psi he calls retroprehensive inclusion. Since process theory holds that every mind has access to the whole past at a deep unconscious level, one might "reach out" into the past, so to speak, and incorporate a particular personality for whom one has affinity. In that case, everything in the past personality—including tastes, knowledge, and skills— would be incorporated into the present personality. This theory does not require survival and means that skills *can* be gained by ESP. He considers that this is a plausible explanation for the Uttara/Sharada case, although he does not claim that it is necessarily the best explanation.[61] Retroprehensive inclusion, however, has problems, which will be discussed below.

Overshadowing

I will use the term "overshadowing" (which has been used by other scholars in somewhat different ways) to apply to cases of apparent spirit influence, usually of a harmful sort, on persons who do not appear to be mediums. Overshadowing cases offer possible insights into haunting apparitions and into painful NDEs involving needy spirit-beings.

Overshadowing might be described as modified possession: the overshadowed person appears to be influenced to some extent by the spirit of a deceased person, while still keeping a sense of her or his own identity. The overshadowed shows, markedly, at least two of the following characteristics of the deceased person: her or his mannerisms, way of speaking, enthusiasms, phobias, pains and illnesses, point of view, and/or psychological problems.

The idea of the overshadowing of a living person by a spirit is found in many times and cultures, becoming prominent in the West in modern times during the Spiritualist movement of the nineteenth century. Enthusiastic experimentation with ouija boards and automatic writing sometimes led to psychological catastrophe, which was interpreted as the work of malicious and/or traumatized earthbound spirits. As we saw in Part II, "rescue circles" were formed by caring persons, including a medium, who would meet to contact a supposed overshadowing spirit (page 118). They were usually reported to be successful.

The disciplined study of overshadowing cases appears in two major phases in the twentieth century. The first phase was pioneered by ASPR stalwart J. H. Hyslop, who investigated several cases of claimed spirit influence in the first decade of the century (see the Gifford/Thompson case below). At his request, his work was taken over after his death by his friend, neurologist/psychotherapist Titus Bull, who encountered a number of cases of apparent overshadowing in his practice during the 1920s and 1930s. Most of his records are lost, except for accounts (one of them evidential) of two impressive cures of schizophrenic persons. Using a medium to communicate with ostensible spirits, over many sessions Bull persuaded them to leave. This approach has become known as depossession. Following the Spiritualist pattern, depossession takes a stance of compassion toward the overshadowing entity as well as toward the client, rather than that of the implacable hostility toward the supposed demon found in traditional Christian exorcism.

A colleague of Bull who, like him, practiced depossession without being fully convinced that spirits were involved was Walter Franklin Prince (whom we met in connection with Mrs. Hand's death, page 166). One of Prince's cases illustrates several typical features of overshadowing. A socially prominent woman whom Prince calls "Phyllis Latimer" came to see him in 1922, reporting that she believed herself to be spirit-possessed (overshadowed) by a cousin and longtime friend named "Marvin" who had died in 1920. Since then she had been hearing his voice, most of the time full of hatred, promising to make her suffer for something she had done (she had written something negative about him to a third party). She reported that the voice was able to make predictions about unpleasant events in her future, which invariably came true. Although she remained calm during her appointments, "Marvin's" threats terrified her and at night she often woke up screaming. Going to Prince's office to keep her appointments required enormous effort against felt resistance.[62]

Prince thought Mrs. Latimer was probably suffering from severe paranoia, but he was willing to consider the spirit hypothesis. With Mrs. Latimer's consent he did a depossession by reasoning and persuasion, showing concern for the overshadower's welfare. Prince gave the Marvin-figure a fifteen-minute homily: Marvin was doing harm to himself as well as to Mrs. Latimer, inhibiting his higher development, and the like. He suggested that Marvin experiment by regarding Mrs. Latimer with his former good will.[63]

In the following days Mrs. Latimer began to feel the problem was breaking. The invisible resistance that had troubled her on her way to Prince's office vanished. The voice stopped speaking, although she could still feel Marvin's presence. A new and helpful personality soon appeared, claiming to be her deceased mother, expressing concern for both her daughter and Marvin. In a few weeks, Prince decided Mrs. Latimer was improved enough to open communication with Marvin. Marvin explained that at the time he had died, his resentment, fresh in his mind, had taken over his consciousness. As he began to torment her, other discarnates were attracted, linked themselves with him, and were vicariously possessing (overshadowing) her through him. Now, however, he felt free and was about to leave.

After Prince failed to hear from Mrs. Latimer for several months, he contacted her and found that Marvin was gone. However, still suffering from battling inner presences, Mrs. Latimer was exhausted. Prince suggested under hypnosis that the mother-personality take away the spirits. Mrs. Latimer improved steadily after this, and after a year and a half was well enough to engage in automatic writing experiments with Prince that showed considerable paranormal knowledge.[64] At about the same time, Prince cured a similar case by the same means of depossession through reasoning and persuasion.

Prince was inclined, although not fully committed, to an overshadowing interpretation of these cases. Comparing the cases with other clients with paranoid schizophrenia, in which the ideas of persecution were generalized rather than focussed on a particular deceased person, he reported that with the generalized paranoia, depossession did not work, probably because there were no spirits present.[65]

One of the most influential psychotherapists using depossession was Carl Wickland, who with the help of his mediumistic wife practiced from the mid-1890s to the mid-1930s. He found that, in many cases, several spirits, sometimes mutually hostile and usually ignorant of having died, were attached to a single person. They were either persuaded to leave or, failing that, were taken in hand by "spirit colleagues" on the order of Mrs. Latimer's mother-personality. Wickland took an essentially compassionate approach to the overshadowers, but he had a more commanding personality than Prince, and held no doubts concerning the spirit hypothesis.

Wickland seems to have been highly successful, rapidly curing hundreds of persons suffering from either physical or mental disorders. But unfortunately he failed to give follow-up information. He did keep full stenographic records. Though he was not interested in trying to confirm the identifying information he received from the claimed spirits, some interested persons investigating three of his cases found confirming evidence.[66] One of these had been a successful case of absent depossession— the overshadowed person was never informed of the seance held on his behalf—thus his subsequent improvement was not due to suggestion.[67]

Wickland's work contrasts interestingly with the findings of most therapists using depossession: very few of his claimed spirits were relatives of the overshadowed persons. Another significant characteristic was that the spirits had negative opinions of organized religion and of reincarnation, as did the Wicklands.[68] More about these findings below in the discussion of personas.

In England in the 1960s and 1970s, Canon John Pierce-Higgins practiced depossession with the help of medium Ena Twigg. Pierce-Higgins judged that only about one in six of the disturbed persons referred to him were in fact possession (overshadowing) cases, the rest having "schizophrenic or hysterical psychopathological problems...."[69] Some of his overshadowing cases involved deceased relatives. His method usually centered on Requiem Eucharist services together with appeals to angels, to send the overshadowing spirit into the divine light. Pierce-Higgins' spirits were not hostile to organized religion, and sooner or later responded favorably to his Christian ministrations. I might add that he is not the only priest-therapist using depossession with success.

Contemporary philosopher-therapist Adam Crabtree expands the list of potential overshadowing entities to include nonpersonal beings, group minds, muses, demons and gods, and fragments of one's own psyche or even of another living person.[70] Crabtree developed the last category as a result of listening seriously to the suggestion of one of his clients, Arthur, that the carping, controlling inner voice that sounded like his mother might in fact *be* a part of his mother (who was alive in another city). Over time Crabtree persuaded the mother-personality to withdraw from her son and reinvest her energies in her own life. What followed was a great improvement not only for Arthur but for the psychological and physical health of the mother (her cancer went into remission). Crabtree does not say whether the mother was informed of this radical new approach, but it seems unlikely. Like Wickland, Crabtree shows little interest in evidentiality.[71]

Hypnotherapist Edith Fiore, who originally followed a conventional approach in her therapeutic practice, began to experiment with both past-life therapy and depossession as a result of some of her clients' descriptions of past lives, some clients' problems with apparent spirit influence, and her own wide reading. Although she was not completely committed to survival, and some of her clients not at all, survival became more and more convincing to her when rapid cures often followed depossession or hypnotic regressions to scenes before conception.

The clients' hypnotic narratives of previous deaths and the state between lives, and the stories told by overshadowing spirits, tend to reflect several of Moody's original elements of the NDE, particularly OBEs, welcoming relatives, and the light. But some spirits did not encounter welcomers or a light (or reported that they encountered and resisted them) and became stuck among the living; during this period they resembled the "earthbound" of Spiritualist tradition[72] (and Moody's "bewildered spirits"[73]). Reasons the deceased may get stuck, says Fiore, include fear of hell, obsessive attachment to the living (especially relatives), vengefulness, attachment to a place, and especially addictions to alcohol, drugs, and food. One addicted spirit usually opens the door to others;[74] "like attracts like."

These spirits are as though "freeze-framed" in the state they were at their deaths, says Fiore: they retain their prejudices, skills, fears, and hangups. Feelings of depression or physical pain or decrepitude continue unchanged by the passage of time.[75] Besides the spirits' own problems inflicted on their hosts, the very act of possession (overshadowing) creates fatigue. It may also lead to difficulty concentrating, memory blanks, mood swings, and inner voices.[76]

Fiore, like Crabtree and Wickland, does little with evidence. She builds her case on several factors often coming together in a client's experience: anesthesia (which, Fiore believes, opens one's aura to invaders), bereavement (she holds that spirits congregate in hospitals, morgues, and cemeteries), the sudden and apparently groundless appearance in a person's life of some of the abovementioned problems, and rapid cures after hypnotic sessions in which spirits agree to leave and enter the light.[77] (This may take some time, as spirits may be fearful or stubborn, and Fiore uses only gentle persuasion.) One cure was particularly impressive after years of different conventional therapies had yielded no result.[78]

Overshadowing and haunting cases are both usually interpreted as the work of earthbound spirits; and when a purported haunting spirit speaks through a medium in trance, he or she does in fact sound much like an overshadower. Both Crabtree and Fiore cite cases in which claimed spirit entities first haunt places, then invade a vulnerable person.[79] But, as we have seen, cultural and personal expectations influence what appears. There are also differences: first, whereas overshadowers are talkative, haunting ghosts seldom speak; secondly, overshadowers do not usually behave like sleepwalkers.

For our purposes, it is unfortunate that therapists doing depossession work tend to be uninterested in following up on the evidence their clients provide. Their accounts of rapid healing of overshadowing cases, especially when the typical features that Fiore cites appear together, are very suggestive.

Inspiration

Cases of apparent inspiration clearly resemble overshadowing cases, but tend to be based more on mutual respect and cooperation; the claimed spirit does not usually drain the host but brings gifts. Thus the spiritual caliber of the inspirer is higher than that of overshadowers. The strongest feature is a skill clearly beyond the host's level of achievement.

A good example is the strongly evidential Thompson/Gifford case, investigated by J. H. Hyslop (who pioneered work in overshadowing). According to his account published in *Proceedings ASPR* in 1909, in the summer of 1905 a goldsmith named Frederic Thompson, who had occasionally done a bit of sketching but soon gave it up in discouragement, "was frequently seized with impulses to sketch and paint in oils." At such times he identified strongly with an artist named Robert Gifford, whom he had met casually a few times but of whose work he knew almost nothing.

During his noon hour one day in January 1906, on impulse Thompson visited an exhibition of Gifford's work and learned that Gifford had died the previous year. He heard a voice saying, "You see what I have done. Can you not take up and finish my work?" Thompson fell into an altered state of consciousness and knew nothing till he found himself back at his job.

After this he began to have visions, especially of landscapes with windblown trees, and painted them. One which especially haunted him was of oaks on a seaside promontory; he entitled his painting "The Battle of the Elements." The urge to paint was now so all-consuming that Thompson's own work of goldsmithing was suffering, leading to serious financial trouble. Fearful that he was losing his mind, he turned to Hyslop for help.[80]

Hyslop took Thompson incognito to visit several mediums to see if they might confirm the connection with Gifford. Medium Minnie Soule picked up many details about Gifford's clothes, tastes, his love of hills and ocean and autumn leaves. She heard him saying, "I will help you, because I want someone who can catch the inspiration of these things as I did, to carry on my work." (Some of this information could, of course, have been absorbed telepathically from Hyslop and Thompson.)

Handing several of his sketches over to Hyslop, Thompson set out to look for the scenes of his visions. He visited Gifford's summer home, met his widow, and saw in his studio a painting that corresponded closely with a sketch he himself had made earlier and given to Hyslop. (Mrs. Gifford certified that Thompson had never had an opportunity to see this painting.) She directed him to the Elizabeth Islands, off the Massachusetts coast, as likely to contain the scenes of his visions.

On Naushon Island Thompson felt led to two places in particular, one of them being the scene of "The Battle of the Elements," which he painted again from the site itself. In the other place, while gazing at a group of trees, he heard a voice telling him to look at the other side of the trees. There he found carved Gifford's initials and the year 1902. There were other correspondences between Thompson's Gifford-inspired sketches, the paintings in Gifford's studio, and scenes on the Elizabeth Islands. After the trip Hyslop and Thompson made several more visits to mediums, and received further confirming details.[81]

Research by D. Scott Rogo shows that Thompson did not return to his goldsmith craft but made painting his permanent career. He became successful, becoming a longterm member of the prestigious Salmagundi Club of professional painters.[82]

When we compare this inspiration-type case with the overshadowing cases above, "Gifford" does resemble the overshadowing personalities in that he intruded into Thompson's life without waiting for his consent, apparently even possessing him at one point, and disrupted his prior career. However, in time Thompson and the Gifford-personality reached a cooperative understanding valuable to both.

Does it establish the survival of Gifford, or would telepathy or retroprehensive inclusion account for it? The explanation must account for three elements: paranormal knowledge, the artistic gift, and purpose/motivation powerful enough to change the course of Thompson's life. Telepathy from Gifford's widow and clairvoyance of the sites might explain the paranormal knowledge, but not the gift. Could the explanation be retroprehensive inclusion of Gifford's life by Thompson? It is true that Thompson wanted to draw and was disappointed, but he quickly gave up and did not seek training. Might he have been unconsciously motivated enough to reach for Gifford's life with its developed gift? It is difficult to say. What he received was so much more than he wanted that it frightened him and left him for a time unable to support himself and his wife.

Retroprehensive inclusion cannot be ruled out as an explanation, but if we judge from appearances, it is strained. It looks very much as though Thompson was hit by the powerful will, purpose, and well-developed talent of someone outside of himself who had unfinished business.

How strong is the evidence from the characteristics of Thompson's drawings and paintings that the "someone" is Gifford? In his discussion of this case Alan Gauld points out that it is obvious that the subject matter of the two artists is very similar; in some cases they clearly painted the very same scenes. Experts at the time differed about how similar the techniques and styles of the two were, but it was clear to them that Thompson's paintings were competent: "few experts could believe that the Thompson paintings were the work of a man who had only been painting a short time and had had virtually no formal training."[83] Unless survival can be proved impossible, it seems to me that inspiration by a surviving Robert Gifford is the most plausible explanation for this case.

Reincarnation

The final category of evidence for survival consists of cases of the reincarnation type. The researcher who has almost singlehandedly put reincarnation studies on the parapsychological map is Ian Stevenson. In intensive research since 1960, he has traveled widely, amassing over twenty-six hundred cases from various countries; in his analysis of each published case he weighs normal explanations.[84] In recent years other scholars have taken up his methods.

Stevenson holds that the apparent memories (after this, only "memories") of former lives in adults are usually inferior as evidence because there are many normal ways for adults to absorb knowledge of the past and forget it. Therefore, he has concentrated chiefly on cases with small children.

Typically, between ages two and four the child tells her parents and siblings of having lived in another time and location, usually in the same culture. She gives detailed information ("imaged memories"), shows strong feelings about it, and behaves accordingly ("behavioral memories"). She begs repeatedly to be taken back to her previous family. At length the parents make inquiries, and reluctantly take her to the town she has named. She is able to guide them to the family's house, to recognize and greet several family members (not usually all) without help. Stevenson prefers to be present to document this meeting, but usually it has already occurred and is described to him by the witnesses.[85] At six or seven the child's memories begin to fade.

A vivid example is the case of Munna/Ravi Shankar of Kanauj in India. On January 19, 1951, the six-year-old son of Jageshwar Prasad and Mano Rama Prasad, nicknamed Munna, was viciously murdered by two neighbors named Jawahar and Chaturi, one a relative of the family who evidently hoped to inherit Jageshwar's property in his place. Munna was enticed from his play and taken to the neighborhood of the Chintamini Temple, where his head was cut off. His body was found buried near the river and the severed head in the vicinity of the temple.[86] Because someone had seen the three go off together, the two men were arrested. Chaturi confessed unofficially but later retracted his confession, and because there were no witnesses to the crime, the case against them collapsed.[87]

Six months afterwards in a neighboring district of the town, a boy named Ravi Shankar was born to Babu Ram Gupta and Ramdulari Ram Gupta. The baby had a long mark like a knife scar on his neck. Between two and three he began to tell his mother and others that he was the son of Jageshwar, a barber of Chhipatti District of the city, that he had been taken to the riverside and murdered in an orchard by a washerman named Chaturi and a barber named Jawahar, who cut his neck with a razor and buried his body in the sand. This caused the mark on his neck. He insisted that his present house was not really his and once tried to run away to his former home.[88] He had things there, he said: a slate, a book bag, an ink pot, a toy pistol, a wooden elephant, a figurine of Krishna, a ball on a string, a watch, and a ring—and he kept asking the Ram Guptas to get them. When he was five he told his story to his teacher, who wrote it down.[89]

Neighbors told Munna's father Jageshwar Prasad, who went to the Ram Gupta house to investigate. Because Ravi Shankar's father would not speak to him, Jageshwar went later, on July 30, 1955, when Babu Ram Gupta was not home. In a 1963 letter to Stevenson, Jageshwar described this meeting: He sat [outside] near the door of the house, the little boy standing about one and a half feet away. He said, "Dear boy, do you know me?" and "Do not be afraid" and "[Y]ou used to take money from me." After hesitating perhaps twenty-five minutes, Ravi Shankar sat on his lap and said, "Father, I used to read in Chhipatti school and my wooden slate is in the [closet]." He also recognized Munna's watch on Jageshwar's wrist. He described the murder, which matched what Jageshwar had reconstructed from the confession of Chaturi, the mutilated state of the body, and his own inspection of the site.[90] Another time when Munna's maternal grandmother (who lived in Kanpur) was visiting a family in the city, Ravi Shankar was taken to the house. Asked who had come, he hesitated and then said, "Nani (mother's mother)....She has come from Kanpur."[91]

Babu Ram Gupta reacted violently to these happenings. He quarreled with his tale-bearing neighbors, insisted that everyone forget the story, and beat the child severely to shut him up. Ravi Shankar became afraid of his father and spoke much less about Munna; he was also afraid of Chaturi. Seeing Chaturi once in a crowd, the boy trembled with terror, although no one had told him who that was (his mother did not know). He was also fearful near the Chintamini Temple, and afraid of razors.[92]

Babu Ram Gupta died not long after these events, but Ravi Shankar did not again talk freely about Munna. Some of the other witnesses were also reluctant to speak, because the murderers were still at large.[93]

Several Indian scholars began investigating the case, one in 1956 and others in 1962.[94] In 1964 Stevenson examined the birthmark and interviewed the witnesses, including Munna's mother and neighbors, Ravi Shankar, his mother and siblings, a classmate, and the abovementioned teacher. Stevenson returned in 1969 and 1971 for further interviews. Among them the witnesses testified to twenty-six correspondences between Ravi Shankar—his claims, behaviors, and birthmark—and Munna's life.[95] Virtually all Ravi Shankar's claims were verified, with only one or two being uncertain.[96] Two sets of witnesses disagreed about whether Babu Ram Gupta had taken his son to Jageshwar's house.[97]

Stevenson considers fraud and forgotten memories as possible explanations. It is very unlikely there was fraud by the Ram Gupta family, who kept having to hear how much the boy preferred his previous family; the wide diffusion of the reincarnation story also made them fearful of the murderers. The gruesomeness of the murder, the murderers' escaping punishment, and Ravi Shankar's further suffering under his father's battering (hardly karmic justice) all make the case very unlike the stereotypical past-life romance. Jageshwar wanted to believe that the child was his lost son reborn, which might have influenced his memories of their meeting in 1955. But much detailed evidence came not from him, but from the Ram Gupta family and their associates early in the case.

Could forgotten memory explain the case? Munna's murder had been well known, and, although the families were barely acquainted, Ramdulari (then three months pregnant with Ravi Shankar) had gone to the Prasad home to offer sympathy. Could Ravi Shankar as a toddler have overheard talk of Munna, forgotten it, then unconsciously formed an identity as Munna? The problem here is that the details of Munna's toys were definitely not public knowledge. The two households were only about half a mile apart, but the intervening roads had many turns; it is very unlikely that a closely guarded Indian child between two and three could have wandered this distance by himself and entered the Prasad house. Therefore, Stevenson concluded that normal explanations for Ravi Shankar's knowledge could be ruled out.[98] Furthermore, the boy's fears of the temple area and of razors, which lasted for years after his imaged memories faded, are hard to explain normally.

Can the unusual birthmark, which supports reincarnation, be explained some other way? There is a folklore idea that an expectant mother who is distressed on seeing or hearing of some injury can cause her unborn child to have a similar mark. Stevenson has gathered substantial documented evidence that this may in fact sometimes happen.[99] More work is needed on this issue, but it is possible that the pregnant Ramdulari, who was distressed about the gruesome murder, was unconsciously responsible for the birthmark. This idea might be developed further to account for Ravi Shankar's knowledge of Munna's toys, his recognitions, and his fears: Perhaps Ramdulari unconsciously wanted to give Munna a new incarnation, and telepathically influenced the infant Ravi Shankar to join her in reaching out to Munna's life in retroprehensive inclusion. If this is what happened, the fact that Ravi Shankar's strong identification with Munna later became a huge liability for the family would not count against it.

Retroprehensive inclusion in this form would account for the paranormal features of the case. But, as Griffin himself points out, there are problems with applying this explanation across the board. In Stevenson's collection of child-cases, as well as those of and his colleagues, the previous personalities often died by violence or left unfinished business—they had lives or deaths of particular vividness. This pattern might be thought to make them attractive enough to be "picked up" later by retroprehensive inclusion, so that one would expect many cases of two or more children claiming to be reincarnations of the same person. But the evidence for this is very scarce and weak.[100] Besides that, there would be no reason why many children would not claim to be reincarnations of persons still living, and evidence for that is virtually nonexistent. The death of the previous personality seems to be essential to substantial reincarnation-type stories.[101]

Could spirit influence be the best explanation? We have seen that some cases, like that of Uttara/Sharada, can be plausibly explained either as reincarnation or as possession/overshadowing. However, two features make reincarnation a better fit to the Munna/Ravi Shankar case. One is the birthmark; if an overshadowing Munna were influencing Ravi Shankar even before birth and causing a birthmark, it might make more sense to see them not as two beings but as one. The other feature is the fading of the memories. Babu Ram Gupta's abuse probably influenced this process, but fading of memories around age six is common in child cases; and, in fact, it would make good sense for an incarnating being, as he or she consolidates a new personality, to relegate memories of the previous one to the background.

Of these several explanations, then, reincarnation seems the simplest and most plausible for the Munna/Ravi Shankar case. (However, traditional ideas of karma are not supported by this and many other cases.)

Strengths and Weaknesses of the Evidence for Survival

Aside from NDE studies, there is a large quantity of evidence of different kinds for survival, and some of it is of very high quality. For the best cases— such as those of Gifford/Thompson, Uttara/Sharada and Munna/Ravi Shankar—normal explanations become very strained. Superpsi in the form of retroprehensive inclusion could explain individual reincarnation-type cases, but it cannot account for the great body of such cases. Though survival has not been proved, it is the simplest hypothesis to explain the strongest evidence. Providing a coherent explanation for several categories of material, survival becomes, in Karlis Osis' term, a metatheory (as is the theory of evolution).[102]

If we assume that survival is a reality, when the various kinds of evidence are taken together there are ways in which they satisfy common sense as well as tend to support and complement one another. Haunting ghosts, overshadowing personalities, and unhappy figures seen in NDEs have traits in common. The existence of such beings (or fragments of beings) in the afterlife is not surprising; one finds no lack of spiritually stunted or even depraved persons on earth. In contrast, there are many living persons who commit themselves to love beyond death; it makes sense that after death they would offer to guide dying friends through the difficult passage, might appear to help living loved ones in crisis, or might try to drop in at seances to send messages. There are people who die young, violently, or with unfinished business; they may well hasten to reincarnate. Even the fact that contrasting cultures may give views of the afterlife that differ substantially (as well as show common elements) does not in itself undercut survival. A little reflection suggests that the state of the dying and deceased will not necessarily be more uniform than that of the living. Predeath expectations might influence what the deceased actually experience.

However, seen from another perspective, different cases and different classes of evidence show tensions or major incompatibilities, especially if we include (nonevidential) radiant and painful NDEs. We noticed tensions among the findings of twentieth-century therapists practicing depossession; most show a high percentage of deceased relatives among overshadowing spirits, whereas in Wickland's cases relatives are rare (page 193). Attitudes toward religion are also in contrast.

Another problematic issue: there are a handful of cases in which mediums present evidential messages from supposedly deceased persons who are afterward found to be still living. Best known is the "Gordon Davis" case, in which psychical investigator S. G. Soal received in a sitting with medium Blanche Cooper a series of impressive and highly evidential messages from an an old acquaintance, Gordon Davis, whom Soal believed to have been killed in the 1914–1918 war. Soal found out later that he was still alive and interviewed him.[103] Soal's reliability has been questioned (in another connection), but there are other cases; for example, that of a man named Reallier, onetime chauffeur of a Canon Douglas, who communicated in a seance of medium Mrs. Halsey in the United States, describing his experiences during World War I and giving a great deal of veridical evidence. Reallier was later found to be very much alive.[104]

There are also difficulties in some of the strongest cases in which the person is undoubtedly deceased. Even very impressive communicators like Mrs. Piper's "George Pelham," with his many recognitions, was unlike the original Pellew in some ways: his handwriting was not like that of George Pellew,[105] and he had trouble getting his name right (an occupational hazard for trance communicators). "Pelham" tended to be evasive, even dishonest at times, and to be confused in intellectual conversation, as Pellew was not.[106] Such behavior is inconsistent with many claims in NDEs and trance communications that the afterlife existence of good people is one of an increase in wisdom and of spiritual maturation.

These challenges are met by the persona theory of Hornell Hart, which builds on the earlier work of William James and Eleanor Sidgwick. Sidgwick held that in seances the sitter is an important part of the communication process, since some sitters receive abundant evidential material from convincing communicators, while other sitters (including herself) never receive any.[107] She proposed that in a seance the surviving spirit is in telepathic contact with his friend the sitter, but the sitter is unaware of it. The medium receives telepathic impressions from the deceased through the (successful) sitter and gives them back to the sitter as the words of a dream-character-like trance personality.[108] James suggested that a communicator may be the product of a discarnate "will to communicate" joined with a "will to personate" in the medium. The "will to communicate" may come from the spirit of the deceased, or from a limited, improvised entity. The mistakes and "rubbish" produced may be due to failures of the trance processes to bring through what the communicator wants to say."[109]

Hart's theory agrees that a mediumistic communicator, or an apparition of the dead, is not the surviving person himself, and that several sources contribute to the communicator. Hart sees the latter, however, not just as a mixture of influences but as a *persona*, a kind of personality in its own right. Hart describes a persona as a personality-structure, developed by the unconscious collaboration of the persons involved in a seance or in an apparitional experience. Some personas may be wholly without self-awareness, while some may be as conscious as the self of an embodied person. "A persona may possess more or less initiative of its own, and may become the vehicle for an 'I'-thinking spirit."[110] Difficulties such as the "moral flabbiness" or intellectual confusion that Mrs. Piper's communicators sometimes showed (or the incompatible attitudes toward religion of the Wicklands' and Pierce-Higgins' communicators), would be due to conditions in which the attempts of the surviving consciousness to speak through the persona were disrupted, and the medium's unconscious tendencies to dramatize led the persona astray.[111] It would be quite likely that at times a persona might simply be the creation of the medium, or of the medium plus the sitter. At other times the apparition or the communicator might be virtually identical with the conscious "I" of a deceased person.

Extending this theory to NDEs, I suggest that the the visionary figures NDErs encounter are personas also. It would explain cultural differences, such as the contrast between the authoritarian guides in medieval cases and the more democratic ones in contemporary cases, without undercutting the evidential nature of some cases. NDE visionary figures as personas would mean that genuine contact with the deceased (or with the divine) could be taking place, with the NDEr contributing, usually unconsciously, to what he or she perceives. NDE visionary figures could also differ in the degree to which the consciousness of the relative or religious being is clear and present (as do apparitions of the living).

In sum, the evidence for survival from NDEs, NCDEs, mediumship, apparitions, spirit-type influence, and cases of the reincarnation type is a massive body of material, much of which cannot be accounted for by materialist worldviews. But if we acknowledge the reality of psi, things become more complex. Superpsi, if there is such a thing, can go a long way (if not all the way) to explain the evidence for survival, as we saw with the theory of retroprehensive inclusion. However, as an alternative to survival, superpsi can be a little too successful and undercut itself. This is because the more omniscient we potentially are, the better our minds can function without dependence on our bodies. Thus, indirectly, superpsi *supports* survival.[112]

It is fair to say that there are no clinching philosophical arguments against survival and that, as a metatheory, it plausibly explains a mass of material of different types.

The various problems in survival evidence can be dealt with by one form or another of the persona theory. But none of these problems are as serious, or as deeply disturbing, as painful NDEs—both the meaningless-void and the hellish types—with their suggestion of a painful afterlife. Can these experiences be reconciled with the implications of universal love and reunion in radiant NDEs? In Part IV I will attempt an answer. I will categorize the different frameworks that have been offered to interpret ideas of life after death. Focussing on the two categories that are most helpful, I will sketch out paradigms derived from myth and romance, from the mystical path and from psychedelic therapy, paradigms that bring together in story form features very similar to those in radiant and painful NDEs. This process yields a metanarrative that suggests a resolution.

PART IV

INTERPRETIVE FRAMEWORKS

Preface to Part IV ⁀

A NYONE WHO HAS SOMETHING TO SAY ABOUT THE SUBJECT of life after death is *interpreting*—interpreting ideas, images, experiences, and/or evidence. These interpretations fall, roughly, into three categories, three mental frameworks. The first framework assumes that there is only one world. The second assumes that there are two or more worlds. The third claims that we don't know.

By a one-world framework I mean a view of the universe as capable of being explored extensively by human minds and means, whether science, philosophy, art, religion, or other disciplines. In that one world, things are related to other things in more or less regular ways of cause and effect. This regularity applies particularly to the moral-spiritual dimension of life: minds are shaped by heredity, environmental influences, their own decisions, and other minds. A one-world view is a *naturalistic* approach. (Naturalistic does not necessarily mean materialistic, as we shall see.)

Multi-world frameworks do not cohere in this way. According to these outlooks, there are hard boundaries, so to speak, between our public physical world and the world or worlds of the afterlife. The gates are controlled by supernatural beings or forces that human minds cannot probe or understand; we can only obey, accept, or try to appease. (Such beings, some hold, may also be at work within our world.)

An agnostic framework is an approach in which the issues of one world or many, survival or extinction, are left open: we do not know. Some hold that we can never know. I will deal with this category first, giving examples in Chapter Ten. (It should be noted that some worldviews do not fit neatly into this typology; some thinkers are not altogether consistent on this issue.)

In Chapter Eleven, "Multi-World Interpretive Frameworks," I will show how, in the Sumerian, Christian fundamentalist, and folk Buddhist views, the world of the afterlife is really cut off from our world and operates in arbitrary ways that we cannot presume to understand.

One-world frameworks may either affirm survival or deny it. Most of those that deny survival are materialistic: they hold that our public physical world is the only world. (Since earlier chapters have shown the inadequacy of such positions, I will not attempt to present them further.) There are some that deny survival while affirming the reality of the spiritual, but as they make no real attempt to deal with survival evidence, they can also be omitted.

The interpretive frameworks given in the last three chapters, which I consider more promising, affirm life after death as operating under the same principles as our familiar world; the two domains are essentially one world. They acknowledge that we are limited in our understanding of the afterlife, but hold that our life here and now is continuous with it in important ways.

Eleven ⁊

AGNOSTIC INTERPRETIVE FRAMEWORKS

LTHOUGH THINKERS WHO REJECT SURVIVAL TEND TO BE hostile to the spiritual significance of NDEs, there are agnostic positions that stress the potentials of NDEs to foster human healing, growth, and transformation. One of these positions is offered by John Wren-Lewis, whose Void experience of "shining darkness" was cited in Chapter Three. Since the experience, Wren-Lewis's mystical consciousness has continued, with enormously transformative effects,[1] and out of these developments he speaks.

Wren-Lewis points out that the OBE and the tunnel–light–welcomers–return sequence actually appear in a mere minority of cases.[2] Furthermore, NDE pictures of the apparent afterlife are in many cases incompatible with one another; it is doubtful that they represent literal glimpses of what lies beyond the grave.[3] Rather they are due to the "play of imagination," but this does not mean that they are unreal. They represent, "a dimension of value, of aliveness...a dimension called eternity"[4] to which we are ordinarily oblivious because we are too anxiously focussed on our individual futures.

The important thing, says Wren-Lewis, is to explore this mystical consciousness and to seek ways that it may become available to all: in short, to break the spell of forgetfulness and heal the soul. Although he does not really expect to survive death, Wren-Lewis does not rule out survival or object to survival research. However, he holds that to prove survival would not achieve much, because when it was widely believed in past times the quality of life was no better than it is now.[5]

Thus Wren-Lewis's position is not agnostic in the more usual sense of holding that it is impossible to know whether or not human beings survive death, but rather that we do not in fact know, and that it is not worth the candle to find out.

It is hard not to sympathize with Wren-Lewis's altruistic concern for soul-healing as having priority over theoretical research into survival. But in context this salvation issue cannot so easily be separated from the question of what lies beyond death. In the modern and postmodern Western world, the widespread materialism understood to be part of Science as authority, with its reductionist view of human consciousness arising from the body and thus ceasing at death, has done much to erode traditional forms of faith. Existing in a world stripped of meaning, many feel that assurance of life after death is crucial if they are to have something to live for. Conviction of survival will not give ultimate fulfillment, but for such people it is a necessary preliminary.

There is another potential problem with Wren-Lewis's agnosticism. Even among NDErs, his kind of ongoing mystical consciousness is rare. Those who long and search for this spiritual fulfillment but have never known more than a glimmering may feel that Wren-Lewis overestimates its availability to the living. If the only real chance for it most people will have is after death, then survival matters absolutely.

Another agnostic position is found in Carol Zaleski's *Otherworld Journeys*. Comparing medieval otherworld journeys with contemporary NDEs, Zaleski points out that not only common elements but marked cultural differences are to be found.[6] Both then and now, she claims, the journey story "is through and through a work of the socially conditioned religious imagination; it is formed in conversation with society, even if it takes place in the solitude of the deathbed...."[7] Thus no spiritual experience is a pure encounter with a "being of light" which the visionary only later interprets as Christ or Krishna.[8] The visionary's worldview is part and parcel of the experience.

Though it cannot be taken literally, says Zaleski, the NDE narrative is an important communication. Its concrete features are symbols, participating in and pointing to a larger reality, but they cannot be translated into conceptual terms.[9] They express an inner psychic world of profound power that opened out to the visionary when he experienced the shock of imminent death. He really did "[experience] something in himself that surpasses death." When we take NDE images in this manner, Zaleski claims, they are immune to reductionist scientific critique, though they prove nothing about life beyond the grave.[10]

Zaleski holds that this immunity is even greater when the narratives are taken as meaningful wholes, dramatic sequences shaped by the telling, "aimed toward a destination."[11] They are conversion stories, telling how the narrator, once caught in a life of sin or spiritual failure, is now transformed and may find the outer world transformed also. Thus the "other world" helps us to find our way through this world. We lose this immunity, however, when we try to isolate veridical elements or make statistical studies. "Paradoxically, the very method that permits us to respect visionary testimony prohibits us from using it to make a case for survival."[12]

Since Zaleski, unlike Wren-Lewis, is saying that NDEs *cannot* give us empirical evidence for survival, she must deal with the fact that they actually seem to do so. She does acknowledge apparently paranormal elements such as Peak-in-Darien encounters and reports of veridical out-of-body perceptions. But she holds that if the counter-explanations of reductionists are taken together, and if telepathy and clairvoyance are added, then the evidence is undercut, leaving the issue a draw between the affirmers and the deniers of survival.[13] (However, Zaleski does not rule out the possibility that survival may be established in other, nonscientific ways, and she affirms that we have a right to believe in life after death as well as to imagine what it is like.)[14]

Two replies to her position can be made. First, we have seen that the claim that NDE accounts are totally shaped by culture is questionable. The reports of "deep" NDEs in small children and infants, and elements akin to foreign religious ideas like the realms of needy and violent spirits seen by the naive Ritchie (page 80), strongly suggest that not everything in NDEs is completely constructed by imagination under the influence of the experiencer's culture.

I am not claiming that this apparent transcendence of culture in certain NDE elements proves survival. We saw in Chapter Seven that the theory of morphic resonance can account for such cases. However, morphic resonance means action at a distance, sometimes the distance between cultures, which would loosen the cultural constrictions that, according to Zaleski, cannot be pried apart to yield evidence for survival. But if we can find a symbolic element in a contemporary NDE that suggests immediate contact with (say) experiences of persons in ancient Egypt, there seems no reason why we cannot compare (say) a Peak-in-Darien welcomer with a drop-in communicator as potential evidence for survival.

A secondary challenge to Zaleski's argument is the fact that not all NDE accounts are otherworld journeys or conversion stories. Some are quite simple, consisting only of one or two elements such as deep peace or out-of-body experience; furthermore, some NDEs do not lead to much spiritual change. If either kind offers evidence that points to survival, Zaleski will have offered us no good reason for not following up on it.

I conclude that paranormal elements in any NDEs may be investigated as potential evidence for survival. Proof may not be forthcoming, but agnostic rejection of such study cannot be justified.

Twelve ☙

MULTI-WORLD FRAMEWORKS

EXAMPLES OF MULTI-WORLD INTERPRETATIVE FRAMEWORKS
have already been given in Part II (pages 125 and following), so here
I will only show their implications. As we saw, according to the story
of Inanna the dying human soul is swept into the Land of No Return, where
the principles of earth-life do not really operate. Previous social or moral
status in the world of the living have no consequences here. Psychological
cause-and-effect may operate for the gods: the rage and sexual frustration
of the Queen Ereshkigal may have been caused by her long-past abduction
from this world to the underworld and by the loss of her husband. But
human souls are cut off from their past.* Bad people suffer, but not because
of any moral degeneration or punishment for their deeds; rather, good and
bad fare alike. Loving relationships in this world are not fulfilled in any
afterlife reunions.

The emergence of Inanna and Dumuzi from the afterworld might seem
to offer some hope of escape to deceased persons who want to identify with
them. But this dying–rising scenario applies only to one goddess and one
human being; ordinary people, created only to be servants to the gods and
discarded when no longer useful, cannot hope for rescue by them. And
divine intervention would be the only possibility, for the realm of the dead
clearly has no transformative power of its own. The only spark of light in
the story is the sacrificial love of Geshtinanna, Dumuzi's sister, who gains

---

*The human Dumuzi was chosen by Inanna to take her place in the underworld because she
was angry at his neglect, which seems to imply punishment for his deeds, and thus moral
connectedness. However, her descent was a one-time affair, and his abduction into the dark
land is the result of his special connection as husband of a Goddess rather than any general
moral lawfulness.

his release for half of each year by taking his place. And this for a person who is meltingly appealing and beautiful but immature, unreliable, and undeserving.

There is something deeply perplexing, as well as revolting, in this grim picture of the afterlife. Why would a whole culture—several ancient cultures—envision a separate world of this kind? One reason, it has been suggested, is the this-worldly religious outlooks before the rise of the so-called Great Religions. Seeing our world as a physical-spiritual whole as ancient cultures did meant that the body was assumed to be integral to the person (rather than a container or even a prison for the heaven-born soul). Therefore, when the body was destroyed by death, the dim surviving consciousness was a mere shade, virtually without energy. Further, burial of the body in the earth suggested the shade's imprisonment underground. A top-heavy class elitism in society probably influenced the picture of human beings as expendable; and with no justice expected in the afterlife, elitism and exploitation in this life was reinforced.

These factors no doubt contributed, but they do not fully explain the situation; after all, in pre-exile Israel there was a tradition of condemning social injustice, and human beings (or at least Israelites) were seen as beloved by God; yet the view of the afterlife was quite similar. And in Egypt the underworld was seen as far more hopeful. The Land of No Return remains a dark mystery.

A Christian Fundamentalist View

Another example of a multiworld framework is the Christian fundamentalist one of Maurice Rawlings. One of its sources is the Calvinist view (based on the earlier Augustinian view) of the afterlife as two worlds, heaven and hell, whose gates are controlled by the will of a just and sovereign God.* It is believed that human beings are born depraved and lead sinful lives, so that we all deserve hell. But God is compassionate; he has made it possible to evade hell and attain heaven if we identify with the

---

*This sketch is not intended to give a portrait of Calvinist or Augustinian Christianity, both of which are complex and multi-leveled. Rather it is a thumbnail account of a single strand of Calvinist-Augustinian thought.

atoning death of Christ, who endured the punishment we deserve. This offer is a source of hope and joy to the Christian.

Anticipating the criticism that this view is arbitrary and unjust, because some non-Christians live obviously good lives, the Calvinist says that God's ways are mysterious to us; we must submit our minds to his will as revealed in the Bible and be grateful for his offer of salvation. Heaven is not, like hell, deserved; it is not a reward for identifying with the work of Christ (which in the fundamentalist view takes place when one is born again). It is completely a gift of divine grace.[1]

Another source for fundamentalist views is the Christian Hellenistic and late-medieval views of the earth as a battleground of spiritual powers. In this world, human beings are the prey of invisible demonic beings, the sources of evil. But God compassionately provides a way for us to be rescued through Christ, who by his death and resurrection is victorious over the Devil and his cohorts, and frees their human prey to become children and servants of God, destined for heaven. It is sin (including failure to acknowledge God) that makes human beings open to demonic control, and thus their plight is their own fault. But there is also a sense in which foolish and unsuspecting (rather than completely depraved) persons are caught by the demons' deceit. Either way, there is no such thing as a human being who is truly self-determining; in the most important sense everyone is controlled, either by evil beings or by God through Christ.

Operating out of this dual framework, Rawlings and other fundamentalist Christians reject as demonic deceptions the encounters with unconditional love by all those NDErs who have not accepted the work of Christ and have experienced being born again according to fundamentalist terms. Good deeds and good character are valued, but do not determine one's fate after death. What matters is which power one submits to, either the God of wrath and compassion who can send one to hell or heaven, or the demons who seek only to drag souls down to hell. Thus Rawlings, especially in *To Hell and Back*, repeatedly urges his readers to submit their minds and souls to his God.[2]

Although the fundamentalist Christian framework has an urgent moral tone and hopefulness very different from the amoral Sumerian view, it is like the Sumerian in that morality is essentially undercut by death. Heaven is admittedly undeserved. Hell is said to be deserved, but since many who lived good lives are expected to end there, from an outside perspective it is a matter of good and bad faring alike. Nor is one's final destiny a continuous unfolding of human deeds and character. The three worlds are separate realms whose gates are controlled by incomprehensible supernatural powers.

Buddhist Multi-World Views

The Buddhist conception of six karmic realms is intended to be a one-world system in which the character and deeds of unenlightened beings unroll their full effects from one life to another. However, we have seen that some ideas about the hells, such as agelong tortures by demons for victimless "crimes," do not fit an impersonal moral universe. These images may stem from the anxieties of religious authorities trying to control society, or, like hellfire Christian evangelists, to frighten listeners into paradise. In any case, these horrors can be better understood as a partial multi-world scheme in which powers representing human religious authority stand between worlds, making self-serving, arbitrary decisions regarding the spirit's fate.

The boundless, heroic compassion of Ti-Tsang also appears to be an arbitrary intervention, having no basis in the karmic status of those in the hells. But if we see it as an appeal to the Buddha-nature of the sufferers, the salvation Ti-Tsang offers makes it possible for sufferers to reject the illusion of selfhood and become enlightened. Ti-Tsang's salvation would then be part of a projectionist framework (see Chapter Fourteen).

Thirteen ⮥

ONE-WORLD FRAMEWORKS: GRADUALISTIC

GNOSTIC FRAMEWORKS TEND TO DISCOURAGE FREE-ranging investigation and philosophical reflection about the afterlife; multi-world frameworks are likely to prohibit them altogether. The next three chapters give one-world approaches, which are much more promising.

These one-world views affirm that life after death is another dimension (or dimensions) of the one world, and closely linked to our world. Thus we can explore the evidence for the afterlife by the same methods of inquiry, ranging from the social sciences to comparative literary analysis. These views hold that there are spiritual principles at work in our physical life that continue to function after death, at least to some extent; that widespread values of earth-life, such as love and beauty, apply also to the afterlife; that the kind of life one has lived will significantly influence one's state in the afterlife. These thinkers do not rule out mystery and surprise, but they insist that we have the right to explore the evidence and ask questions, and may find some answers.

Gradualism in Spiritualism and Theosophy

The basic principle in a gradualistic one-world view is that the kind of consciousness developed in physical life continues and develops in afterlife experience. The Spiritualistic view sketched in Part II is a good example. For Spiritualists, not only is there continuity, but the afterlife sharply reveals the deepest traits and principles of human nature. Good consciousness and bad, which in incarnate life are sometimes hidden by misleading faces and manners, are intensified in the afterlife because people of like mind are drawn together. Multi-world concepts of an authoritarian judge meting out punishment are emphatically rejected by Spiritualists. The evil and the addicted either become earthbound or tend to gravitate to dark realms of desolation or violence where they suffer the effects of what they have become. But compassionate spirits are always available to encourage and support them in choosing to change. Likewise, good people are drawn to realms akin to their own love of truth, goodness, and beauty, where they enjoy what they have become as they continue to grow spiritually. Eventually they will be united with the Divine Source.

This satisfying view does admit that there are moral ambiguities in which the afterdeath processes of self-unfolding become clogged. Innocent persons who suffered abuse or died violent deaths may also become earthbound due to ignorance, becoming entrapped in reenacting their traumas. They also can be helped by compassionate beings living or discarnate.

However, there is really no place in Spiritualist schemes for the most troubling moral ambiguity of all: the possibility that a good and spiritually aware person may plunge at death into a scene of meaninglessness or alien horror, as certain painful NDEs suggest may happen. This gap suggests that the Spiritualist framework, though it makes sense of much of the material of parapsychology and Near-Death studies, by itself is not adequate.

Like Spiritualism, Theosophy affirms that the afterlife experience of a human being is a continuation of her spiritual and moral development while incarnate, to culminate finally in union with the Divine from which she (as the Pilgrim) originally issued. Also like Spiritualism, Theosophy might have some difficulty with the issue of painful afterdeath experiences happening to good and spiritually knowledgeable persons.

However, Theosophy has more potential than most forms of Spiritualism for dealing with painful NDEs because of its emphasis on initiations. By this term Theosophists mean experiences of consciousness-expansion, pleasant or painful, that the Pilgrim undergoes in both incarnate and discarnate conditions. Initiations build upon earlier initiations as the Pilgrim develops deeper levels of experience and insight. Although at lower levels of understanding some initiatory experiences may come as unwelcome surprises, at the Pilgrim's higher levels of conscious participation in the Divine all initiations are voluntary. Thus Theosophy's teachings regarding the afterlife could potentially accommodate the possibility of painful afterdeath experiences happening to good people.

Despite its initiatory theme, however, Theosophy is clearly gradualistic, with experiences of many kinds strung like beads on the agelong U-shaped journey of the Pilgrim.

Gradualism in Aurobindo's View

Aurobindo's Vedantic view is also gradualistic, and, as we have seen, fits rather well as the philosophic backdrop for many radiant NDEs with their sense of remembering that which had been forgotten. We recall that in his view it is not matter but the Divine consciousness, Being-Awareness-Bliss, that is primary, choosing to descend into the conditions of limited existence. This is the process of involution or partial forgetting.

At the lowest point of the descending arc is the level of matter and energy; in them, consciousness is asleep, unaware of itself.[1] As in human slumber, in this metaphorical sleep the Divine consciousness is not suspended but is gathered inward, unable to respond to external things.[2] The level of matter and energy is also the beginning of the ascent, of evolution; there is an elementary form of will and desire even in the atom.[3] At the level of plants exists life or "vital consciousness," a less-than-mental awareness that is capable of a kind of seeking-for and shrinking-away.[4] There is no sharp division between plants and animals, but the same forces are more conscious in the animal.[5] In the animal or bodily level, the bliss of the Eternal is sensed, not as something possessed, but as longed for: all-pervading desire and hunger. It is the violent level at which everything devours or is devoured.[6]

In the human being we have this level plus a further level of awakening: (individualized) Mind, capable of reflection and religious and ethical feeling.[7] Mind is aware of itself as ego, but in most cases unaware of the full depths of consciousness within.[8] This hidden self is the Purusha or spiritual Person, one in nature and being with the divine Self, the Source and guide.

What becomes of human consciousness, with its hidden divine Self, after death? Afterdeath experience, which is an integral part of the soul's evolution, varies according to the degree of spiritual development of the individual. There are various powers and planes of nonphysical reality—powers that help or hinder our evolution even now on earth—through which the surviving individual must go. The lowest ones may be molded by the imagination to seem like a re-creation of familiar earth-conditions, and the individual that was preoccupied with bodily life may linger there. But the nonphysical planes, especially the higher ones, are not created by the individual, though he or she may perhaps add something to them.[9]

The afterlife planes include powers of darkness and evil, existing more purely and fully than on earth. Aurobindo does not explain why a particular deceased person might experience one of them, but his general principle is that "the post-mortal state of the soul must correspond in some way to the development of the being on earth."[10] This implies that it is darkness in the soul that draws him or her to a dark plane. However, Aurobindo acknowledges the possibility that painful situations on earth are not necessarily the result of karmic retribution but may have been chosen by an advanced soul because of their potential for spiritual growth.[11] It seems possible, then, that the same may be true of painful afterlife experiences.

In Aurobindo's view, reincarnation, under the guidance of one's own divine Person (who is one with the cosmic Person) is important to the individual self's evolutionary awakening.[12] Having crossed to the higher spiritual planes, the discarnate self evaluates the life completed, detaches himself from the past personality's ties and motives, and selects his inner potentials to be developed by the new personality in the next life.[13] However, some unevolved individuals may not get beyond their earth-like lower planes, but reincarnate again unreflectingly.[14]

Through many embodiments the vast potentials of the self are unfolded, until finally the self attains the full flowering of the divine Spirit in the embodied human being.[15] For Aurobindo, human beings may hasten this process by conscious cooperation with the Spirit, or may delay it by refusing to transcend their addictions and egotism.[16] Eventually, however, the individual overcomes the limitations caused by ignorance and hunger, achieves unity with the divine Person within as well as harmony with other persons and the physical world.[17] This next stage of evolution takes place on earth.

This Aurobindo calls the Life Divine, in which the transformed being wills only that the Spirit express itself.[18] There is an ascetic phase, in that one turns away from ego gratifications, but once the Spirit-directed life is achieved, the world is affirmed. This transformation can take place among relatively isolated individuals, which fosters further awakening to divine consciousness in others.[19] But, notes Aurobindo, it begins to make a difference for universal evolution when it takes place on a group level, establishing on earth a race of people ready for it. Aurobindo is clear that he

Yes

does not mean a biological race, but a category of awakened people of many different types and styles. In such a community of transformed human beings, one operates out of a sense that the self in one is the self in all.[20] One feels the presence of the Divine in every center of one's consciousness, every cell of one's body; one has a spontaneous sympathy with all in the universe,[21] (like St. Francis' brother- and sisterhood with all things). The return to oneness with Being-Awareness-Bliss is not a dissolving of the individual into formlessness, but a conscious attainment of the One while still part of the many.

Gradualism in NDEs and NCDEs

Radiant NDEs that express the themes of being one with perfect Love, knowing all things and recognizing the Divine reality that one has forgotten, of coming "home" after a brief stint on earth, both do and do not suggest a gradualistic outlook. They do in that they imply that that which was hidden deep within is being unfolded by a natural process. But they do not in that the mystical experience is very often a huge jump from the person's ordinary spiritual and moral state of self-preoccupation and trivial concerns.

Of painful NDEs and NCDEs, Ritchie's NDE clearly assumes gradualism, in view of the obvious cause-and-effect connections he witnessed between unhealthy or evil earth life and afterdeath states. Considering his youth and supernatural-resurrectionist Christian view at the time, this situation is significant, strongly suggesting that his experience was not totally (or even primarily) shaped by culture. Angie Fenimore's dark plain of despairing suicides (page 64) and Marietta Davis's unhappy socialites at infernal parties (page 66) also show gradualistic continuity. Fenimore's experience fits with the gradualism of her Mormon worldview, but Davis's does not fit the nineteenth-century evangelical Protestantism of her community; thus it does not seem to be culturally shaped. Several of the experiences of OBE pioneers show gradualism: Muldoon's attack by F. D. (page 77), Fox's crucifixion, assuming it is not a past-life scene (page 88), perhaps also Monroe's struggles in the "inner ring," (page 65). These OBEs may have been influenced by Theosophy and kindred movements.

Fourteen

ONE-WORLD FRAMEWORKS: PROJECTIONIST

IN THIS CHAPTER I WILL USE THE TERMS "PROJECTION," "creation," "co-projection," and "co-creation" to refer to the power of mind to project its images so that they seem to be independent, "out there." "Creation" emphasizes that they do apparently become partly independent. "Co-projection" and "co-creation" emphasize the cooperation of two or more minds in this process.

Projectionism in Tibetan Buddhism

The Tibetan Buddhist view expressed in the *Bardo Thodol* has both gradualistic and initiatory elements, but its central theme is co-projectionist. The message is that the radiant and frightening Buddhas and other visionary figures are formed by mind. This mind is first of all that of the deceased person, who as a Tibetan has been focusing on these cosmic deities in meditation during physical life and thus has participated in putting them there.[1] If the person has led a selfish and harmful life, his bad karma causes him to project the frightening scenes of the third Bardo: tornadoes, avalanches, the judgment of Yama, and the like; if he or she has led a good life, paradisal scenes will appear.

But the deceased does not act alone, since she is in fact not a separate being but one expression among many of the cosmic field of consciousness, the One Mind. This is the Store Consciousness, made up of shared impressions from past group and individual experiences. The Store Consciousness causes individuals to see what appear to be things and beings existing in their own right, whether in the public physical world or in the Bardo.[2] But they are in fact co-projections, like reflected images in a hall of mirrors.

These perceived figures keep their power to frighten or attract only so long as the deceased is ignorant that they are mind-creations. When he recognizes this process and overcomes fear, revulsion, or desire, both the radiant and the terrifying figures are seen as expressions of transcendent compassion, offering opportunities for liberation. When he acknowledges them as his own and unites with them, he is freed from the illusory ego with its entrapping passions, and enters the Clear Light/Void which is Nirvana, Infinity. The processes of karma are then transcended.

Although welcoming spirits of the deceased do not appear in the *Bardo Thodol*, according to its principles such figures in contemporary Western NDEs would not be persons existing in their own right as they appear, but projections offering the possibility of liberation. Whether one has a radiant or a painful death experience is not crucially important, for both have the same potential, and after death most persons will encounter both kinds of experiences.

Partial Support for Mind as Creator or Projector

Some of the NDEs and NCDEs cited in Part I above have (or were interpreted as having) elements of mind-as-creator. Examples are Atwater's deliberate creation of a house, tree, and town (page 50), Whiteman's lion-figure that became harmless when he responded to its threat with love (page 69), and the tiger that shrank down to a domestic cat when the visionary conquered fear and faced it (page 68). The element of cooperation does not appear in these cases.

There are signs of co-creation in the imagery of haunting, particularly the Cheltenham case; remember that twice the ghost appeared to Rosina's sisters, but when Rosina entered the ghost manifested only to her, as though she were the preferred source of energy (page 182). G. N. M. Tyrrell's and Eileen Garrett's theories of apparitions as formed by both surviving spirit and percipients are also co-creationist (page 185).

·Co-creation is at the heart of the persona theory of Hornell Hart. Hart shows that only if the medium's trance personalities (which would include the visual figures that the control sees) are understood to be created jointly, by medium, sitters and deceased, can all the material of mediumship, both positive and negative for survival, be plausibly explained (page 204).

Projectionism in Ring's Thought

In *Life at Death* Kenneth Ring draws on holography to sketch out a co-creationist theory similar to that of the *Bardo Thodol*. The holograph is a three-dimensional image formed when a laser beam illuminates an interference pattern. Ring suggests that NDErs' perception of the tunnel and the light may reflect a shift in consciousness from our familiar world to what might be called a fourth dimension. This "dimension," pure reality, is a domain of frequencies, where time and space are collapsed and everything is happening all at once. In ordinary body-based consciousness, the brain is the laser beam that illuminates the interference pattern of these frequencies, forming the three-dimensional world we see. As consciousness begins to function independently of the physical body, it becomes aware of the frequency domain itself, which (to some extent) it still interprets holographically. The tunnel effect is the way the mind experiences this shift. The light seen by the NDEr, and the "world of light" reported by many mystics, may be the way mind experiences a higher range of frequencies. If so, we do not need to die or nearly die to experience this level of consciousness; it is potentially available to the living who learn to loosen consciousness from the body.[3]

Ring goes on to suggest that the light as Presence is the NDEr's total self or "higher self," an awesome and loving reality from which the individual personality is a split-off fragment. Because the personality is ignorant of this larger whole, it may fail to recognize this identity. The higher self has total knowledge of the individual personality, both past and future, and thus can initiate the life review. Ring does not rule out the possibility that the higher self is in fact an aspect of God or the divine.[4]

According to Ring, the beautiful paradisal world and the spirit-forms the NDEr sees may be, in holographic terms, "a realm that is created by the *interacting thought structures*" of minds already deceased. Accustomed to physical life but now attuned to this higher frequency domain, these minds combine to form the pattern seen; the newly-arrived NDEr contributes to this creative process.[5] Hellish experiences can be interpreted as the "lower frequency domain" creations of minds of a different caliber; since this domain appears to be closer to our public physical world, some NDErs may become "stuck" there for a time. Ring speculates that in some cases the tunnel "serves as a shield to protect the individual from an awareness of this domain."[6]

In an essay on painful NDEs, Ring develops these ideas further, dealing not only with the formation of images but with finite minds as projections. Drawing from *A Course in Miracles,* Ring theorizes that the only thing that is real is "the Light," the realm of total love and universal knowledge. The ego, on the other hand, is illusory, rooted in fear, vulnerable because it believes itself to be a separate reality. NDErs who strongly identify with and cling to their egos enter the dying experience with a good deal of fear, a state that tends to generate fearsome images. The person will feel threatened with extinction—as indeed she is, insofar as she is separate. But when she begins to surrender to the Light, she finds out that the ego was an empty illusion, that it kept her consciousness screened off from an awareness that the splendor of one's being is an aspect of the Light itself.[7] There are instances in which "inverted" NDEs have converted to radiant ones when the experiencer gave up resistance; Ring suggests that this is also the case with hellish ones. He cites the case of Howard Storm as an example (acknowledging that it is the only known example).

Thus, according to Ring, what is experienced in a painful NDE is unreal (though the pain is really felt); its images are projections that vanish when the ego is given up. In contrast, the light and love encountered in a radiant experience are ultimate reality. Then what of the religious figures in radiant experiences: Christ, Amida, Krishna? In *Heading Toward Omega* Ring records his belief that while the Light is universal, the particular religious figures seen are determined by culture (as Osis and Haraldsson's study suggests)[8]—in effect co-projected. About whether the landscapes and welcomers in radiant experiences are real, Ring gives his opinion elsewhere that the answer depends on

> the *state of consciousness* from which the question is addressed. From the level of an enlightened consciousness...I think the beings of these realms are all projections in the sense that they are mind-generated from either the individual or collective psyche. However, from a more ordinary state of consciousness in which dualism reigns with a false supremacy, it is almost impossible not to believe in a world of self-existent spirits, good, bad and boring, including angelic and demonic creatures, with various degrees of self-awareness. In this respect, the

spiritual world reflects pretty much the same sort of folks and preoccupations as we find here below....[T]his, however, is not to deny that living persons, even when near death, can still project their own hallucinatory beings into this realm, so in that sense it may still be a mix of things, real and phantasmagorical....[B]eyond the shadows and simulacra...there is only Light Inexpressible and Love Unending.[9]

Thus Ring holds that from our limited human viewpoint, the figures in radiant experiences may be varyingly real or unreal, whereas from a truer enlightened perspective all figures are unreal in the sense of being projections. It would follow that, like the threatening figures in painful NDEs, these loving beings also offer opportunities for overcoming the illusion of ego.

Ring's view differs from the ancient Tibetan outlook in his affirmation of ultimate reality as Love, which would not be the case in the world of the *Bardo Thodol*. We saw that the Clear Light/Void is not described as love, and in most cases the dying person, it is assumed, will seek to avoid it or will fail to focus on it.

The theory does not cover all painful NDEs, as Ring himself admits, citing the case of "Vera" who encountered the devil in a church in paradise (pages 90–91); any given NDE has multiple influences behind it.[10] Another difficulty, pointed out by Christopher Bache and acknowledged by Ring, is that almost everyone has some attachment to ego and fear of death, which makes it hard to see why there are so few reports of painful NDEs in proportion to the peaceful ones.[11]

To clarify: the idea that the images and beings encountered in NDEs (or after death) are co-created and projected by minds does not mean that the figures are illusory in the sense of being figments of the imagination, for they may have their own thoughts. It means only that they, as well as all other particular beings, do not exist in their own right as they seem to do.

The solution to the problem of painful NDEs offered by projection theories is not simply that bad people in the grip of karma project terrifying images and therefore deserve their pain. We saw that the wrathful Buddhas in the *Bardo Thodol* also cause terror and pain for ordinary decent people whose only crime is being attached to ego. The solution the theories offer lies rather in the potential outcome when ego is given up: salvation as enlightenment.

The gradualistic and projectionist frameworks are not necessarily incompatible with one another, and both offer helpful insights. The next chapter will present a third category of views, the initiatory, with further answers. Initiatory frameworks are quite compatible with projectionist ones (in fact Ring combines them), though they tend to be in tension with gradualistic views.

Fifteen

ONE-WORLD FRAMEWORKS: INITIATORY

THE INTERPRETIVE FRAMEWORKS THAT FOLLOW DIFFER from the gradualistic and projectionistic ones in that they do not arise from actual death crises, but all have close similarities to elements in NDEs, whether radiant or painful. They all have the shape of a story in which the central event or events are painful experiences out of which develop joy and transformation. They are seen as examples of a cosmic pattern of initiation that is necessary to ultimate fulfillment.

We should notice first that there is an overlap between projectionist and initiatory frameworks. The projectionist theories (of painful NDEs) given above generally follow an initiatory pattern, but not all projectionist or co-creationist views are initiatory (and vice versa). For example, if a dying Tibetan has already largely overcome the illusion of ego as a result of meditation, it is possible for him to enter the Clear Light directly after death, without undergoing the pain of encountering his own terrifying projections. In the initiatory one-world views that follow, however, the destructive forces one meets are in most cases assumed to be real in their own right.

The Hero's Adventure

In fabulous stories in various genres—myth, folk tale, romance, and novels and motion pictures of adventure, fantasy, and science fiction—certain thinkers have traced out a widespread initiatory pattern of undying appeal: a hero of high ancestry but humble birth goes on a journey, experiences painful ordeals and challenges, meets them successfully, and returns to claim a reward or reclaim his or her true identity. Probably the scholar best known for this kind of work is mythologist Joseph Campbell, whose book *The Hero With a Thousand Faces* has been mined to interpret NDEs.

Certainly Campbell has many valuable insights, and criticisms of the validity of his work can, I believe, be partly answered. But for lack of space to do so, I will turn rather to the less controversial work of literary critic Northrop Frye, whose ideas are essentially complementary with Campbell's. I present Frye's analysis of the adventure scenario in romance literature, with its dreadful ordeals and typical happy ending, as a potential framework to integrate painful and radiant afterlife experiences into a meaningful and hopeful metanarrative.

Frye was influenced by Jung's analysis of the archetypes of the collective unconscious (as was Campbell). Jung has a great deal to say about the universality of the hero and his adventure, and has substantial passages on various of the motifs that Frye traces. However, it would not really be appropriate to cite Jung as an authoritative source for a metanarrative that brings together painful and radiant NDEs, at least if it is to be applied to the afterlife. For one thing, Jung does not give a consistent picture of life after death. In one passage he implies a vastly expanded existence before and after death,[1] but in another place he gives his opinion that the dead do not gain infinite knowledge but know no more than they did at death, so that for further insight they must turn to the living.[2] Jung asserts that he does not anticipate any sort of mystical union or attainment of universal consciousness.[3] More significantly, perhaps, he repeatedly insists that the archetypes, especially the hero archetype, are not to be identified with human individuals; to do so is inflation, an unbalanced state in which one sees oneself as a divine or semi-divine being.[4] The story of the hero symbolizes the psychological process of individuation, but the hero is not a human being undergoing physical death and survival.

Frye's Hero: The U-Shaped Journey

In his book *The Secular Scriptures* Northrop Frye traces out a hero-adventure pattern in "naive and sentimental romance"[5] literature in the West from late Roman times to the twentieth century. Though romance is an identifiable genre in a more or less continuous cultural tradition, it also has a spontaneous quality; it is a basic human product. Descended from folk tale;[6] a romance is the kind of story that centers on adventures and erotic love, with a happy ending. Romance literature keeps turning up mostly outside the literary establishment, without much regard for that establishment's usual disapproval.[7] Frye proposes that romance may form "a single integrated vision of the world,"[8] the ultimate human view of reality: "how the world looks when the ego has collapsed,"[9] and subject and object are one. It is a sharing of God's view of the world on the seventh day in the Hebrew creation story: "God saw everything that he had made, and behold, it was very good."[10, 11]

The map of the universe on which Frye traces the hero's journey is vertical rather than horizontal, with three levels. The hero comes originally from heaven or the divine dimension. He (less often she) descends in two stages: from the upper world to our "middle earth," and from here into the world below, followed by a return in a corresponding two-stage ascent. (There is a clear resemblance to the U-figure in the thought of Theosophy and Aurobindo.) All of these levels are symbolically ambivalent, says Frye. Usually the world or worlds above are the place of God, or Paradise, but they may also be represented by stars with malevolent influence. Our world is an obvious mix of good and bad, and in romance tends to be sexualized. The lower world is considered to be wholly demonic in Christianity, but in much of romance it contains, hidden within its horrors, treasures of wealth or wisdom.[12]

The idea that the hero's origin is the upper world may be represented by the motif of his birth in the context of a love-triangle: divine or royal father, human mother, and a human foster-father who is jealous and hostile. The infant hero may be threatened by violence and put out to die of exposure before being rescued and raised in a humble rustic setting.[13] It is not surprising that this motif should have appeared frequently in romances in the Roman world, since exposing unwanted babies was an accepted practice. But Frye considers it significant that fifteen centuries later, Victorian writers are as preoccupied as ever with the motif of the mysterious birth,[14] even though the ancient romances "nearly all remain unknown to modern readers."[15]

Another mode of representing this first descent is some kind of disruption in continuity of the hero's identity near the beginning of the story. It may be a break in consciousness: perhaps it is amnesia, induced by a love potion or a curse; "[i]t may be externalized as a disaster like capture by pirates, or a wandering into the land of the fairies,"[16] entering a dream-atmosphere, exile of some kind. It is a sharp loss of social status, "from riches to poverty, from privilege to a struggle to survive, or even slavery."[17]

The dream world often takes the form of a deepening forest which the hero enters, perhaps becoming lost, as he hunts an animal. The forest becomes sexualized, suggesting an enveloping female body. Hunter and prey may be identified, with the hero metamorphizing into a beast, thus losing the power of communication. Even if loss of identity is not carried this far, there may be disguise or change of name. A motif of mirror images or twins may appear, indicating that the hero, moving in a world of constriction, is alienated from his or her true self.[18]

There may be a deity behind the action in a romance, who speaks through oracles or prophecies, giving the message that the ultimate outcome is predetermined. Parallel to this theme is the twin who retains his or her identity, a Higher Self who watches the adventures of her double in the mirror world, or a dreamer watching her dream-self, sometimes with the ability to help.[19]

The second descent is into a night world, "often a dark and labyrinthine world of caves and shadows where the forest has turned subterranean, and where we are surrounded by the shapes of animals."[20]* The hero may have an animal or silent ghost as a companion, representing the reduction of person to thing. The night world is a place of ritualized cruelty and horror.[21] At its lowest point may be the sacrifice of a youth or maiden offered to be swallowed by a monster, again suggesting the identification of human being and animal.[22] Or, as a prisoner of pirates or some other outlaw society, the hero may be sentenced to death, may be killed or prematurely buried. Caves, devouring, and burial are all linked, says Frye, to "an earth-mother at the bottom of the world."[23] If the entire mythological universe is seen as a macrocosmic body, the organs of generation and excretion are at its bottom, organs whose function is "emphasized in proportion as this part of the mythical universe is made demonic. Devils are associated with blackness, soot, and sulfurous smell, besides having the horns, hoofs, and tails of the sort of fertility spirit that is close to the sexual instinct."[24] Thus Frye shows a linkage between the destructiveness, the exaggerated sexuality, and the potential for rebirth found in the lower world.

---

*In the movie *Titanic,* this theme is vividly represented by Rose's desperate search through the lower corridors of the sinking ship, especially when the lights dim and a deep, growling roar of collapsing steel is heard.

The theme of judgment is represented in a trial, in which the prisoner knows nothing yet is totally known by those who hold him captive. Frye holds that this situation (represented in Kafka's *The Trial)* is so horrifying that many romances mitigate it by making the trial center upon an unjust charge or mistaken identity.[25] But the essence of this theme, says Frye, is that the hero has forgotten his true identity, so that the world presents itself to him as absurd. However, the very fact of telling a story, with its meaningful shape, its beginning and (happy) ending, gives an answer; it is part of a counter-absurdity, "the vision that comes...[to those who have forgotten who they are]...and ends with finding one's identity in the body of the god...."[26] *The narrative shape of romance is itself an insistence that meaning has the final word.*

The hero's ascent reverses the preceding movement: escape from a dungeon, or a breaking of the evil enchantments, and, especially, *remembering.* Unreflective awe and terror give way to laughter, as tragedy turns to comedy. Ideally the reversal "is both a surprise to the reader and yet seems...an inevitable development of events up to that point."[27] The feeling that the ascent is inevitable may be supported by an appeal to fate or prophecy; what appeals to the reader, says Frye, is the archetype of death and rebirth. In everyday life we feel that death is inevitable, but now it is new life that is inevitable.[28]

The restoration of memory marks the return to the surface of the earth. A story may represent this return as a recognition of the hero's identity via a birthmark or memento from her or his earlier life, which would mean that he is on his way up the second stage, toward an actual recovery of original identity. The upper world may be represented as an ideal society in which nature is in harmony with humanity, perhaps with imagery of the garden of Eden.[29]

A frequent and important motif of ascent is the hero driven by his love to climb or fly to a higher world, with imagery of mountains, spiral stairs, ladders, towers, and arrows. Reversing the twin- and mirror-image themes of the descent, the ascent is a movement toward resuming one's unfallen state. This state may be symbolized by marriage, by virginity (suggesting renewed youth and freshness), by a dance as representation of universal harmony, by sleeping beauties waking or statues coming to life.[30] Traditional romance tends to suggest that this upward journey is the return of a creature to its creator.

Frye's Hero: Interface with NDEs

The literary theme of the hero's origin in an upper world, descent to our earth, and ultimate return to the paradisal or divine realm, is reflected in the claims of NDErs that the light is not something new but is "home," that "it's like I was always there and I will always will be there, and that my existence on earth was just a brief instant."[31] We have seen that the descent theme of romance may be expressed by stories of the birth of a child with one human and one divine (or noble) parent; in a Christian context this theme echoes the Virgin Birth of Christ, the one descent of God to incarnate on earth. When we compare this romance motif to the momentous recognition in the radiant NDE of one's true identity, the story of romance suggests that all human beings (or all sentient beings) descended from such a state, and this particular human being is at the moment enjoying a brief "visit home" (a visit not part of the scenario of romance).

When romances represent the descent by a break in consciousness, such as evil enchantment, we have a quite literal analogy to what certain home-visiting NDErs have described: the cosmic insights, or total knowledge, are "something I had always known and managed to forget."[32] They are forgotten again after the visit ends, but are, presumably, remembered once more at the final ascent.

The theme of twins or mirror images corresponds to the situation of the NDEr who enjoys the guardianship or guidance of a wise figure that can be interpreted as the Transcendent Self. This could apply both to paradisal scenes in which the NDEr is given insights into his or her life and sent back ("This is not your time,") or to a menacing situation in which the guiding figure protects and reassures—such as those of Cathy Baker (page 67), Luisa Vazquez (page 66), and Grey's "chapel" suicide (page 89). The divine oracles and prophecies in romance that give a sense of a predetermined outcome also resemble the wisdom of the NDEr's guide. Still another element of NDEs that fits the idea of predetermined outcome is the "personal flashforward" portion of the life overview: that is, glimpses of events to be expected in the NDEr's future after return.

I suggest that the animal theme and the forest (resembling an enfolding female body) that darkens around the hero, correspond to the dimming of consciousness that, according to a U-shaped journey of the soul, would happen with incarnation as a fetus. Disguise, change of name, and descending from wealth to poverty could also represent separating from the light to take up a new restricted identity (or resume it at return to earth-life after an NDE).

So far, I have been comparing Frye's first stage of the descent to the process of incarnation that certain radiant NDErs are convinced they have undergone. Frye's second stage of descent, however, corresponds to actual painful NDE narratives of descent into hell. To begin with, those who undergo hellish NDEs tend actually to experience their directional movement as a descent—through a sloping tunnel, vortex, or the like. (Of course the idea of hell being downward is influenced by a long tradition of popular thought in the West.) The dark underground realm of the hellish NDE is unmistakably like the caves and dark labyrinths of romance. Imprisonment, cruelty, and horror threatened or committed by an outlaw society of demonic beings certainly appear in such NDEs, in some instances with a suggestion or outright action of sexual abuse (for example Storm [page 82], Patricia [page 78], Ritchie [page 80]). Such treatment as a sex object is an example of the "reduction of person to thing" symbolized by the animal companion.

In romance, this monstrous sexual destructiveness precedes the hero's rebirth as though from the womb of a Cosmic Mother. But there is not much evidence that such ego-death results in blissful renewal during the NDE itself. As Kenneth Ring pointed out, so far we have only one case, that of Howard Storm (and even Storm was rescued; ego-death was probably not total). Others who escaped or were rescued before full ego-death have described gradual renewal during the months and years following the experience (for example Patricia, [page 78], Thomas Welch, [page 86]).

The romance motif of a nightmare trial in the underworld in which the hero knows little or nothing yet is totally known appears infrequently in contemporary NDEs. A good example is Grey's attempted suicide in the "chapel" (page 89); Barbara Rommer also presents a few tribunal cases. They resemble the traditional Christian image of the Throne of Judgment, and the Weighing of the Heart in the *Going Forth by Day* [page 126].

We saw that for Frye the essence of the trial motif is that the hero has forgotten his original identity. Thus the trial gives "the vision of the absurd, the realization...that nothing before or after death makes sense." Frye's interpretation may apply not only to certain tribunal cases, but may resolve the meaningless-void NDE: it puts the dreadful experience that has presented the universe as random, shapeless, and unreal into a *story*, a story that begins with identity lost and ends with remembering and regaining that lost identity.[33] If we trust the story, we thereby claim that the all-knowing tribunal and the meaningless-void NDE do not have the last word. For contemporary survivors of painful NDEs, who tend to be stunned and confused and to need a considerable period for recovery, the first stage of ascent—the return to "the surface of the earth"—is seldom marked by laughter as it is for the romance hero. But, as we have seen, transformation and renewal do eventually take place for some.

The second stage of ascent would be the flight (at full death) upward toward Home: to the Garden (nature in harmony with humanity), to the City (the ideal society), and especially to the Light, oneness with the Divine. Here, of course, we are throwing a bridge over the gap.

If the romance scenario is applied to possible painful experiences after full death, one might ascend directly from the hellish world to a paradise or the light (as Patricia thought she would have done if she hadn't revived [page 79]), or one might first ascend to earth for another incarnation, or perhaps to some level similar to earth with its mixture of good and evil. However, since Frye's four-stage plot is an ideal type and not an exact fit, we cannot expect a neat fit to situations after death.

Campbell and Frye are of course not the only thinkers who have analyzed the tale of the hero's journey and applied it to the soul. But they are willing to interpret the tale not only as a here-and-now psychological process but a cosmic one. This means that their work is particularly friendly, so to speak, to the search for an initiatory story to make hopeful sense of the possibility that painful NDEs may foreshadow painful afterdeath experiences.

Other Commentary on the Heroic Journey

Several thinkers have made the connection between the journey narrative and NDEs. Prominent among them is Carol Zaleski, but, since she rejects the idea of evidence for survival (see pages 211–212),[34] it would be inappropriate to use her discussion to support my case.

Michael Grosso's concept of the Archetype of Death and Enlightenment (ADE) is potentially more helpful for my purpose. The ADE is a passage from darkness to light, enclosure to disclosure. He describes this passage as essentially a two-stage journey, and, in NDEs, the darkness or enclosure is the pain and terror of dying, from which one emerges into the light that is the Self, wholeness.[35] The out-of-body state expresses the emergence from the body as cave or tomb into freedom. The guide with his wisdom, and the life overview (especially when it includes scenes of what is to come), represent the emergence from the unenlightened ego into the light of the whole Self.[36] Grosso sees the NDE as one context among others, such as mystical experiences and myths, in which the ADE appears,[37] but does affirm NDEs as foreshadowing life beyond physical death.

Another supportive thinker on this issue, F. Gordon Greene, compares various well-known works of quest fiction to NDEs and finds some of the same parallels. In various literary fantasies including *Peter Pan*, *The Wizard of Oz*, and *The Lion, the Witch and the Wardrobe*, Greene traces NDE features such as tunnel imagery, flying, and encounter with spirits. He notes the presence of demonic figures and certain heroes' struggles with evil.[38] He makes explicit reference to painful NDEs when he compares Odysseus' descent to Hades and meeting the "lifeless, mournful shades" to Moody's "bewildered spirits" and the unhappy spirit-beings Monroe met when out-of-body.[39] Greene suggests that the many obstacles of Odysseus' journey, particularly frightening ordeals such as the near-drowning in a shipwreck, are like a shamanic initiation which brings about "a higher, more evolved state of being." Odysseus' successful return to his wife and retaking of his kingdom represent this transformed state.[40] One might add that his disguising himself as a beggar when he first returns, then showing himself as a powerful king, also symbolizes this transformation. However, his massacre of the suitors and even the servant maids is hardly the work of one in touch with unconditional love.

The Psychedelic Rebirth Scenario

The second kind of narrative framework comes from LSD studies. For several decades Stanislav Grof and colleagues have explored the deeps of human consciousness through various means: in recent years breath techniques, dancing and body work, originally the taking of large quantities of LSD. I will focus on his reports of the psychedelic studies, drawn from at least five thousand LSD sessions. Finding astonishing material that would not fit the mechanistic model of the universe, Grof develops and offers the makings of an alternative model.[41] He notes that it can be applied to Near-Death experiences.[42]

Grof's LSD voyagers encountered different levels of the unconscious. As the LSD voyager crosses from the daylight world into the beyond, she sees or hears rather abstract phenomena: geometrical forms, beautiful buildings, chimes, buzzing, other noises.[43] Theese phenomena may be appealing but have little significance for the process of self-exploration.[44] Some who take LSD in small quantities may go no further than this. But the explorations that lead to transformation occur in the deeps of the individual's own unconscious and vast transpersonal realms, often intertwined in complex ways.

The LSD experiencer vividly *relives in clusters* those past experiences that carry emotional weight, particularly physical traumas. Most of these clusters, or systems of condensed experience (COEX systems), are connected to aspects of the birth process, and may transcend individuality.[45] Remarkably, when reliving childhood trauma scenes the person may feel a complete identification with all those who participated, either at the same time or alternately. While doing so he largely loses his own identity.[46]

The different scenes in a cluster may actually come to consciousness simultaneously, with the experiencer able to choose whether to explore them all at once, or to alternate them.[47] A particular cluster, centering in the core experience that happened first in her life, is worked through in a series of sessions. Once the core experience is resolved, that cluster no longer reappears; another may take its place.[48]

1. The Perinatal Matrices

The themes of birth and death are very important in most of the clusters, with feelings of being born including specific changes that happen at birth. Both birth and death aspects involve such intense emotional and physical pain that the person may feel he or she has gone beyond individual limits and identified with entire populations of sufferers (such as persecuted Jews or accused witches), or even all life. Grof refuses to explain these reductionistically as merely a reliving of birth, for there are profound spiritual dimensions as well. The birth/death theme appears in four patterns of experience corresponding to four stages of biological birth, patterns which Grof calls Basic Perinatal Matrices. They are (in simplified terminology): Matrix One, ongoing life in the womb; Matrix Two, contractions when the cervix is closed; Matrix Three, passage through the birth canal; and Matrix Four, emergence.

Matrix One takes both peaceful and disturbed forms. In a peaceful form, besides actually feeling herself to be living serenely in the womb, the person may be conscious of other boundaryless states: undersea life, interstellar space. There may be a sense of cosmic unity;[49] ego is gone, consciousness encompasses the whole universe. The experiencer may use paradox as she tries to describe the indescribable.[50] Everything is perfect, is as it should be; evil is unimportant or nonexistent.[51] In contrast, in disturbed Matrix One states the experiencer may have a sense that someone is trying to abort her. She may sense underwater dangers or pollution, nausea and tremors, or the presence of evil forces.[52] She may see demons, perhaps scenes from past lives that carry bad karma.[53]

Matrix Two is painful. The experiencer feels the birth process beginning; he is attacked by alarming chemicals and by powerful contractions, and feels there is no escape. Grof notes that there may be a cosmic engulfment, "a three-dimensional spiral, funnel, or whirlpool, sucking the individual relentlessly toward its center."[54] There may be scenes from the hells of Christian tradition,[55] descent into an underworld or labyrinth,[56] a terrifying monster that attacks or swallows the person. In all these images, free-floating movement gives way to life-threatening entrapment.[57]

Another variant of Matrix Two is situations of meaninglessness, with feelings of insanity and/or of terrible loneliness and hopelessness.[58] The background may be a barren moonscape, a black dangerous cavern, or nightfall.[59] There may be a soulless world of mechanical gadgets; the person may feel an ultimate insight that the world is absurd.[60] Human distinctions mean nothing; the rich and the famous are no different in death from beggars. The person has not herself become soulless but desperately longs for meaning.[61] She will relive any personal memories, such as air raids, in which an overwhelming force left her no escape; she identifies with prisoners in dungeons, concentration camps, or insane asylums.[62]

In Matrix Three the experiencer as fetus feels the contractions continue, but the cervix is open. No longer helpless and hopeless, he is active; there is direction and a goal; it is more like purgatory than hell.[63] He struggles to survive under crushing pressures, unable to get oxygen. There may be scenes of natural disasters: storms, volcanic eruptions, earthquakes.[64] Symbolic themes include nuclear bombs, the Last Judgment, and the Witches' Sabbath; images such as bloody sacrifice, rape, and murder appear. There may be worship of a terrible goddess like Kali, or identification with Christ crucified.

Energy builds up and discharges explosively in sexual and aggressive feelings. The subject identifies with both parties in a conflict, feeling both the anguish of the victim and the fury of the aggressor. When the pain passes bearing it becomes rapturous ecstasy; aggression and love, pain and pleasure become indistinguishable.[65] There may be a carnival atmosphere, uniting a sexual charge with the bizarre or macabre.[66] Any very intense personal experiences of sex or combat will be relived.[67]

There is a repulsive and nauseating element that appears just before birth or rebirth: the experiencer feels overwhelmingly confronted with pus, urine, and feces; there may be mountains of garbage or corpses. This theme merges into fire imagery that purifies her and consumes the filth. Images such as medieval witch-burnings or the self-immolation of the Phoenix may appear.[68] The person relives any rescues, any survival of accidents from her past.[69]

At the point of breakthrough to Matrix Four, the experiencer feels a huge catastrophe is about to take place.[70] It unfolds as annihilation, utter defeat and humiliation, the death of the ego. Afterwards, says Grof,

> [the experiencer] is struck by visions of blinding white or golden light and has the feelings of enormous decompression and expansion of space. The general atmosphere is that of liberation...and forgiveness....He experiences overwhelming love for his fellow men... accompanied by humility and a tendency to engage in service and charitable activities...exaggerated ambition, craving for money...or power appear...to be absurd and childish desires...."[71]

The experiencer may identify with dying-rising gods such as Christ or Osiris, may be united with mother goddesses like Isis.[72] Typical imagery of Matrix Four would be huge halls with decorated columns and crystal chandeliers.[73]

Grof's experiencers do not necessarily go through these four matrices in order; they may return again and again to one of the first three matrices, deepening their experience of it. A painful session may shift to a fourth-stage liberation when the particular issues involved are resolved. But there will be a need to return later to matrices Two or Three until all material relating to birth and death has been completely explored. Then, having undergone total ego death, the person emerges once and for all into the fourth stage.

The outcome of the therapy is a deep transformation of life. Reborn individuals are characterized by a heightened ability for enjoyment, for living the simple life, and for living in the present moment.[74] The experiencer's senses are keen, all things are fresh and exciting; natural beauty is greatly appreciated.[75]

2. The Transpersonal Dimension

Grof tells of instances of apparent ESP occurring as experiencers expand beyond the boundaries of embodied ego. A sense of leaving the body is frequent in LSD sessions, with the person seeming to observe his body from another vantage point in the room.[76] He may have a strong sense of dual unity with a particular person who is either present in the session or elsewhere.[77] He may identify very authentically with animals, gaining accurate information regarding animal psychology and zoology. (This is not the same as symbolic animal transformations.) A subject may identify with plants, finding herself a geminating seed going through cell division.[78] There may be a sense of oneness with all life—from humans to single-celled organisms—throughout time, bringing insights into the processes of evolution and ecology.[79] There are reports of identifying with the consciousness of supposedly inorganic bodies such as the ocean. Rarely, an LSD experiencer may during advanced sessions undergo an expansion of consciousness to include all aspects of the planet, inorganic and organic, as a living being. In these Gaia experiences, all aspects of evolution seem to be a Gaian attempt to reach a higher level of self-realization.[80]

There may also be a narrowing and focussing of consciousness, with participation in the experiences of one's own organs, tissues, or cells. It is common for an experiencer to identify with the sperm and ovum at the time of her conception; she may perceive the cell nucleus and chromosomes. These inner-space explorations are often accompanied by impressive insights into bodily physiology and chemistry, unknown to the experiencer before.[81]

Some forms of such expanded consciousness transcend the ordinary limits of time. Experiencers may witness scenes from the past; one woman, for example, saw many evidential scenes from the life and violent death of a seventeenth-century aristocrat whom she later learned was an ancestor. There may be reincarnation-type experiences showing a strong tie with another person.[82] On a collective level, experiencers can participate in elaborate sequences in the past life of an alien culture, with insights into its social structure, religion, art, and technological development. They often describe the culture in accurate detail, and show skills such as dance and yoga postures.[83]

Besides these transpersonal experiences that have reference (at some level) to the public physical world, there are otherworldly experiences. One type seems to involve spirits of the deceased. For example, an experiencer named Dana relived her ordeal at age ten of watching her father deteriorate and die. In the reliving, her consciousness fused with his, to share his death agony and enter with him into a world filled with a macabre, glowing mist. Countless souls of the deceased were suspended there, barraging her with telepathic messages of urgent need, causing her to panic.[84] Other examples of spirit-figures are beneficent guides, teachers, and protectors. The experiencer seldom sees the guiding spirit, but rather feels his or her protecting presence while undergoing harsh experiences. The spirit guide may be unrecognized, may be identified with a religious figure, or may be seen as one's higher self.[85]

According to Grof, various deities and supernatural beings, such as Isis, Krishna, or Kali, appear in LSD sessions. Sophisticated experiencers have been able to identify some of them, while the unsophisticated have been able to describe them in such detail that they could be identified with ancient mythological figures.[86] One of the most profound occurrences in LSD sessions is the transpersonal identification with Universal Mind, in which, Grof says, "the illusions of matter, space and time...have been completely transcended....This experience is boundless, unfathomable, and ineffable....All the questions that have ever been asked seem to be answered...."[87] Some experience the Supracosmic Void, which underlies the public physical world. "It is beyond time and space, beyond form...and beyond polarities such as good and evil...." It also transcends cause and effect. The Universal Mind emerges from the Void and returns to it; "they are different aspects of the same phenomenon."[88]

One phenomenon appearing many times in LSD sessions is kundalini awakening. This sometimes happens to ignorant persons, whose informal descriptions clearly describe the processes and underlying theories.[89]

Interface of LSD Rebirth and NDEs

In the LSD material one can find many similarities to NDEs. In both cases, as experiencers move "between worlds," they may hear sounds—chimes, buzzing, or other noise—with no apparent significance. Feeling out of body and watching the surrounding scene is also common in both. The empathic life overview (ELO) in NDEs is like the "dual unity" of LSD subjects who relive scenes from their personal pasts, sharing the consciousness of all participants. The sense of union with animals, plants, and supposedly inorganic matter as well as persons is another shared element (page 98).[90] The ELO is usually limited to sharing in the effects on others of one's own thoughts, words, and acts, but LSD dual unity and the LSD experiencer's union with animals and plants do not seem to be limited in this way. Scenes apparently from past lives also appear both in ELOs and LSD sessions.

Experiencing one's own body at the level of cells is still another experience found in both fields. Frequent in LSD therapy, especially as the reliving of one's own conception, it is rare in NDE reports; one instance is Atwater's dialogues with her cells during the aftermath of her second NDE[91] (page 150).

The appearance of religious figures and symbols alien to one's own culture or experience (particularly Mellen-Thomas Benedict's visions of various deities [page 37] and Nancy Evans Bush's yin/yang circles [page 75]), rare in the records of NDEs, are supported by the more frequent appearance of such figures in LSD therapy.

Our chief concern, of course, is the LSD–NDE overlap of painful experiences, especially those leading to renewal. Encounter with unhappy spirits is one instance. The dual-unity case of Dana cited above reveals wretched, needy spirits similar to those appearing in Angie Fenimore's limbo of suicides (page 64) and Moody's case with dull, hopeless beings (page 56). However, cases of unhappy spirits seem to be less frequent in both LSD therapy and NDEs than are benevolent and wise spirit guides.[92]

The images in hellish and meaningless-void NDEs are overwhelmingly like those in Grof's matrices Two and Three. Funnels and vortices in painful NDEs, serving as downward-oriented tunnels (see the Gloria Hipple case, page 72), function like the cosmic whirlpools in Matrix Two that entrap the experiencer in a hellish no-exit situation. A notable difference is that in NDE cases there tends to be a quick reversal of the terrifying downward plunge, whereas Matrix Two experiences appear to be very drawn-out.

Unutterably evil beings like those in Matrices Two and Three appear in painful NDEs; for example, the evil presence encountered by Cathy Baker in the wind tunnel (page 67) and Patricia's unspeakable presence approaching from behind (page 79). Threats of violence from wild beasts appear both in NDEs and an NCDE.

A savage struggle between active antagonists, including elements of sexual abuse (as in Matrix Three), appears in important NDEs (page 79). There are also a good many NDEs that involve catastrophic upheavals and global wars, presented as inevitable or alternative future scenarios.

The similarities between radiant NDEs and Matrix Four are obvious, especially white or golden light, scenes of splendor and wealth (as in the celestial cities in NDEs), and the sense of cosmic unity. After-effects are also very similar, particularly the conviction that the drives for wealth, prestige, and power are empty, and that love and service to others are what matters. The pattern of emerging from the dark nether world into the light also appears in NDEs, though at present cases of complete ego-death (perhaps Howard Storm [page 83] and the electroshock patient [page 88]) are few and uncertain.

Besides Grof himself, two major scholars in NDE research affirm the application of Grof's psychedelic rebirth paradigm to NDEs. Kenneth Ring, though acknowledging the need for caution, compares Matrix Two experiences of meaninglessness with everlasting-void NDEs. In the context of interpreting painful NDEs as encounters with one's own projections, Ring comments that the NDErs who report them tend to be left with "a pervasive sense of emptiness and fatalistic despair," which fits Grof's findings about Matrix Two psychedelic subjects whose experiences remain unresolved.[93] These feelings are not the last word on the experiences, but result when the proper course of the cycle of experiences is aborted. Such a painful NDE, says Ring, is an incomplete experience.[94] Ego has not yet been dissolved.

Christopher Bache carries the issue further by suggesting that all three types of painful NDEs—"inverted," meaningless-void, and hell—correspond to Grof's birth model. He proposes that void and hellish NDE experiences be classed together as essentially akin, for both involve meaningless suffering. Further, some void NDErs spontaneously refer to their experience as hell.[95] Inverted NDEs may be interpreted as milder forms of hellish ones. If we apply them to the birth model, particularly Matrix Two, all three types would then be intermediate stages of a process climaxing in the transpersonal radiant experience. Bache agrees with Ring that both inverted and hellish NDEs convert to radiant ones when the experiencer gives up ego. By implication, radiant and painful experiences are not opposites as they appear, but "two aspects of an underlying, organic process."[96] NDErs get brief glimpses of what LSD experiencers encounter repeatedly and at length.

The only obstacle to this proposal, says Bache, is the fact that we do not yet have a case in which the meaningless void converts to the radiant experience.[97] However, it might be argued that Storm's case qualifies, if the period during which he lay alone in the darkness (page 82) is in fact the experience of meaningless void. Storm describes this desolation in darkness as so much worse than being tormented by the entities that he even hoped one or two of them might come back. Barbara Rommer also reports a case that, arguably, might qualify.

Bache does not, like Ring, interpret the tormenting figures and landscapes in painful NDEs as projections, but he agrees that the crucial thing linking the second and third matrices to the fourth is ego-death. One must, says Bache, give up the idea of separate existence and die to self in order to be reborn into cosmic consciousness. The perinatal matrices are certainly not merely a return of memories of physical birth, as Sagan claims, but are the meeting place between the limited personal consciousness and the transpersonal.[98]

Bache asks a significant and provocative question regarding the meaning of the spiritual birth process that Grof describes. Grof affirms that the transpersonal elements in LSD sessions are real, but he sees the transformational process as an individual's adventure. But an important question remains: Why should the individual's reliving of unresolved birth and other trauma involve such vast collective suffering? The process is clearly a healing one for the individual, and Grof explains *how* it takes place—through the clustering of similar events—but not *why* such huge transpersonal anguish should be part of it.[99]

Assuming that this collective pain appears for a purpose (since it happens so regularly), Bache suggests that the healing process in question is not only an individual but a collective one. To explain, he draws upon Rupert Sheldrake's concept of morphic fields, specifically the field called "the group mind." As we saw in Chapter Seven, this field is conceived as existing on various levels nesting within one another: family, community, nation, race, and species. Sheldrake conceives the group mind as collecting and incorporating into itself the new experiences of its members and synthesizing them at a central level. The implication is that just as the individual remembers his or her past traumas and uses choice in integrating them, the group mind can remember the sufferings of all its members and attempt to deal with them. Bache speculates that

> just as problematic experiences can collect and block the healthy functioning of the individual, similar blockages might also occur at the collective level....[T]he unresolved human anguish of history might still be active in the memory of the species-mind, burdening its life....[I]f conscious engagement of previously unresolved pain brings therapeutic release at the personal level, the same might also occur at the species-level.[100]

In other words, the group mind takes advantage of the return to consciousness of the individual's past pain, together with the collective pain with which it is linked, to heal itself by a similar process of rebirth.

Bache compares this process to that suggested by Ring in *Heading Toward Omega*. Just as the individual's transformation of consciousness as a result of a radiant NDE might have an enlightening effect on the entire species, the frightening NDE, says Bache, "might have a small cleansing effect on the entire species mind." In this way the individual sufferer is in the tradition of the "suffering servant": of Jesus seen as one whose death is a sacrifice for others, of the Buddhist bodhisattva (such as Ksitigarbha, page 135) undergoing whatever experience is necessary in order to bring about the enlightenment of all sentient beings.[101]

What might be the nature of such a collective healing and transforming process? Bache projects from the crucial factor in individual transformation, ego death. When a person gives way to the seemingly

John Woolman

merciless attacks of the forces of rebirth, she is released from the prison of isolation, and restored, says Bache, to "the larger flow of life itself."[102] Must the group mind also undergo something like ego death? This may well be the case, considering the many levels of group mind—levels apparently reflected in perinatal LSD experiences, in which one may feel oneself to be all animals being slaughtered, all victims of the Spanish Inquisition, all mothers and children dying during birth, and the like,[103] or all human beings, even all living creatures. At every level, a group mind may be partially blocked and closed off by past pain, needing to be broken open by re-experiencing and releasing this pain in order to be restored to "the larger flow of life itself." In *Dark Night, Early Dawn* Bache explores the possibility that the looming ecological crisis, with the enormous suffering that it will bring, may function as an NDE of humanity, awakening supposedly isolated human minds to little-known functions and powers in the collective unconscious.[104]

The Western Mystical Path

The third narrative framework, offered by Evelyn Underhill, I have called the Western Mystical Path.

A mystical experience is one that is interpreted, by the experiencer, as direct union or communion with the Ultimate or with all things. Scholars have discussed at great length whether accounts of mystics from different religious tradition describe essentially the same experience or are thoroughly culture-bound. There is no doubt that understanding mysticism is important to the study of NDEs, but I will not discuss the issue of whether these experiences of union or communion really are what they seem. My focus is NDEs; my intent is to explore a metanarrative into which they can fit. For this, it is enough here and now to point out that there are strong similarities between certain typical mystical experiences and typical radiant NDEs, as well as between painful experiences mystics tend to undergo and painful NDEs. Evelyn Underhill in her 1911 book *Mysticism* puts the mystic's painful and radiant experiences into the framework of a journey ending in joyful union with the Divine. Another form of the death-and-rebirth narrative, this framework can help to make hopeful sense of painful NDEs.

Underhill's work in *Mysticism* shares the limitations of her times. Around the turn of the twentieth century, scholarship on Taoist, Hindu, and Buddhist mysticism was not widely available, and her rare comments on them are uninformed. Most of the mystics Underhill studies are Christian, a few are Muslim; Jewish mysticism Underhill virtually ignores. She leaves no doubt about her conviction that Christian mysticism is superior to all other. Robert Ellwood claims that her five-stage model applies to much of Eastern mysticism as well,[105] but lacking space to deal with this issue I will present it as a helpful paradigm of Western mystical life that may cast light on afterdeath states.

Underhill's model is an expansion of the major one in Western Christian mystical tradition (which also influenced Jewish mysticism), the three-stage ladder originating with the Hellenistic mystic Plotinus: Purgation, Illumination, and Union.[106, 107] To this model Underhill adds, at the beginning, Awakening, and between Illumination and Union, the Dark Night of the Soul. This development is particularly helpful for us, for it is in her two additional stages that the resemblances between NDEs and mystical experiences are especially evident.

Underhill makes it clear that the five-stage pattern is an approximation. Some mystics do not go beyond Illumination; some undergo certain stages in reverse order, or skip a stage, or move rapidly back and forth between two stages Underhill compares her oversimplified map to the somewhat artificial division of human life into infancy, adolescence, maturity, and old age; for what it is worth, she says, it can give insight.[108]

1. Awakening

In the first stage, Awakening, the future mystic gradually, or more often suddenly, becomes aware of a marvelous splendor in the world, perhaps a loving divine presence. The splendor is in many cases literal. For example, the fourteenth-century monk Henry Suso, as a teenager, saw it as he sat alone in the chapel of his monastery. Writing in the third person, he reports " [T]he Friar could do naught but contemplate this Shining Brightness; and he altogether forgot himself and all other things." Some have perceived the splendor in nature: "It was like entering into another world....Natural objects were glorified....I saw beauty in every material object in the universe. The woods were vocal with heavenly music."[109] Others, without use of sight or hearing, experienced Awakening in the form of an awareness of Divine Love within themselves. This was the case with the medieval

English hermit Richard Rolle, who felt this overwhelming love accompanied by a literal burning heat in his heart.[110]

2. Purgation

The Awakening experience ends, leaving the mystic feeling deeply unworthy, aware that her life, out of keeping with this sublime beauty and love, is muddled, shaped by false values and ego-centeredness—rust that blocks her soul's mirror from freely reflecting the divine light she has experienced. Therefore, she sets out on a program of Purgation. This process has two aspects, Detachment and Mortification. Detachment means renouncing all cravings and possessiveness, for one can truly love only what one does not own; if one owns nothing, loving only God in all things, one eventually becomes a free citizen of the world. Attachments divide one's energies and complicate life, and the mystic longs to be rid of them. Yet giving up everything to which one is attached means a rigorous, painful discipline. However, the important point is not that the *things* are banished, but rather the *desire* for them. Outer poverty is helpful, but only the inner poverty confers true freedom.[111]

Detachment may take different forms, depending on the mystic's personal style. The nineteenth-century Cure d'Ars refused to let himself smell a rose, but Francis of Assisi (who had walked away from his old life in literal nakedness) had his brothers plant roses near their chapel so that visitors might be reminded of the divine sweetness.[112] Teresa of Avila gave up her stimulating conversations with friends from the town to focus her energies wholly on God. Though quite innocent, these talks led to thoughts that distracted her at prayer, so that she could enjoy neither.[113]

The other aspect of Purgation is Mortification. Detachment clears the ground; Mortification, as Underhill describes it, seeks to destroy the "lower centre of consciousness" to make way for the "higher centre."[114] In short, the mystic seeks to dismantle the ego. He may do this by setting terrible tasks for himself, like the originally very fastidious Margery Kempe and Francis of Assisi, who served and kissed lepers. Such compassionate actions, self-denying and loving at once, could be seen as a necessary sharing in the birth pangs of the world.[115] (Not all mortifications were this socially valuable, and many were motivated significantly by a conviction that the human body is vile and sinful.)[116] Among Christian mystics it is understood to be a matter of following Christ in the Way of the Cross.[117] Suggestively, one mystic compares the deliberately accepted pain of mortification to the "heroic plunge into Purgatory" by the deceased.[118]

Like artists, mystics tend to be intense, unstable people, given to extremes, says Underhill. Late in this stage, the privation of mortification may alternate with periods of the joy of Illumination, as "[i]ncreasing control of the lower centres, of the surface intelligence and its scattered desires, permits the emergence of the transcendental perceptions."[119] Medieval Christian mystics call this the "Game of Love" that God plays with the passionate soul, a form of hide and seek. It might be called a rollercoaster of pain and joy.

3. Illumination

The Game comes to an end when the conflicting, struggling levels of consciousness come to their first unity, the state of Illumination,[120] when the mystic enjoys deep fellowship with the "great life of the All." The transcendent self or divine spark, until now largely hidden in the unconscious, expands into the conscious field. The mystic enjoys an intimate relationship, but not yet union; he remains aware of himself as an individual "I," aware of the Absolute as the object of his love. A favorite image for this relationship is betrothal.[121]

There are three main styles of experience in this stage. The first, introvertive type is a sharp and joyful awareness of the Divine presence even in the midst of daily life. It may cause the beginner to become so absorbed in this inner communion that he fumbles in his tasks; more mature mystics, however, learn to integrate the elevated consciousness with the mundane task, so that they become more efficient.[122]

The second, extravertive kind of experience is a heightened sensitivity to the physical world. As the senses and appetites cease to dominate consciousness, the doors of perception are cleansed and a divine splendor is continually perceived in all things, especially in nature.[123] (Compare the second kind of Awakening above.) Thus George Fox, after he had passed through the "flaming sword" of purgation, found that the world about him was the Paradise of God, with all things giving forth an unutterable new fragrance. He understood the inner healing powers of herbs and other creatures; he felt that all things were opened to him, so that he could know "the hidden unity in the Eternal Being."[124] As this quotation implies, inward-looking and outward-looking spirituality often coexist in a self that, as

Underhill describes it, "turns and sees all about it a transfigured universe, radiant with that same Light Divine which nests in its own heart...."[125]

The third kind of experience in Illumination involves psychic manifestations: trances, visions, voices, perhaps automatic writing. Interpreting these phenomena, Underhill avoids the rationalist view that they are pathological, and, at the other extreme, the view of "materialistic piety" that takes them as literal messages from God. She holds rather that they are symbols, shaped by the visionary's mind out of its own raw materials. Although some of them come purely from the visionary's imagination and contribute nothing to her life; others stem from "real transcendental activity," bringing wisdom, peace, and guidance. Underhill's view is similar to the persona theory presented in Part III: the life-giving phenomena are co-created by the visionary and higher powers.[126]

In this position, Underhill is supported by the critical outlook of many visionary mystics themselves: they often voice suspicions that their spectacular phenomena are illusory or ensnaring. In effect, they are acknowledging that, despite their conviction of direct communication with the Ultimate, there is also a middle level. The heart of the message may come from God, but not every voice or vision is exactly what it seems. Visions are also likely to pose a temptation to egotism, and thus one is not to seek them.

Underhill's test to distinguish which experiences are merely the result of imagination and which come from transcendent powers is whether or not they promote life. In their highest forms, visions and voices are systematic and goal-directed; they guide the soul through the process of transformation. They are manifestations of a secret, permanent, and higher personality—in other words, the transcendent self.

However, Underhill acknowledges that even the great mystics sometimes have seemingly pathological visions that are not life-enhancing, such as the freckled red fiend seen by Julian of Norwich. Underhill attributes such visions to a reappearance of "forgotten superstitions" made possible by "exhaustion and temporary loss of balance...which allowed [the mystics'] intense consciousness of the reality of evil to assume a concrete form."[127] Eventually, however, even the fiends may serve to promote life, as we shall see.

4. The Dark Night of the Soul

The Dark Night of the Soul is, of course, particularly relevant to painful NDEs, and requires longer treatment.

In this stage, everything goes wrong in the mystic's life, both within and without. Physical illness attacks; friends and companions may turn against the mystic, as happened for example with Brother Henry Suso (the one who saw the divine light in his chapel). Timid and reclusive, Suso was forced by circumstances to leave his cell for a rough world; he was unjustly accused of having fathered a child, and suffered agonies of humiliation.[128]

Worse yet, the awareness of the Divine Presence, so long the center of the mystic's life, disappears, and he feels abandoned forever. Not only the Beloved, but even the soul's own Divine Spark seems to be gone, leaving a terrible thirst for that which has been lost. This extreme desolation is expressed in images of the desert or wilderness, of the fire of hell, of the abyss, the darkness, the tomb, of being suspended in unreachable aloneness between heaven and earth.[129] "The great wastes to be found in this divine ground...have neither image or form...a fathomless Abyss...."[130] "It is intensely cold here; it is intensely dark; and yet you will find nothing but flames and light."[131]

The concepts of desert, void, and fire are particularly important and need closer attention. The term "the Dark Night of the Soul" comes, of course, from the writings of John of the Cross, who describes this state in poetry and analyzes it extensively as comprised of several substages. Among them are the Active Night of the Spirit, in which one gives up rewarding devotional practices, all concepts or inner images of God, even refusing visions of Christ and of the light, and regards them as appropriate only for beginners. In the Active Night of Memory and Will, the mystic courts amnesia, willing to forget all knowledge of all things gained through the senses. In the Passive Night of the Senses, the mystic finds herself in the state of emptiness referred to as "dryness" and "desert," when nothing interests or comforts her. This boredom strikes at the heart of her long-cherished identity as a lover of God. The "Passive Night of the Spirit" is the hardest of all: there is, writes John, "a certain inflowing of God into the soul," but it is perceived as torment. "The soul begins to burn in the darkness," experiencing both God's love and her own frustrated love at the same time as the fire of hell. The intensity of desire for God is such that the mystic may disregard social rules, and do strange and extravagant acts.[132] John of the

Cross expresses this state in his poem "Dark Night" by the risky illicit affair of the narrator. Sometimes the mystic feels the fire as a literal burning pain, as did Teresa of Avila who experienced being both "burned and dismembered" in a hellish dark enclosure.[133]

It is worthwhile looking a little more deeply than Underhill does into the imagery of fire, since it is so important in certain painful NDEs. In the writings of Jacob Boehme, fire not only expresses the mystic's suffering but is at the heart of all reality; it represents the basic energy of all life and all creation.[134] In the Godhead, the true divine nature, fire is united with the light that symbolizes total consciousness and blissful peace. But somehow there is a separation even in the Godhead; fire is first of all the impassioned longing of the Godhead as formless Nothing for itself as Something. In creation and especially in the Fall, the fire and the light also become separated.* Both exist in every human being, the fire expressing itself as intense desires for physical things, for prestige, power, and other vanities, often leading to violence. The person who follows this route eventually experiences the fire within as divine wrath.

However, the inner light remains hidden in the soul until Sophia, the divine light and the face of God, comes to the soul, kisses him, and offers to be reunited with him in blissful love. After this betrothal, she withdraws, leaving the mystic to live by faith. Now he must learn to detach himself from desire for all physical things, as the fire of his longing increasingly focuses on Sophia, the light, who will be his bride after this life.[135]

Although Boehme does not speak of the fire as found in a fourth stage in the soul's journey, his discussion of the soul's painful separation from his betrothed is evidently very close to what John of the Cross says about the Passive Night of the Spirit. Boehme's overall discussion goes further than John's, however, in showing the mystic's movement between joy and frustrated longing to be an individual expression of cosmic process.

To return to Underhill's analysis of the Dark Night: On the level of intellect and will, the mystic finds herself off-center during the Night, in a state of stagnation similar to the boredom and dryness of the feelings. The powerful self-discipline gained during Purgation vanishes into confusion and inability to focus on God, or even on reading a book. Old temptations

---

*Compare Aurobindo's concept of the semi-conscious Being-Awareness-Bliss existing as hunger at the Vital stage of evolution.

of the senses return; evil thoughts obsess her, perhaps taking the form of tormenting demonic visions or voices. Catherine of Sienna, for example, endured a crowd of demonic figures making obscene gestures and suggestions; they followed her even into church.[136] George Fox experienced long trances in which he was surrounded and attacked by violent beings he called "men-eaters."[137] One might add the twentieth-century mystic Padre Pio, who suffered violent attacks that left physical wounds, with poltergeist phenomena others could hear.[138] When such states are greatly prolonged, the mystic is terribly tempted to despair.[139]

The Dark Night, which to the mystic seems everlasting while it is going on, in fact has an end. Looking back on it, mature mystics see it as a purgation that goes deeper than Stage Two, as a necessary total abolishing of ego. When the mystic completely accepts the hellish pain of the Dark Night, he surrenders his dependence on spiritual joys, and the last shreds of the right to his own life are burned away. He now sees that the Spark of the Soul has not gone out but, unrecognized by him, has taken over his entire being. Similarly, he now understands that the darkness is an unrecognized form of the Divine Light, which he perceived as darkness because his eyes were still too weak to bear it.[140] The darkness of the Night might be compared to a photographic negative, whose bizarre reversal of values is necessary to the formation of the true picture.[141]

5. The Unitive State

Slowly or abruptly, the mystic emerges from the Dark Night no longer as an individual self enjoying fellowship with the Divine, but transformed into Divine Humanity, unified within itself, and in seamless Union with the life of God.[142] Mystics describe their new life in two kinds of language, impersonal and personal. Impersonal language speaks of "deification," of the self being submerged in God as the sponge by the sea, the coal by the fire. Shining in the divine light, sinking in the divine abyss, it is one with the larger reality: not only still itself but more really itself than before.[143] Personal language speaks of love, the favorite image being the spiritual marriage in which God and the soul are wholly given to one another and dwell within one another's hearts.[144]

The effects of Union are far-reaching, says Underhill. In accordance with their reborn state, unitive mystics are marked by a childlike lightheartedness. They have great vitality, endurance, and creativity. Far

Dali Lama

from remaining mostly withdrawn in contemplation, they go out into in the world to break new ground: as administrators, as founders of churches, as social reformers. The marriage with God also leads to spiritual parenthood, in that the mystics attract likeminded persons who come to share the vision and the work.[145]

According to Underhill, some of the characteristics of the Dark Night persist in the Unitive State, supporting (if not clearly explaining) mystics' view that the darkness and the light are somehow the same reality. The ego that died so painful a death remains dead; the mystic's lost identity, as a religious person in a particular religious slot, is not regained. The transcendent self that now carries the day has a continuity with the deceased ego: it is not, yet is, the same person. Significantly, the imagery of fire and void is still used, although now it has connotations of joyous love rather than anguished isolation.

Undoubtedly, Underhill's picture of transformed humanity is essentially accurate, closely resembling Aurobindo's account of the Life Divine. I feel reluctant to introduce a dissonant note, but there is evidence that even great saints in fact fall short of being completely unstained mirrors of divine light. For example, Bernard of Clairvaux and Catherine of Siena, inspired singers of divine-human love, preached crusades;[146] my own spiritual forebear George Fox, impassioned preacher of universal equality in the divine light, declined to condemn slavery in Barbados.[147] If these transformed persons were acting upon guidance from their transcendent selves at these points, the guidance was clearly wrong. We cannot always know whether some individual egoism is still there, or whether it is ethnic egoism, moral failure to transcend distorted cultural values. Although empowered by the Infinite, mystics remain limited human beings. To my mind, therefore, the distinction between Illumination and the Unitive State is better seen as a matter of degree. What is crucial is the ongoing transmutation of spiritual death into transformed life.

Interface of the Western Mystical Path with NDEs

Since the five-stage path is not absolute, one cannot expect to find an exact correspondence with the lives of NDErs. However, there are undoubtedly many similar themes, including painful elements, as Judith Cressy[148] and Christopher Bache have shown.[149] The resemblances are enough to show that we are in the same country, and that we may expect or at least hope that the proposed narrative shape of the one will probably fit the other, at least in part.

There is little question that some mystical awakenings resemble typical radiant NDEs: one finds feelings of the Divine presence, visions of light, auditions of angelic music, and perceptions of luminous beauty (in nature in the case of the mystic, of an Edenic otherworld in the case of NDErs). The effects often found in both kinds of experiences are also similar: the experiencer re-evaluates his past life, rejecting patterns of egocentricity and possessiveness regarding persons and things. While it would not be accurate to say that returned NDErs usually embark on active purgative programs of detachment and mortification of the ego, a spontaneous tendency to detachment on their part has been noted, especially as part of a reorientation away from materialistic gain and competitiveness, and toward generosity, compassion, and service.[150]

I do not find a distinct period corresponding to Illumination among returned NDErs, though some of its characteristics are prevalent simultaneously with those comparable to Purgation. The sense of fellowship with the Divine that is central for Underhill's Christian mystics has the same priority among many NDErs—for example George Ritchie, who tells that in his daily time of prayer he again feels the loving presence of the Christ.[151] It may also take the form of a sense of impersonal oneness.[152] P. M. H. Atwater, who has interviewed thousands of NDErs, has no doubt that it is widespread: "Most survivors fall head over heels in love with God."[153] Thus, although there are definitely manifestations of Illumination, it is not easy to connect them to a distinctly bounded period.

A sense of communion with the rest of the physical world, akin to George Fox's "hidden unity in the Eternal Being," is also unmistakable among NDErs.[154] Even more conspicuous is the appearance of psychic phenomena like that of the mystics. Beginning with Moody's original book, numerous works on NDErs refer to psychic events: telepathy, clairvoyance, precognition, apparitions, healings, kundalini phenomena. Although messages from God for others are not as frequently reported by NDErs as by mystics, both frequently experience guidance from the transcendent self or guardian.

Many survivors of radiant NDEs go though painful experiences like the Dark Night, especially feeling misunderstood or rejected by friends and family, a stranger in a strange land burning with desire to return to the divine presence felt during their NDEs. I have heard no reports of a sense of permanent abandonment by the Divine, though cases may exist among isolated experiencers, particularly children.   *why?*

The closest similarities to the Dark Night are of course found in painful NDEs, especially the meaningless-void and hellish types, which correspond to three elements of the mystics' Dark Night: images of the desert, abyss, or void; images of fire; and persecution by demonic beings. For NDErs, outer space as the Void seems to be the equivalent of the mystics' Desert. As described by by Nancy Evans Bush (page 73), Peggy Holladay (page 75), and the NDEr in childbirth after she reached the shadow of the bridge (page 76), the suspension in the darkness of space was agony, total loneliness, with an intense pitch of desire for the meaningful world that has been lost.

That this painful void is potentially a void of blissful fulfillment for NDErs as well as mystics is suggested by the "inverted" experiences, particularly those that change from terror to peace, and especially by the "shining darkness" NDEs in which the experiencers found themselves suspended in a wonderful darkness that to them meant union with the all. (Others have spoken of it as wonderful and perfect without mentioning union with all things.)

We have seen that some NDErs, like mystics in the Dark Night, find themselves in fiery hells. Unlike the mystics, seldom do NDErs of the present or medieval times describe being actually burned in the fire;* in most cases they witness it from close at hand, sometimes uncomfortably feeling the heat. NDErs do not have the mystics' sense of the fire as agonizing desire for God; but then, conscious desire for God cannot fairly be expected from ordinary, this-worldly people suddenly plunged into a fiery otherworldly scene.

Complicating matters is the fact that some NDErs experience the fire as cold,[156] which suggests isolation from the source of life, but not passionate desire or purgation. We should be cautious, therefore, in supposing that all hellfire visions symbolize the cosmic fire as Boehme conceives it. However, at least some hellfire NDErs do have the *tremendum et fascinans* ambivalence that would support such an interpretation. One is Kenneth Hagin who found the orb of fire in hell magnetically attractive despite his fear (page 86); another is the electroshock patient (page 88).

---

*Rawlings cites one case in which an NDEr reported a dry, dehydrating, very painful heat, in the midst of a darkness that felt like heavy pressure.[155]

There is unmistakable resemblance between the demonic entities who "welcome" some NDErs and the demons who torment mystics. The sexually perverted or violent entities who tormented Catherine of Siena, George Fox, and Padre Pio have much in common with those in the painful NDEs and NCDEs of George Ritchie (page 80), Patricia (page 78), Cathy Baker (page 67), Howard Storm (page 80) and Gary Wells (page 79). It is possible that the reason the NDErs were rescued from without whereas the mystics were left to endure is, again, that the NDErs were beginners in their Awakening and, unlike the mystics, were not ready to follow the Dark Night fully into the Unitive State.

We have seen that the Unitive State is not an absolute matter. Likewise, though I see impressive signs of transformation in certain survivors of painful NDEs, I am not in a position to show that any have reached this ultimate condition. I intend only to show that, because the Dark Night does often lead to transformation in the lives of mystics and NDErs, there is reason to believe that any painful experiences of void, fire, or demonic entities after real death will likely also transmute into a state of joy and spiritual power.

The Mystical Path as first developed by Plotinus, and as adapted by many Christian Neoplatonists, especially Johannes Eckhart, has a U-shaped form: the soul has a virtual existence in union with the Divine, moves downward and outward into separate existence and exile, finally returning to union.[157] But Eckhart, though he influenced many, was condemned as a heretic, and the general tenor of Christian thought (as with Judaism and Islam) has been to emphasize that the human soul has no eternal existence but rather is created by God in God's image. This distinction is a relative one for some Christian Neoplatonists, but for mainstream Christians the Path might better be represented not by a U-figure but a J-figure. But the difference is not crucial to my purposes of showing that the Western Mystical Path supports the expectation that painful afterdeath experiences will transmute into love and light.

I suggest that the Western Mystical Path is another form of the metanarrative, the dramatic movement from joy to sorrow to joy that I have traced in the hero adventure and the four perinatal matrices of psychedelic therapy. All three of these patterns are generalizations based on many individual stories and accounts of experience. In all three we are partly dependent on the insightfulness of the scholars who formulated the scenarios, which undoubtedly oversimplify and to some extent distort the variety and complexity of their sources.

The Question of the Genuineness and Meaning of the Metanarrative

We must also address the question of how independent of each other the three scenarios are. Certainly many mutually similar experiences and fictional stories are independent of each other, with unsophisticated NDErs and LSD takers describing Void or light experiences that are, unknown to them, very close to elements of the mystical tradition. But the three narrative structures that interpret the experiences and tales by anchoring them in cosmic process are not independent. Grof is familiar with Underhill's work and with NDE studies, and Campbell and Frye, as we have seen, were both influenced by Jung, himself an NDEr (though sometimes unsympathetic to mysticism). If the three scenarios do convince, it must be because they are each convincing in their own right, cumulative perhaps but not providing out-of-the-blue confirmation for one another.

Furthermore, even if we grant that the three kinds of journeys do point to a single reality, this is not to establish that the true explanation is in fact the U-shaped journey of the human soul (or, in Aurobindo's philosophy, of all finite things) from union to separation and pain back to union, either in the body, or at death, or much later. The metanarrative may be interpreted purely psychologically, as an image for the individual's potential and unfolding; it may be seen reductionistically as a projection of universal human wishes and fears.

I suggest that a strong reason for taking the metanarrative seriously as a possible or likely account of the soul's journey is the cumulative weight of the evidence for survival of death. While the evidence does not prove survival, or give us a map of the afterworld, it cannot be responsibly dismissed; and for some cases it is the most plausible explanation.

Survival means that consciousness transcends the body to some extent. What survives is not necessarily the Higher Self or the Divine Spark; neither heaven nor hell necessarily follows. But once it is granted that the soul very likely does transcend the body, reductionistic interpretations of the metanarrative are no longer compelling; the message of union with the Divine in radiant NDEs must command, at least, equal respect. Spiritual death followed by renewal is a much-used image for the crisis in the basic scenario. If survival is a reality, it seems quite possible, even likely, that what is true metaphorically is also true literally. Imaginative or experiential stories of otherworldly visits to paradisal or hellish realms may well be representations of something real to be known after death.

And the metanarrative is hopeful—it gives due weight to hellish experiences while giving the first and final word to joy. We are not compelled to believe that this is the key to painful NDEs—we may choose to believe something else—but we have the right to believe that, in the deepest sense, this story is true.

Conclusion ⁀

I F THERE IS ONE THING THAT IS SELF-EVIDENT ABOUT NEAR-
Death Experiences, it is that the explanation for them is not self-
evident. The initial challenge presented by NDEs was to confirm,
explore and explain the widespread "Moody-type" pattern—particularly
OBE, peace, tunnel, meeting others, life overview, light, other worlds,
return. Paranormal happenings such as Peak-in-Darien welcomers showed
that reductionistic explanations were inadequate, and reinforced the
apparent message: this is what death is like to the dying.

We saw that within and alongside this pattern there is considerable
variety, including significant cultural differences, so that we cannot speak of
"the NDE." But there are also common motifs found cross-culturally that
are almost surely not due to the ordinary spread of ideas. The common
themes cannot be dismissed, but neither can the cultural inconsistencies.
The theory of morphic resonance from earlier mental fields could explain
the cross-cultural motifs without requiring survival (though it is
compatible with survival), but it does not explain why the pattern should
appear in so many situations near death. The pattern remains a challenge;
it strongly suggests survival without compelling one to believe it.

Another challenge comes from the powerful life-transforming
aftereffects (including psychic gifts) experienced by NDErs, even by many
who have had painful experiences. These aftereffects make it especially
difficult to explain NDEs away as physiological changes or psychological
fantasies to cope with the prospect of death, especially if the picture of the
afterlife they give is sometimes so painful. Whether the NDEr is undergoing
the death process or not, he or she is tapping into some extraordinary
source of inner power, as Zaleski says.

That this source of empowerment is within does not mean that NDEs cannot give us evidence for survival. In Chapter Ten we saw that the survival hypothesis is impressively supported by evidence of various kinds, to which Peak-in-Darien NDEs, NDEs in the blind, and veridical OBEs may be added. Survival becomes a metatheory that makes good sense of several categories of material; it becomes probable. This gives us permission, so to speak, provisionally to accept the obvious: that the "classic" NDE scenario, or something similar, is what really happens after death.

But how are individual and cultural differences and inconsistencies to be explained? A good candidate explanation is the processes of unconscious co-creation—among individuals and cultures, among the living and the deceased—leading to variations on the death-journey themes that recur over centuries. What (and whose) intentions such products of cooperation might serve are left open. An uncomfortable alternative is the possibility of an essentially chaotic situation in which some dying persons may, for superficial reasons, miss the well-traveled route and enter upon little-traveled byways—some of which go downward into darkness, hellish suffering, or chaos—paths with no necessary connection to the travelers' personality and character. This latter interpretation could not finally be squared with the message of many radiant NDEs that all things work together for good. Some ancient cultures such as Sumeria were apparently willing to accept such ultimate moral and spiritual breakdown, but, perhaps as a result of the influence of the Great Religions (which sought to build an all-encompassing view of reality), present-day minds seek to find a coherent explanation. We search for meaning, I believe rightly so.

I have sketched two types of explanatory frameworks that have been offered by various thinkers. The multi-world view of fundamentalist-Calvinist-Augustinian Christianity comes close to the moral nihilism of Sumeria on this issue: whatever one's character—whether one strives to be a good person doing good deeds or is exploitative and violent—if one has not submitted to the authority of the fundamentalist God, one can expect endless misery after death. There is a sense in which Rawlings' fundamentalist view is harshly honest, giving full place to the implications of the most disturbing painful NDEs—that cruelty and injustice appear to claim their victims in the afterworld as they do on earth. We can admit also that Rawlings shows both courage and compassion in presenting his unwelcome message. But when he and other fundamentalists insist that this situation of (everlasting) damnation serves the intentions of a good and just God, they are no longer being coherent. The incoherence is compounded when they then claim that radiant NDEs with their good news of unconditional love are demonic deceptions, in spite of their usually good aftereffects.

There are other, more serious objections to this position. The Father of Wrath who punishes brief temporal sins in everlasting hell (sins being both wrongs against others and the victimless crime of failing to submit to him) and the Compassionate Father who provides a way of escape to heaven provide an implicit model for human beings, especially males.[1] Although fundamentalists urge males as well as females to submit to this masculine God, sociologically this model encourages human beings to imitate his ways. This means that authority, power, and control are reinforced as the appropriate ways for males to relate to presumably lesser beings (women, children, animals, the earth).[2] Compassion is valued, but it is one option within a power-over approach. From a feminist, egalitarian viewpoint (supported by sociological evidence), this authoritarian outlook is unhealthy; it fosters interpersonal violence[3] and ecological disaster.[4] Furthermore, a view that places great stress on conflict between God and demonic forces also encourages the assumption that warfare is an underlying reality in every earthly situation. This outlook tends to support militarism and imperialism.[5]

The conviction that a person can be saved from the threat of divine wrath and the forces of hell only by submission to the God of the Bible as interpreted by Christian fundamentalists leads to a fearful and rigid outlook. Not only the message of radiant NDEs but all non-fundamentalist religious and spiritual claims, and even much that seems neutral in education, psychology, and popular culture, become masks for demonic deceit and subversion. As with the fundamentalist claim that the experience of the light in radiant NDEs is a demonic deceit, very little evidence is presented to support the sweeping accusations that Rawlings and others make.[6] It does not take profound psychological analysis to see that this position encourages alienation and suspicion at almost every turn. For these reasons, both logical and pragmatic, the fundamentalist multi-world position will not do.

We are left with the three classes of one-world frameworks, the gradualistic, projectionist, and initiatory, all of which have much to recommend them. We have seen that a certain amount of overlap between them is possible; for example, the Theosophical gradualistic position includes initiations along the way, and Ring's projectionist position includes both gradualistic and initiatory elements.

But when the three views are taken at the deepest level, they have incompatible elements. When the projectionist theory goes beyond explaining particular elements of individual NDEs and is applied to the whole public world, as in the worldviews of Kenneth Ring and the *Bardo Thodol,* the assumptions of the other positions (as well as much that we assume in daily life) are undercut. The crux of the difficulty is in the issue of whether time, and thus the many things that come into existence and pass out again, are real. In the full projectionist position only the Ultimate, the Light, is really real; to find salvation from suffering and evil is to penetrate the illusion of separateness, and to realize for oneself that the Oneness (or the Light/Void) is all there is. Narratives of any sort may be useful in bringing about this realization, including the gradualistic story of the eons-long U-shaped journey of the pilgrim soul, or the LSD adventurer's birth-passage from the anguish of Matrices II and III to the cosmic joy of Matrix IV. But they do not themselves describe a real process or real entities.

Since even the experiencer is not real, the positive cosmic energy embracing all beings that is felt in radiant NDEs is better seen as compassion than love, for love affirms the real selfhood of the beloved, whereas compassion can coexist with a will that the other's illusion of selfhood be done away. The problem posed by the psychological and quasi-physical suffering in painful NDEs is dissolved (as are other forms of evil and suffering) by the projectionist position. (The problem of why there should be illusions of separate selfhood remains, however.) Thus to the NDEr enduring tormenting beings or chaos or cosmic loneliness, and to the story's anxious listener, the projectionist response is: When you see with clear consciousness, there is nothing to fear; the situation isn't real; you are already "home."

For some whose approaches are essentially gradualist or initiatory, however, the NDEr, the journey and some or all of the beings encountered along the way are real. The Ultimate may be understood as the Creator, or perhaps as the Source from which they flow out and to which they return, or as that of which nothing concrete can be said. Such realist approaches do not necessarily take a simplistically literal view. In some realist outlooks, much of what a person believes about herself in ordinary life may be illusory; the vision of Christ or a demonic being in an NDE may be co-projected by the visionary and others. But, essentially, conscious beings are more than projections; they have an existence in their own right. They may be aware of their Creator/Source, or may be ignorant or partially asleep. Their decisions make a difference; they can become evil, can do harm to others and themselves. They can suffer terribly; they can help and heal. But there is a cosmic pattern to which they belong, a J-shaped or U-shaped story with a happy ending. From these perspectives the response to evil and to the prospect of cosmic pain is: With your eyes on the prize, control your fear, choose to love; you will be "home" in the morning.

Logically, one has to choose between the non-realist and realist approaches. Some NDErs, on the basis of their experience, take a paradoxical position balancing projectionist and realist positions. This is very interesting, and apparently is pragmatically very workable, but to support it philosophically would take more space than we have here.

I do not claim that any one or any combination of the three one-world frameworks is a fully satisfactory response to painful NDEs. These three alternatives, especially the initiatory, depend heavily upon metaphors and symbols, whose meanings cannot be clearly explained to the rigorous intellect. None of these approaches is presented as the final word on the meaning of painful Near-Death Experiences, but rather as sources for hopeful exploration.

Notes ⤳

JNDS: *Journal of Near-Death Studies* (at one time called *Anabiosis*)
PSPR: *Proceedings of the Society for Psychical Research*
JASPR: *Journal of the American Society for Psychical Research*

Introduction

1. Nancy Evans Bush, "The Near-Death Experience in Children: Shades of the Prison-House Reopening," **Anabiosis: JNDS** 3, No. 2 (Dec. 1983), 186–87.

2. Ibid., 187.

3. G. N. M. Tyrrell, *Science and Psychical Phenomena* in *Apparitions/Science and Psychical Phenomena,* two books in one volume (New York: University Books, 1961), 9.

4. Ibid., 25.

5. Rhea White, "An Experience-Centered Approach to Parapsychology," *Exceptional Human Experience: Background Papers* 2, No. 2 (Dec. 1993), 18–20.

6. David Griffin, *Parapsychology, Philosophy, and Spirituality* (Albany: SUNY Press, 1997), 29–33.

7. William James, *William James on Psychical Research,* ed. Gardner Murphy, and Robert Ballou (New York: Viking Press, 1960), 31; cf. William James, "The Will to Believe," in *To Believe or Not to Believe: Readings in the Philosophy of Religion,* ed. E. D. Klemke (Fort Worth: Harcourt Brace Jovanovich, 1992), 501, 504–05.

8. Susan Blackmore, *Dying to Live* (Buffalo: Prometheus Books, 1993), 115–16.

9. Tyrrell, *Apparitions,* 22.

10. Walter Franklin Prince, *Noted Witnesses for Psychic Occurrences* (New Hyde Park, NY: University Books, 1963), 130.

11. Charles A. Garfield, "The Dying Person's Concern with Life After Death," in Craig R. Lundahl, ed., *A Collection of Near-Death Research Readings* (Chicago: Nelson-Hall, 1982), 161; Ian Stevenson, *Twenty Cases Suggestive of Reincarnation* (Charlottesville: University Press of Virginia, 1974), *passim.*

One: Moody's Work: "The NDE"

1. Raymond Moody, *Life After Life* (Atlanta: Mockingbird Books, 1975), 19.

2. Ibid., 26–43. This arrangement of Moody's fifteen elements into early, middle, late, and aftermath is for convenience of presentation; it is not part of his original analysis.

3. Ibid., 43–54.

4. F. Gordon Greene and Stanley Krippner, "Panoramic Vision: Hallucination or Bridge to the Beyond?" in Gary Doore, *What Survives? Contemporary Explorations of Life After Death* (Los Angeles: Jeremy Tarcher, 1990), 64.

5. Moody, *Life After Life,* 54–62.

6. Ibid., 25–26, 62–76.

7. Ibid., 79–125.

8. Raymond Moody, *Reflections on Life After Life* (New York: Bantam Books, 1978), 10–11.

9. George G. Ritchie, *My Life After Dying* (Norfolk: Hampton Roads, 1991), 22–23; George G. Ritchie with Elizabeth Sherrill, *Return From Tomorrow* (Old Tappan, NJ: Fleming H. Revell, 1978), 57. *Return From Tomorrow* contains many details not found in *My Life After Dying,* some of them inconsistent with the text of the latter. They appear to be embroidery added by co-author Elizabeth Sherrill.

10. Moody, *Reflections,* 9–28.

11. Ibid., 35.

12. David Lorimer, *Whole in One* (London: Arkana, Penguin, 1990), 47–104.

13. Andrew MacKenzie, *Riddle of the Future* (New York: Taplinger Publishing Co., 1974), 81–87, 95–98.

14. Luisa Vazquez, "Death and I," Seattle IANDS Newsletter (Sept–Oct 1993), no pagination.

15. John Wren-Lewis, "The Darkness of God: An Account of Lasting Mystical Consciousness Resulting from an NDE," **Anabiosis: JNDS** 5, No. 2, 53–66.

Two: Precursors in Modern Times

1. Albert von St. Gallen Heim, "Remarks on Fatal Falls," trans. Roy Kletti, in Russell Noyes, Jr., and Roy Kletti, "The Experience of Dying From Falls," **Omega** 3 (1972), 50.

2. Ibid., 47.

3. Osis, Karlis, and Erlendur Haraldsson, *At the Hour of Death* (New York: Hastings House, 1986), 167–68.

4. Ibid., 168.

5. Heim, "Remarks," 51–52.

6. D. Scott Rogo, *NAD, A Study of Some Unusual Other-World Experiences* (New Hyde Park, NY: University Books, 1970), 53.

7. Ibid, 52, 64–65.

8. Ibid., 26.

9. Ibid., 63.

10. William Barrett, *Death-Bed Visions* (Wellingborough, England: The Aquarian Press, 1986), 99–101.

11. Ibid., 106–07.

12. Rogo, Vol. 2, 119–33.

13. "Psychic ether" is a term taken from philosopher H. H. Price, referring to a posited level of reality consisting of persisting, dynamic images created by the mind and capable of being perceived by certain persons. Rogo. Vol. 2, 67.

14. Rogo, *NAD*, 50–53, 147–48.

15. Frances Power Cobbe, *The Peak in Darien* (London: privately published, 1882), 297.

16. Ibid., vi.

17. Ibid., 278.

18. Ibid., 302–03.

19. Emma M. Pearson and Eliza Quinton, letters, cited in Frederic W. H. Myers, *Human Personality and Its Survival of Bodily Death*, Vol. 2 (New York: Longmans, Green, 1954), 333–34.

20. Mary Wilson, cited in J. H. Hyslop, *Psychical Research and the Resurrection* (Boston, MA: Small, Maynard & Co., 1908), 102–04. This account first appeared in **PSPR**, volume no., date and page no. not given.

21. Barrett, *Visions*, 81–84.

22. George C. Ritchie (sic), "The Pseudodeath of Private Ritchie," in David Knight, ed., *The ESP Reader* (New York: Grosset & Dunlap, 1969), 397.

23. Ibid., 397–98.

24. Ibid., 398.

25. Ibid.

26. Ibid., 400.

27. Cobbe, *Peak*, 296–97.

28. C G. Jung, *Memories, Dreams, Reflections* (New York: Pantheon, 1961), 289.

29. J. H. M. Whiteman, *The Mystical Life* (London: Faber & Faber, 1961), 12–14.

30. J. H. M. Whiteman, *New and Old Evidence on the Meaning of Life, the Mystical World-View and Inner Contest*, Vol. I (Gerrards Cross, Buckinghamshire, England: Colin Smythe Ltd., 1986), 18–19. In this book Whiteman further elucidates several of the terms employed in his 1961 *The Mystical Life*.

31. Whiteman, *Mystical Life*, 51–52.

32. Ibid., 151, 124–25.

33. Ibid., 35–36.

34. Ibid., 38.

35. Yram [Marcel Louis Forhan], *Practical Astral Projection* (New York: Samuel Weiser, Inc., 1969), 27.

36. Ibid., 33.

37. Ibid., 35–36.

38. Ibid., 220–22.

39. Mrs. Howard W. Jeffrey Sr., letter, cited in Robert Crookall, *The Study and Practice of Astral Projection* (New Hyde Park, NY: University Books, 1966), 72.

40. Heim, in Noyes and Kletti, "Experience," 50.

41. Sylvan Muldoon, *The Case for Astral Projection* (Chicago: Aries Press, 1936), 119.

42. Ibid., 283.

43. Ibid., 283–86.

44. Ibid., 24, italics Muldoon's.

45. Whiteman, *Mystical Life*, 96, 99–100, 101.

46. Jung, *Memories*, 290.

47. Charles T. Tart, *Transpersonal Psychologies* (New York: Harper & Row, 1975), 39–41.

48. Sylvan Muldoon and Hereward Carrington, *The Projection of the Astral Body* (London: Rider & Son, 1989), 76–80.

49. Ibid., 114.

50. Ibid., 101.

51. Crookall, *Study and Practice*, 94, 129.

52. Frederic W. H. Myers, *Human Personality and Its Survival of Bodily Death*, Vol. 2 (New York: Longmans, Green & Co., 1954), 315–18. Myers' account, slightly abridged, is taken from **PSPR** 8, 180ff.

53. Robert Monroe, *Journeys Out of the Body*, 170.

54. Crookall, *Study and Practice*, 176.

55. Hornell Hart, "ESP Projection: Spontaneous Cases and the Experimental Method," **JASPR** 48, No. 4, 124.

56. Celia Green, *Out-of-the-Body Experiences* (New York: Ballantine Books, 1968), xvii.

57. Ibid., 16–17.

58. Ibid., 21–22.

59. Glen O. Gabbard and Stuart W. Twemlow, *With the Eyes of the Mind: An Empirical Analysis of Out-of-Body States* (New York: Praeger, 1984), 13–21.

60. Green, *Experiences*, 112.

61. Crookall, *Study and Practice*, 162; Caroline D. Larsen, *My Travels in the Spirit World* (Rutland, VT: Tuttle Co., 1927), page no. not given, cited in Sylvan Muldoon, *The Case for Astral Projection* (Chicago, Aries Press, 1936), 93–94.

62. Whiteman, *Mystical Life*, 206.

63. Osis and Haraldsson, *At the Hour*, 51–52.

64. Ibid., 55–56.

65. Ibid., 66, 112.

66. Ibid., 88.

67. Ibid., 69, 71.

68. Ibid., 91–92.

69. Ibid., 164–84.

70. Robert Ellwood, personal communication, August 24, 1997.

71. Ibid., 163–65.

Three: Studies Confirming and Exploring The NDE

1. Moody, *Life After Life*, 10–11, 123–24.

2. Kenneth Ring, cited in Evelyn Elsaesser Valarino, *On the Other Side of Life: Exploring the Phenomenon of the Near-Death Experience* (New York: Insight Books/Plenum Press, 1997), 85–86.

3. Kenneth Ring, *Life at Death* (New York: Coward, McCann & Geoghegan, 1980), 32–34.

4. Ibid., 39.

5. Ibid., 39–66.

6. Ibid., 67–68.

7. Kenneth Ring and Stephen Franklin, "Do Suicide Survivors Report Near-Death Experiences? in Craig R. Lundahl, ed., *A Collection of Near-Death Research Readings* (Chicago: Nelson-Hall, 1982).

8. Margot Grey, *Return From Death* (London: Arkana, 1985), 30–32.

9. Ibid., 59–72.

10. Michael Sabom, *Recollections of Death: A Medical Investigation*, New York: Harper & Row, 1982, 9, 56.

11. Ibid., *passim*.

12. Bruce Greyson, "The Near-Death Experience Scale: Construction, Reliability, and Validity" *J. Nervous and Mental Disease*, 171 (1983), reprinted in Bruce Greyson, ed., *The Near-Death Experience: Problems, Prospects, Perspectives* (Springfield, IL: Charles C. Thomas, 1984) 48–51, 56–57.

13. Mellen-Thomas Benedict, "Through the Light and Beyond," Lee W. Bailey and Jenny Yates, eds., *The Near-Death Experience: A Reader* (New York: Routledge, 1996), 42.

14. Carol Zaleski, *Otherworld Journeys: Accounts of Near-Death Experience in*

Medieval and Modern Times (New York: Oxford University Press), 1987, 188–89.

15. Ring, *Life at Death*, 133–34.

16. Ibid., 134.

17. Sabom, *Recollections*, 194, 57.

18. Evans Bush, "Prison-House." **Anabiosis: JNDS**, 177–78.

19. Ibid., 179–92.

20. Gabbard and Twemlow, *Eyes*, 154–66.

21. Melvin Morse, "Parting Visions: A New Scientific Paradigm," Bailey and Yates, *The NDE*, 207–08.

22. Ibid., 309–10.

23. Joan Peter, prod., *Transcending the Limits: The Near-Death Experience*, Seattle: Video Resource Center (for Seattle IANDS), 1993. Mark and Carol Botts first recounted their story at the Pacific Northwest IANDS Regional Conference, 1991. The reference to aftereffects was part of their narrative but was not included in the videotape.

24. P. M. H. Atwater, "Second Birth: What Really Happens When Children Have an NDE," Perpetual Motion Audiotape, 1997 IANDS North American Conference.

25. Ibid.

26. P. M. H. Atwater, "Children and the Near-Death Phenomenon: Another Viewpoint," **JNDS** 15, No. 1 (Fall 1996), 7–11.

27. Ibid., 14–15.

28. Ring, *Heading Toward Omega*, 53–54.

29. Ibid., 57–58.

30. Ibid., 64–66.

31. Ibid., 71–72.

32. Benedict, "Through the Light," 44–45.

33. John Wren-Lewis, "The Darkness of God," **Anabiosis: JNDS**, 51–64.

34. M.H. Atwater, *Coming Back to Life* (New York: Dodd, Mead & Co, 1988), 32–37.

35. Ring, *Heading Toward Omega*, 99–111.

36. Ibid., 111–114.

37. Ibid., 130–31.

38. P. M. H. Atwater, "What Is Not Being Said About the Near-Death Experience," Bailey and Yates, *The NDE*, 241.

39. P. M. H. Atwater, *Coming Back to Life* (New York: Dodd, Mead, 1988), 65–73.

40. Ring, *Heading Toward Omega*, 157–162.

41. Kenneth Ring, *The Omega Project: Near-Death Experiences, UFO Encounters, and Mind at Large* (New York: Morrow, 1992), 179–82.

42. Sabom, Michael, *Light and Death: One Doctor's Fascinating Account of Near-Death Experiences* (Grand Rapids: Zondervan, 1998), 140.

43. Gibson, Arvin, *Glimpses of Eternity* (Bountiful, UT: Horizon, 1992), *passim*; Gibson, *Echoes from Eternity* (Bountiful, UT: Horizon, 1993), *passim*.

44. Ibid., 144–56, 317.

45. Ring, *Heading Toward Omega*, 139–141.

46. Atwater, *Coming Back*, 72.

47. Cherie Sutherland, *Transformed by the Light* (Sydney: Bantam Books, 1992), 207–28.

48. Ibid., 57–68.

49. Ring, *Omega Project*, 153–54.

50. Ibid., 156–64 .

51. Ibid., 164–66, 278–79.

52. Barbara Harris Whitfield, *Spiritual Awakenings* (Deerfield Beach, FL: Health Communications, Inc., 1995), 32, 85–86.

53. Yvonne Kason, *A Farther Shore* (Toronto: HarperCollins Ltd.), *passim*.

54. Ring, *Heading Toward Omega*, 166.

55. Ibid., 165–80.

56. Lee W. Bailey, "Black Elk: Seeing in a Sacred Manner," Bailey and Yates, *NDE Reader*, 85.

57. Kason, *Farther Shore*, 83.

58. Ring, *Heading Toward Omega*, 175–76.

59. Bruce Greyson, "Increase in Psychic and Psi-Related Phenomena Following Near-Death Experiences, **Theta** (issue not specified), cited in Ring, ibid., 180–81; Richard Kohr, "Near-Death Experience and Its Relationship to Psi and Various Altered States," **Theta**, 10 (1982), 50–53, cited in Ring, ibid., 181.

60. Sabom, *Recollections*, 100–04.

61. Kimberly Clark, "Clinical Interventions With Near-Death Experiencers," in Bruce

Greyson and Charles Flynn, eds., *The Near-Death Experience: Problems, Prospects, Perspectives* (Springfield, IL: Charles C. Thomas, 1984), 242–43. Kimberly "Kim" Clark Sharp prefers that her married name be used. Kimberly Clark Sharp, personal communication, August 1996. (This helps prevent confusion with another NDEr named Kim Clark.)

62. Kenneth Ring and Madelaine Lawrence, "Further Evidence for Veridical Perception During Near-Death Experiences," **JNDS** 11, No. 4 (Summer 1993), 226–27.

63. Kenneth Ring, "NDEs in the Blind: Can They Actually See?" Presentation at 1995 IANDS Annual Conference, Hartford, Conn., Aug. 5, 1995.

64. Kenneth Ring and Sharon Cooper, *ND & OBEs*, 31–47. See also (Vicki Umipeg), "Vicky [sic]: A Blind Woman's Two Near-Death Experiences," **Vital Signs** 13, No. 2 (Spring 1994), 1,3–6, 8.

65. Ibid., 66, 68.

66. Ibid., 92–104.

67. Ring, *Heading Toward Omega*, 183–92.

68. Ibid., 193–218.

69. P. M. H. Atwater, *Future Memory*, 31, 41.

70. Ibid., *passim*.

71. Ring, *Heading Toward Omega*, 242–43.

72. Yvonne Kason, *A Farther Shore*, 206–07.

73. Ring, *Heading Toward Omega*, 240–41; Kason, *A Farther Shore*, 207.

74. Wren-Lewis, "Darkness of God," 60.

75. Kason, *A Farther Shore*, 203–06; Gibson, *Echoes*, 168–69.

76. Whitfield, *Spiritual Awakenings*, 36–38.

77. Ring, *Omega Project*, 137–50.

78. Ring and Cooper, *NDEs & OBEs*, 82–83, 107–08.

79. Ibid., 128–30.

80. Ibid., 138–42.

81. Atwater, *Coming Back*, 32–37.

82. Raymond Moody with Paul Perry, *Reunions: Visionary Encounters With Departed Loved Ones* (New York: Ballantine, 1993), 65–66.

83. Ibid., 90, 146.

84. Ibid., 90–91.

85. Raymond Moody, "Family Reunions: Visionary Encounters with the Departed in a Modern-Day Psychomanteum," **JNDS** 11, No. 2 (Winter 1992), 111–12.

86. Moody with Perry, *Reunions*, 16–18.

87. Ibid., 18–22, 109, 113–14.

88. Moody, "Family Reunions," 116.

89. Cited in Alister Hardy, *The Spiritual Nature of Man* (Oxford: Clarendon Press, 1979), 59.

90. Arvin Gibson, *Fingerprints of God* (Bountiful, UT: Horizon, 1999), 128–31.

91. Grosso, *The Final Choice: Playing the Survival Game* (Walpole, NH: Stillpoint Publishing, 1985), *passim*.

92. Ibid., 13–15.

93. Ibid.

94. Ibid.

95. Ring, *Heading Toward Omega*, 255, italics in original.

96. Ibid., 258–59.

97. Ibid., 261–63.

98. Ibid., 252–53, 260.

99. Kenneth Ring, *Omega Project*, *passim*.

100. Ibid, "Religious Wars in the NDE Movement: Some Personal Reflections on Michael Sabom's Light and Death," **JNDS** 18, No. 4 (Summer 2000), 226; Michael Grosso, *The Millennium Myth*, Wheaton: Quest, 1995, *passim*.

101. Lorimer, *Whole*, 10, 20.

102. Ibid., 37–38.

103. Ibid., 83–93.

Four: A Challenge to the Peaceful NDE:

1. I owe the identity of this NDEr to Kenneth Ring, letter, April 19, 1995.

2. Moody, *Reflections*, 19–20.

3. Tom Mace, personal communication, March 1995.

4. Ritchie, *My Life*, 21–23.

5. Whiteman, *Mystical Life*, 79.

6. Ibid.

7. Monroe, *Out of the Body*, 160–63.

8. Ibid.

9. Robert Monroe, *Far Journeys* (New York: Doubleday, 1985), 239–40.

10. Moody, *Reflections*, 22.

11. Ritchie, *My Life*, 22–23.

12. Muldoon and Carrington, *Projection of the Astral*, 259–61.

13. Ibid., 261.

14. Ibid., 261–63.

15. P. M. H. Atwater, *Beyond the Light: What Isn't Being Said About Near-Death Experience* (New York: Birch Lane Press, 1994), 41–43.

16. Elaine Winner, cited in Charles Flynn, *After the Beyond: Human Transformation and the Near-Death Experience* (New York: Prentice-Hall, 1986), 82–83.

17. Reinee Pasarow, "Near-Death Experience," presentation in Los Angeles, California, January 11, 1992.

18. Elizabeth d'Espérance [Elizabeth Hope], *Shadow Land or Light From the Other Side* (London: George Redway, 1897), 351–67.

19. Ibid., cited in Crookall, *Study and Practice*, 39–41.

20. Atwater, *Coming Back*, 14–15.

21. Angie Fenimore, *Beyond the Darkness: My Near-Death Journey to the Edge of Hell and Back* (New York: Bantam, 1995), 94–103, 129–30.

22. Monroe, *Out of the Body*, 120.

23. Ibid., 121.

24. Robert Monroe, *Ultimate Journey* (New York: Doubleday, 1994), 126–27.

25. Robert Monroe, *Far Journeys* (New York: Doubleday, 1985), 239–40.

26. Gordon Lindsay, ed., *Scenes Beyond the Grave: Visions of Marietta Davis* (Dallas: Voice of Healing Publications, n.d.), 61–66.

27. Vazquez, "Death and I," no pagination.

28. Cathy Baker, "A Glimpse," Seattle IANDS Newsletter (July–Aug. 1995), no pagination.

29. Ring, *Life at Death*, 249–50.

30. Grey, *Return From Death* (New York: Routledge & Kegan Paul, 1986), 63.

31. Ibid., 192.

32. Grey, *Return*, 192–93.

33. Ibid.

34. Fox, *Astral Projection*, 92–93.

35. Ibid., 29–30.

36. Whiteman, *Mystical Life*, 193.

37. Maurice Rawlings, *Beyond Death's Door* (New York: Bantam, 1978), 89–90.

38. Gibson, *Echoes From Eternity* (Bountiful, UT: Horizon, 1993), 155.

39. Grey, *Return*, 72.

40. Ibid., 58.

41. Ibid., 68–69.

42. Kenneth Ring, "Solving the Riddle of Frightening Near-Death Experiences," **JNDS** 13, No. 1 (Fall 1994), 7.

43. Bruce Greyson, and Nancy Evans Bush, "Distressing Near-Death Experiences," *Psychiatry* (Feb. 1992), 100.

44. William Serdehely, "Variations From the Prototypic Near-Death Experience: The 'Individually Tailored' Hypothesis," **JNDS** 13, No. 3 (Spring 1995), 189.

45. William Dudley Pelley, "Seven Minutes in Eternity—With Their Aftermath," (brochure) (Collier, city and date not given), cited in Muldoon, *Case*, 135–37.

46. Gloria Hipple, letter, 14 April 1992. See also P. M. H. Atwater, *Beyond the Light* (New York: Birch Lane Press, 1994), 29–33. Both of Hipple's experiences are originally from my own files.

47. Yram, *Practical Astral Projection*, 102–03.

48. Raynor Johnson, *The Imprisoned Splendour* (New York: Harper & Bros., 1953), 343.

49. Atwater, *Coming Back*, 44.

50. Greyson and Bush, "Distressing NDEs," 100.

51. Atwater, *Beyond the Light*, 44.

52. Greyson and Bush, "Distressing NDEs," 102–03.

53. Pamela Kircher, *Love is the Link* (Burdette, NY: Larson Publications, 1995) 116–17.

54. Peggy Holladay, "My NDE" (unpublished essay), no pagination.

55. Greyson and Bush, "Distressing NDEs," 104.

56. Ibid., 132.

57. Muldoon and Carrington, *Projection of the Astral*, 292–93.

58. Monroe, *Out of the Body*, 142–43.

59. Ibid., 119–20.

60. Patricia, personal communication, 1994.

61. Gary Wells, personal communication, June, 1994.

62. Ritchie, *My Life*, 24–25.

63. Edward Smith, "From Hell to Eternity: The Float Home," Edward Smith and Kenneth Ring, **Exceptional Human Experience: Studies of the Unitive/Spontaneous/ Imaginal**, 15 No. 2 (Dec. 1997), 196.

64. George Ritchie, personal communication, May 5, 1995.

65. Judith Cressy, *The Near-Death Experience: Mysticism or Madness?* (Hanover, MA. Christopher Publishing House, 1994), 19–20. I first heard Storm's experience at the IANDS conference at Rosemont, PA, in 1989, and questioned him further.

66. Ibid., 21.

67. Ibid., 21–23.

68. Ibid., 23, 25.

69. Ibid.

70. Ibid., 25.

71. Ibid., 25–26.

72. Ibid., 26–32.

73. Wilson Van Dusen, *The Presence of Other Worlds: The Psychological/Spiritual Findings of Emanuel Swedenborg* (New York: Harper & Row, 1974), 120–22.

74. Ibid., 123.

75. Lindley, Bryan, and Conley, "Evergreen Study," **Anabiosis**, 114.

76. Norman Van Rooy, unpublished MS, n.d., no pagination; *idem*, personal communication, 1994.

77. Matt. 25:31–46.

78. Van Rooy, ibid.

79. Otto, *Holy*, 12–24.

80. Barbara Rommer, "Less Than Positive Experiences of Children," **Vital Signs** 18, 3, 1999, 14.

81. Thomas Welch, "Oregon's Amazing Miracle," no pagination, no date (10–13),

cited in Maurice Rawlings, *Beyond Death's Door*, 86–89.

82. Welch, "Miracle," no pagination.

83. Kenneth Hagin, "My Testimony," no pagination, no date, cited in Rawlings, *Death's Door*, 91–92.

84. Rawlings, *Death's Door*, 101–03.

85. Keith Floyd, "ECT: TNT or TLC? A Near-Death Experience Triggered by Electroconvulsive Therapy," **JNDS** 14, No. 3 (Spring 1996), 187–95.

86. Oliver Fox, *Astral Projection*, 106–07.

87. Julian Ries, "Cross," in Mircea Eliade, ed., *The Encyclopedia of Religion*, Vol. 4, 156, 161.

88. Fox, *Astral Projection*.

89. Margot Grey, *Return*, 65–66.

90. Ibid., 66–67.

91. A. J. Ayer, "What I Saw When I Was Dead," *National Review* (Oct. 14, 1988), 38–39.

92. Ibid., 39.

93. Harvey Irwin and Barbara Bramwell, "The Devil in Heaven: A Near-Death Experience with both Positive and Negative Facets," **JNDS** 7, No. 1 (Fall 1988), 41–42.

94. Ibid., 42.

95. Maurice Rawlings, *To Hell*, 73.

96. Charles A. Garfield, "The Dying Patient's Concern with Life After Death," in Craig R. Lundahl, ed., *A Collection of Near-Death Research Readings* (Chicago: Nelson-Hall, 1982), 161.

97. Ibid., 161–62.

98. Lindley, Bryan and Conley, "Evergreen Study," 113.

99. Ibid.

100. Ibid., 114.

101. Ibid., 107, 108.

102. George Gallup, with William Proctor, *Adventures in Immortality* (New York: McGraw-Hill, 1982), 76.

103. Ibid., 79–83.

104. Grey, *Return*, 30, 59.

105. Ibid., 58.

106. P. M. H. Atwater, "Is There a Hell?" **JNDS** 10, No. 3 (Spring 1992), 150.

107. Atwater, *Beyond the Light,* 27, italics in original.

108. Rommer, *Blessing in Disguise: Another Side of the Near-Death Experience,* (St. Paul: Llewellyn, 2000).

109. Grey, *Return,* 179.

110. Atwater, *Beyond the Light,* 46.

111. Ibid., 62.

112. Rommer, *Blessings,* 26, 27.

113. Evans Bush, "Frightening NDEs," cited in Rommer, ibid., 27.

114. Arvin Gibson, *Glimpses of Eternity* (Bountiful, UT: Horizon, 1992), 154–55, 261.

115. Atwater, *Beyond the Light,* 51–53.

116. Ibid., 58–60.

117. Rogo, *Return From Silence,* 136.

118. Ibid., 137.

119. Starr Daily, *Release* (New York: Harper & Bros, 1942), 35–36.

120. Atwater, *Coming Back,* 36–37.

121. Ibid., 46–47.

122. George Ritchie, personal communication, May 6, 1995.

123. Sidney Saylor Farr, *What Tom Sawyer Learned from Dying* (Norfolk, VA: Hampton Roads, 1993), 32–34.

124. Ibid., 34–35.

125. Ibid., 35.

126. Betty Eadie, *Embraced by the Light* (Placerville, CA: Gold Leaf Press, 1992, 113.

127. Lorimer, *Whole in One,* 7–105, 256–87.

128. Rommer, *Blessings,* 215 in MS.

129. Ibid, 227.

130. Ibid, 134.

131. Ibid, 133–34.

132. Atwater, *Beyond the Light,* 119–23.

133. Nancy Evans Bush, personal communication, 1994.

134. Patricia, personal communication, 1994.

Five: A Challenge to Transcendence: This-Worldly Interpretations

1. Schnaper, "Comments Germane to the Paper Entitled 'The Reality of Death Experiences,' by Rodding," **J. of Nervous and Mental Diseases** 168 (1980), 268–70, cited in Christopher Cherry, "Are Near-Death Experiences Really Suggestive of Life After Death?" in *Beyond Death: Theological and Philosophical Reflections on Life After Death,* ed. Dan Cohn-Sherbok and Christopher Lewis (New York: St. Martin's, 1995), 153.

2. David Hume, "On the Immortality of the Soul," in Richard Wollheim, ed., *Hume on Religion* (London: Collins, 1963), 238–39, cited in Cherry, ibid., 149.

3. Cherry, ibid., 149–154.

4. Carl B. Becker, *Paranormal Experience and Survival of Death* (Albany: SUNY Press, 1993), 93.

5. Russell Noyes and Roy Kletti, "Depersonalization in the Face of Life Threatening Danger: A Description," **Psychiatry** 39 (Feb. 1976), 19–27, reprinted in Craig R. Lundahl, ed., *A Collection of Near-Death Research Readings* (Chicago: Nelson-Hall Publishers, 1982, 51–64. Although the original publication of this essay is dated the year after Moody's 1975 book, it actually appeared only about two months later, and reflects work done independently of Moody's.

6. Ibid., 24.

7. Russell Noyes, Jr. and Donald Slymen, "The Subjective Response to Life-Threatening Danger," in Greyson and Flynn, *The Near-Death Experience,* 27.

8. Noyes and Kletti, "Depersonalization," 62–63.

9. Ibid., 61–64.

10. Russell Noyes, Jr., "Near-Death Experiences: Their Interpretation and Significance," in Robert Kastenbaum, ed., *Between Life and Death* (New York: Springer, 1979), 73–88, cited in Bruce Greyson, "The Psycho-dynamics of Near-Death Experiences," in Greyson and Flynn, *NDE,* 164.

11. Ibid., 62–64.

12. H. J. Irwin, *An Introduction to Parapsychology* (Jefferson, NC: McFarland & Co, 1989), 196.

13. Osis and Haraldson, *At the Hour,* 198.

14. Ibid., 208.

15. Gabbard and Twemlow, *Eyes of the Mind,* 56–57.

16. Ring, *Life at Death,* 207–08.

17. Russell Noyes, "The Human Experience of Death," **Omega** 13, 251–59, reprinted in Greyson and Flynn, *NDE* 267–77.

18. Greyson, "The Psychodynamics of Near-Death Experiences," in Greyson and Flynn, *NDE,* 164–70.

19. Ibid., 163, 170–71.

20. Carl Sagan, "The Amniotic Universe," in Greyson and Flynn, *NDE,* 145–47.

21. Carl Becker, "Why Birth Models Cannot Explain Near-Death Phenomena," in Greyson and Flynn, *NDE,* 159–60.

22. Ibid., 156.

23. Ronald K. Siegel, "Psychology of Life," in Greyson and Flynn, *NDE,* 102.

24. Ibid., 109.

25. Blackmore, *Dying to Live,* 70–71.

26. Moody, *Life After Life,* 116–18.

27. Ibid., 55–56.

28. Siegel, "Psychology of Life," 100.

29. Ibid., 101.

30. Ibid., 81–90.

31. Ibid., 51.

32. Susan Blackmore, "Near-Death Experiences in India: They Have Tunnels Too," **JNDS** 11, No. 4 (Summer 1993), 215.

33. Allan Kellehear, Ian Stevenson, Satwant Pasricha, and Emily Cook, "The Absence of Tunnel Sensations in Near-Death Experiences from India," **JNDS** 13, No. 2 (Winter 1994), 110–111.

34. Daniel Carr, "Pathophysiology of Stress-induced Limbic Lobe Dysfunctions," in Greyson and Flynn, *NDE,* 127–31.

35. Ibid., 133.

36. Melvin Morse et. al., "Near-Death Experiences in a Pediatric Population," **American J. of Diseases of Children**, Vol. 139 (June 1985), 599.

37. Ibid.

38. Melvin Morse with Paul Perry, *Transformed by the Light* (New York: Villard, 1992), 145.

39. Blackmore, *Dying to Live,* 111–12.

40. Griffin, *Parapsychology, Philosophy,* 243.

41. Siegel, "Psychology of Life," 94–95, 99.

42. Blackmore, *Dying to Live,* 75, 77.

43. Moody, *Life After Life,* 102–03.

44. Michael B. Sabom, *Light and Death* (Grand Rapids: Zondervan, 1998), 43.

45. Ibid.

46. Ibid., 45.

47. Moody, *Life After Life,* 102–03.

48. Sabom, *Light and Death,* 46.

49. Blackmore, *Dying to Live,* 117–19.

50. Griffin, *Parapsychology, Philosophy,* 249–50.

51. Susan Blackmore, personal letter, June 1996.

52. Blackmore, *Dying to Live,* 127–28.

53. Ibid., 119.

54. Hayden Ebbern et al., "Maria's Near-Death Experience: Waiting for the Other Shoe to Drop," **Skeptical Inquirer** 20, No. 4 (July/Aug. 1996), 32–33.

55. Kimberly Clark Sharp, personal communication, Aug. 1996.

56. Susan Blackmore, *Beyond the Body* (Chicago: Academy Chicago Publishers, 1992) (1982), 243.

57. Ibid., 128–135.

58. Jule Eisenbud, *The World of Ted Serios* (New York: Morrow, 1982) (1967), 152, 160, 237, 323.

Preface to Part Two

1. Joachim Wach, *The Sociology of Religion* (Chicago: Univ. of Chicago Press, 1944), *passim*.

Six: Some Afterlife Views in Religions of the West

1. Slater Brown, *The Heyday of Spiritualism* (New York: Pocket Books, 1970), 57–58.

2. Arthur Conan Doyle, *The History of Spiritualism* (New York: Arno Press, 1975) (1926), 280–82.

3. Ibid.

4. Ibid., 55.

5. Ibid., 282–86.

6. James R. Lewis, *Encyclopedia of Afterlife Beliefs and Phenomena* (Detroit: Visible Ink Press, Gale Research Inc., 1995), 352.

7. Leslie A. Shepard, ed., *Encyclopedia of Occultism and Parapsychology*, Vol. 2, 1692–94; Rosemary Ellen Guiley, *Harper's Encyclopedia of Mystical and Paranormal Experience* (San Francisco: HarperSan Francisco, 1991), 611–14.

8. Robert S. Ellwood, *Theosophy* (Wheaton, IL: Theosophical Publishing House, 1986), 102–04.

9. Ibid., 108–14.

10. Ibid., 115.

11. Ibid., 113.

12. Annie Besant and C. W. Leadbeater, *Thought-Forms* (Wheaton, IL: Theosophical Publishing House, 1971), *passim*.

13. James R. Lewis, "Christianity," *Encyclopedial of Afterlife Beliefs and Phenomena* (Detroit: Visible Ink Press, 1995), 75–77. See also Robert S. Ellwood, *History and Future of Faith* (New York: Crossroad, 1988), 44, 48.

14. Alan F. Segal, "Paul and the Beginning of Jewish Mysticism," in John J. Collins and Michael Fishbane, eds., *Death, Ecstasy and Otherworldly Journeys* (Albany, NY: SUNY Press, 1995), 95–12.

15. Luke 11:19; Matt. 18:10.

16. Luke 15:19–31.

17. Matt. 28:9, John 20:27, Luke 24:43.

18. Acts 1:9, Mark 16:19 (in the addendum to Mark).

19. I Thess. 4:13–17.

20. Rev. 19, 20, 21, 22.

21. Peter Brown, *The Cult of the Saints: Its Rise and Function in Latin Christianity* (Chicago: Univ. of Chicago Press, 1981), *passim*.

22. J. H. Crehan, "Purgatory," *Man, Myth and Magic*, Vol 17, 2305–07. The scriptural citations are II Maccabees 12, I Cor. 3:13–15. The book of Enoch (22:12), a Jewish work taken over by Christians, holds out a prospect of release for certain sufferers in Gehenna. In addition, II Tim.

1:18 and Luke 11:58–59 were interpreted as referring to afterdeath states.

23. Zaleski, *Otherworld Journeys*, 28–32.

24. Ibid., 69–74.

25. Robert Ellwood, *Alternative Altars* (Chicago: Univ. of Chicago Press, 1979), 91.

26. Gallup, George Jr., with William Proctor, *Adventures in Immortality*, (New York: McGraw-Hill, 1982), 27.

27. See Maria Simma, *My Personal Experiences with the Poor Souls* (Chicago: Franciscan Herald Press, 1979), *passim*.

28. Zaleski, *Otherworld Journeys*, 54–55, 136–37.

Seven: Some Afterlife Views in Nonwestern Religions

1. S. G. F. Brandon, *The Judgment of the Dead* (London: Weidenfeld & Nicolson, 1967). 14, 15.

2. Ibid., 20–21.

3. Raymond, Faulkner and Ogden Goulet, *The Egyptian Book of the Dead: The Book of Going Forth by Day* (San Francisco: Chronicle Books, 1994), 143.

4. Ibid., 149, 150.

5. Ibid., 18.

6. Ibid., Plate 3.

7. Ibid., 157.

8. Ibid., 153.

9. Ibid., 161.

10. Ibid., 163.

11. Ibid., 154.

12. Ibid., 151.

13. Ibid.

14. Ibid., Plate 8, Chap. 17.

15. Ibid., Plate 37, and 170.

16. Brandon, *Judgment*, 44.

17. Ibid., 43–44.

18. Atwater, *Coming Back*, 36.

19. Brandon, *Judgment*, 147.

20. Ibid., 45.

21. Ibid., 50.

22. Ibid., 50–51.

23. Ibid., 51.

24. Diane Wolkstein and Samuel N. Kramer, *Inanna: Queen of Heaven and Earth* (New York: Harper & Row, 1983), 6–8.

25. Ibid.

26. Ibid., 52–89, 157–168.

27. John Hick, *Death and Eternal Life* (San Francisco: Harper & Row, 1976), 55–60, and Michael Grosso, "Fear of Life After Death," in Gary Doore, *What Survives? Contemporary Explorations of Life After Death* (Los Angeles: Jeremy Tarcher, 1990), 242–45.

28. Richard Robinson and Willard Johnson, *The Buddhist Religion: A Historical Introduction* (Belmont, CA: Wadsworth, 1982), 19.

29. Ibid.

30. J. B. Long, "Asura," in Keith Crim, ed., *Abingdon Dictionary of Living Religions*, Nashville: Abingdon, 1981), 75.

31. Pierre Grimal, ed., *Larousse World Mythology* (London: Paul Hamlyn, 1965), 241.

32. J.B. Long, in *Abingdon Dictionary*, 75.

33. Seami, "Tsunemasa," in Arthur Waley, tr., *The No Plays of Japan* (New York: Grove Press), 1957, 82–87.

34. Dharmika Subhuti, *Sadgatikarika*, in John S. Strong, ed. and tr., *The Experience of Buddhism: Sources and Interpretations* (Belmont, CA: Wadsworth, 1995), 30.

35. Robinson and Johnson, *Buddhist Religion*, 19.

36. Keith Crim, "Preta," in *Abingdon Dictionary*, 581.

37. Laurence G. Thompson, *Chinese Religion: An Introduction* (Belmont, CA: Dickenson, 1969), 29.

38. Crim, *Abingdon Dictionary*, 581.

39. Winston L. King, *A Thousand Lives Away* (Cambridge, MA: Harvard Univ. Press, 1964), 90.

40. Robert S. Ellwood, *Many Peoples, Many Faiths* (Engelwood Cliffs, NJ: Prentice-Hall, 1992), 187.

41. Wolfram Eberhard, *Guilt and Sin in Traditional China* (Berkeley: Univ. of California Press, 1967), 30–40.

42. William Theodore De Bary, *The Buddhist Tradition in India, China & Japan* (New York: The Modern Library, 1969), 322–324.

43. Winston L. King, *Thousand Lives*, 90.

44. Subhuti, "Sadgatikarika," in Strong, *Buddhism*, 29.

45. Miriam Levering, "Ksitigarbha," in Mircea Eliade, ed., *The Encyclopedia of Religion*, Vol. 8 (New York: MacMillan, 1987), 392–393. See also Heng Ching, trans., *Sutra of the Past Vows of Earth Store Bodhisattva* (San Francisco: Institute for the Advanced Study of World Religions, 1974), 76–89; Vessantara, *Meeting the Buddhas* (Glasgow: Windhorse, 1993), 198–201; and Alice Getty, *The Gods of Northern Buddhism* (Rutland, VT: Tuttle, 1962), 103.

46. King, *Thousand Lives*, 91.

47. Eberhard, *Guilt and Sin*, 74.

48. King, *A Thousand Lives*, 92.

49. Ibid., 93–95.

50. Ibid., 93.

51. Alan Andrews, *The Teachings Essential for Rebirth: A Study of Genshin's Ojoyoshu* (Tokyo: Sophia University, 1973), 9–11.

52. Vessantara, *Meeting the Buddhas*, 95–96.

53. Carl Becker, "The Centrality of Near-Death Experiences in Chinese Pure Land Buddhism," **Anabiosis: JNDS** (1981), 163.

54. Francesca Fremantle and Chonyid Trungpa, *The Tibetan Book of the Dead* (Boston & London: Shambhala, 1987), 35.

55. Ibid., 37.

56. Ibid., 38.

57. Ibid., 40–42.

58. I owe the interpretation of *Sambhogakaya* as analogous to Jung's conception of the archetypal level of reality to Robert Ellwood Jr., personal communication, 1996. See also Ken Wilber, "Death, Rebirth, and Meditation," in Doore, *What Survives?*, 185.

59. Fremantle and Trungpa, 48–49.

60. Ibid., 57–71.

61. Ibid., 72–74.

62. Ibid., 74–76.

63. Thurman, *Book of the Dead,* 174–75.

64. Ibid., 90–93, 196–97.

65. Moody, *Life After Life,* 84–85.

66. Greyson and Bush, "Distressing NDEs," 100; Kenneth Ring, "Solving the Riddle," 14–16.

67. Eberhard, *Guilt and Sin,* 35, 51.

68. Andrews, *Teachings,* 5, 7.

69. Greyson, "Psychodynamics," in Greyson and Flynn, *NDE,* 170.

70. Rupert Sheldrake, "Can Our Memories Survive the Death of Our Brains?" in Doore, *What Survives?* 118–21. Ring, *Toward Omega,* 261–63, applies Sheldrake's ideas to the next evolutionary step.

71. Rupert Sheldrake, *The Presence of the Past* (New York: Vintage Books, 1989), xvii–xix, 370–71.

72. Ibid., 199.

73. Ibid., 285–89.

Eight: The Possibility of Survival: Body and Mind

1. David R. Griffin, *Parapsychology, Philosophy, and Spirituality: A Postmodern Exploration* (Albany: SUNY Press, 1997), 25–26.

2. Ibid., 26–27.

3. Ibid., 22.

4. Griffin, *God and Religion,* 55.

5. Ibid., 1–3, 21–23, 30–34.

6. Paul Churchland, *Matter and Consciousness* (Cambridge, MA: The MIT Press, 1984), 26.

7. Ibid., 27–28.

8. Ibid., 139.

9. Ibid., 140, 153.

10. Ibid., 16–17.

11. Atwater, *Coming Back,* 41. I have a second account from Atwater of a later instance of X-ray vision, again upon herself, followed by self-healing of a severe injury. *Idem,* Personal communication, March 1992.

12. Thomas Nagel, *The View From Nowhere* (New York: Oxford Univ. Press, 1986), 9.

13. Thomas Nagel, "What is It Like to Be a Bat?" *Mortal Questions* (Cambridge: Cambridge Univ. Press, 1979), 166.

14. Nagel, "Panpsychism," *Mortal Questions,* 188.

15. Nagel, "Bat," 166–67.

16. Ibid., 168–73.

17. Ibid., 176–77.

18. Ibid., 32–34.

19. Ibid., 42.

20. Ibid., 40, 43.

21. Ibid., 30.

22. Ibid., 48.

23. Ibid.

24. Ibid., 30.

25. Ibid., 31.

26. Nagel, "Panpsychism," 182, 193; Nagel, *Nowhere,* 49–50.

27. Nagel, *Nowhere,* 12.

28. Ibid., 194–95.

29. Griffin, *Unsnarling the World-Knot* (Berkeley, Los Angeles & London: Univ. of California Press, 1998), *passim.*

30. Karl Popper and John Eccles, *The Self and Its Brain* (Berlin: Springer-Verlag, 1977), 36–50, 56–57.

31. Ibid., 127–30.

32. Ibid., 125.

33. Ibid., 362, italics added.

34. Ibid., 384–85.

35. Ibid., 104–05.

36. John Searle, *The Rediscovery of the Mind* (Cambridge: MIT Press, 1992), 49, cited in Griffin, Ibid.

37. McGinn, *Problem,* 2; Nagel, *Nowhere,* 10.

38. Aurobindo, from *Arya,* Sarvepalli Radhakrishnan and Charles A. Moore, eds., *Sourcebook in Indian Philosophy* (Princeton, NJ: Princeton Univ. Press, 1957), 578.

39. Aurobindo, from *The Life Divine,* in *Sourcebook,* 596–98.

40. Aurobindo, *The Life Divine,* Vol. 1 (Calcutta: Arya Publishing, 1939), 184.

41. Ibid., 600.

42. Ibid., 709.

43. Ibid., 344.

44. *The Life Divine,* Vol. 2, Pondicherry: All India Press, 1973, 759.

45. Ibid., 757.

46. Ibid., 787.

47. *Life,* Vol. 1, 293–99.

48. *Life,* Vol. 2, 896–97.

49. Ibid., 759–61.

50. Ibid., 762–63.

51. Ibid., 914–15.

52. Ibid., 972.

53. Ibid., 89–90.

54. Charles Hartshorne, "Physics and Psychics: The Place of Mind in Nature," in John B. Cobb, Jr., and David Griffin, eds., *Mind in Nature* (Washington, DC: Univ. Press of America, 1977), 92.

55. F. C. S. Schiller, *Riddles of the Sphinx* (London: Swan Sonnenschein, 1891), 293–95, cited in David Lorimer, *Survival? Body, Mind and Death in the Light of Psychic Experience* (London: Routledge & Kegan Paul, 1984), 131–32, italics in original.

56. William James, "Religion and the Problems of the Soul," in Gardner Murphy and Robert Ballou, eds., *William James on Psychical Research* (New York: Viking, 1960), 291, italics in original.

57. Ibid., 291–92.

58. Ibid., 257–61.

59. Ibid., 230, n.

60. Grosso, *Final Choice,* 107–12.

Nine: The Probability of Survival: Empirical Arguments

1. Walter N. Pahnke, "Drugs and Mysticism," **Int'l J. of Parapsychology,** 8, No. 2 (1966), reprinted in Bernard Aaronson and Humphrey Osmond, *Psychedelics: The Uses and Implications of Hallucinogenic Drugs* (Garden City, NY: Doubleday, 1970), 145–65.

2. Oliver Sacks, *The Man Who Mistook his Wife for a Hat* (New York: Harper & Row, 1987), 149.

3. Ibid., 150–52.

4. Wilder Penfield, *The Mystery of the Mind: A Critical Study of Consciousness and the Human Brain* (Princeton, NJ: Princeton Univ. Press, 1975), *passim.*

5. Ibid., 157.

6. Oliver Sacks, *Man Who Mistook,* 141–42.

7. Studies by Nancy C. Andreasen and Kay Redfield Jamison reaching this conclusion were described in "Madness and Creativity: Scientists Hunt for Links," *Los Angeles Times,* (Sept. 30, 1989).

8. Sacks, *Man Who Mistook,* 97–100.

9. Ibid., 8–22.

10. van Dusen, *Other Worlds,* 120–135.

11. E. R. Dodds, "Why I Do Not Believe in Survival," **Proc. SPR,** Part 135 (1934), 152–53.

12. Ibid., 158–60.

13. David Griffin, personal communication.

14. Viktor Frankl, *Man's Search for Meaning* (New York: Washington Square Press, 1963), 117–21.

15. Blair Justice, *Who Gets Sick* (Houston: Peak Press, 1987), 62–63.

16. A careful study of such phenomena with many examples is Herbert Thurston, *The Physical Phenomena of Mysticism* (London: Burns Oates, 1952).

17. D. Scott Rogo, *Miracles: A Scientific Exploration of Wondrous Phenomena* (Hammersmith, London: 1983), 17–21. Rogo's account is partially dependent on Thurston's.

18. "Power of Prayer," presentation at Medjugorje Peace Conference, Irvine, Calif., 1990, (audiotape, Huntington Beach: Follow Me Communications, Inc., 1990).

19. John Sutherland Bonnell, *Do You Want to Be Healed?* (New York: Harper & Row, 1968), 20–23, cited in H. Richard Neff, *Psychic Phenomena and Religion* (Philadelphia: Westminster Press, 1971), 98.

20. Adam Crabtree, *Multiple Man: Explorations in Possession and Multiple Personality* (New York: Praeger Publishers, 1985), 95–97, 100–01.

21. Stephen Braude, *First Person Plural* (London: Routledge and Kegan Paul, 1991), *passim*.

22. C. D. Broad, "The Relevance of Psychical Research to Philosophy," in Fabian Gudas, ed., *Extrasensory Perception* (New York: Scribner's, 1961), 102–03.

23. W. F. Prince, **JASPR** 17 (1923), cited in Gardner Murphy, *Challenge of Psychical Research: A Primer of Parapsychology* (New York: Harper & Brothers, 1961), 31–35.

24. Ibid., 33–35.

25. Ibid., 38–39.

26. Ibid., 39–43.

27. Griffin, *Parapsychology*, 11.

28. Ibid.

29. Naomi A. Hintze and J. Gaither Pratt, *The Psychic Realm: What Can You Believe?* (New York: Random House, 1975), 117–20. For a fuller account see William G. Roll, *The Poltergeist* (New York: New American Library, 1974), 104–57.

30. Hintze and Pratt, *Realm*, 120–22.

31. Ibid., 121–29.

32. Ibid., 82–83.

33. Griffin, *Parapsychology*, 41–43, 83–85.

34. Rosalind Heywood, *Beyond the Reach of Sense* (New York: E. P. Dutton, 1961) 53–58, 77–90, 95–107; Harmon Hartzell Bro, *A Seer Out of Season: The Life of Edgar Cayce* (New York: Signet, 1990); Lawrence LeShan, *The Medium, the Mystic, and the Physicist: Toward a General Theory of the Paranormal* (New York: Ballantine, 1966),16–40.

35. Jenny Wade, *Changes of Mind: A Holonomic Theory of the Evolution of Consciousness* (New York: SUNY Press, 1996), 29.

36. Helen Wambach, *Life Before Life* (Toronto: Bantam, 1979), 98–121.

37. Michael Gabriel, *Voices From the Womb* (Lower Lake, CA: Aslan Publishing, 1992), 46–50.

38. David Chamberlain, *Babies Remember Birth* (Los Angeles: Jeremy Tarcher, 1988), 103.

49. Ibid. 46.

40. Ibid.

41. Ibid., 52–56; Wambach, *Before Life, passim*; Gabriel, *Voices*, 121–29.

42. William Wordsworth, "Intimations of Immortality From Recollections of Early Childhood," Oscar Williams, ed., *Immortal Poems* (New York: Washington Square Press, 1952), 262.

Ten: Documented Evidence for Survival

1. Alan Gauld, *Mediumship and Survival* (London: Paladin, 1983), 42–43.

2. Ibid.

3. Ibid., 34.

4. James Munvies, "Richard Hodgson, Mrs. Piper and 'George Pelham': A Centennial Reassessment," **JASPR** 62 (No. 849) (Oct. 1997), 147.

5. Richard Hodgson (title not given), **PSPR** 13 (1897–98), 328, cited in C.J. Ducasse, *The Belief in a Life After Death* (Springfield, IL: Charles Thomas, 1961), 181.

6. David C. Knight, introductory note to Richard Hodgson, "G.P.," in Knight, ed., *ESP Reader*, 67.

7. James Munvies, "Reassessment," 143, 147, 149–50.

8. Michael Polanyi, "Tacit Knowing," *Review of Modern Physics* 34 (1962), 601–16, cited in Ian Stevenson, *Twenty Cases Suggestive of Reincarnation* (Charlottesville: Univ. of Virginia Press, 1974), 335–36.

9. Stevenson, ibid., 348.

10. Hart, *Enigma*, p. 83.

11. Drayton Thomas, "A New Hypothesis Concerning Trance-Communications," **PSPR** 48 (1947), cited in Hart, *Enigma*, 92.

12. Arthur S. Berger, *Aristocracy of the Dead: New Findings in Posmortem Survival* (Jefferson, NC: McFarland & Co., 1987), 61–72, 102–09.

13. Jean Balfour, "The 'Palm Sunday' Case: New Light on an Old Love Story," **PSPR** 52 (Feb. 1960), summarized in Andrew MacKenzie, *The Unexplained: Some*

Strange Cases in Psychical Research (London: Arthur Barker Ltd., 1966), pp. 117–32; in Susy Smith, "Lord Balfour's Lost Love," in Susy Smith, ed., *Adventures in the Supernormal* (New York: Pyramid Publications, 1968), 213–16; and Renee Haynes, *The Society for Psychical Research 1882–1982: A History* (London: MacDonald & Co, 1982), 72–73.

14. Berger, *Aristocracy*, 100–01.

15. G. N. M. Tyrrell, *Science and Psychical Phenomena* (New Hyde Park, NY: University Books, 1961), 249–50.

16. Ian Stevenson, "A Communicator Unknown to Medium and Sitters," **JASPR** 64, No. 1 (Jan. 1970), 54–56.

17. Ibid., 56.

18. Ibid., 56–57.

19. Ibid.

20. Ibid., 57–58.

21. Ibid., 60–63.

22. Ibid., 63–64.

23. Nancy-Lou Patterson, personal communication.

24. F. W. H. Myers, *Human Personality and Its Survival of Bodily Death*, Vol. 2 (New York: Longmans, Green, & Co., 1954) (1903), 327–29.

25. Gauld, *Mediumship*, 235.

26. R. C. Morton (Rosina Despard), "Record of a Haunted House," **PSPR** 8, 311–32, cited in Myers, *Human Personality*, Vol. 2, 389.

27. Ibid., 390–93.

28. Ibid.

29. Ibid.

30. R. C. Morton [Rosina Despard], "Record of a Haunted House," **PSPR** 8 (1892), 314, cited by Gracia Fay Ellwood, "The Cheltenham Haunting: An Interpretation," **JASPR** 63 (April 1969), 185–96.

31. Ibid., 321.

32. Ibid.

33. Morton in Myers, *Human Personality*, 394–95.

34. Andrew MacKenzie, "The Weeping Ghost of Cheltenham," *Fate,* Vol. 41, No. 9 (Sep. 1988), p. 41.

35. Ibid.

36. Ibid., 39.

37. Ibid., 40.

38. Ibid., 40–41.

39. Lorimer, *Whole in One*, 34.

40. Morton, "Record," 323.

41. Eileen J. Garrett, *Many Voices: The Autobiography of a Medium* (New York: Dell Publishing Co., 1968), *passim*. See also Eileen J. Garrett, *Adventures in the Supernormal* (New York: Paperback Library, 1968) (1949), *passim*.

42. G. N. M. Tyrrell, *Apparitions,* 142.

43. F. W. H. Myers, in **PSPR** 6 (title and pagination not given), cited in MacKenzie, *Apparitions and Ghosts,* 174, Tyrrell, *Apparitions,* 144–45; and H. H. Price, "Haunting and the 'Psychic Ether' Hypothesis," **PSPR** 45 (1939), 317–28, cited in Hart, *Enigma,* 197–98. Price suggests that the fragment split off during the time the historical person lived in the house, an idea which fits most somnambulistic-type ghosts but not the Cheltenham ghost (who wore widow's garb but was not a widow during her residence).

44. Myers, *Human Personality*, Vol.I, 292–94.

45. Tyrrell, *Apparitions,* 34–35.

46. Laura A. Dale et al., "A Selection of Cases from a Recent Survey of Spontaneous ESP Phenomena," **JASPR** 61, No. 1 (Jan. 1962), 28–29.

47. Hornell Hart et. al., *Six Theories About Apparitions,* **PSPR** 50, Part 185 (May 1956), 153–65.

48. Alan Gauld, *Mediumship,* 258.

49. V. V. Akolkar, "Search for Sharada: Report of a Case and Its Investigation," **JASPR** 86, No. 3 (July 1992), 209–47, and Ian Stevenson, *Unlearned Language* (Charlottesville: Univ. Press of Virginia, 1984) 73–153.

50. Akolkar, ibid.; Stevenson, ibid.

51. Ibid., 95.

52. Ibid., 102–03.

53. Ibid., 112.

54. Ibid., 120–21.

55. Ibid., 124–27.

56. Ibid., 143–44.

57. Ibid., 146–47.

58. Stevenson, 152–53.

59. Akolkar, 244.

60. Stevenson, 160–61.

61. David Griffin, *Parapsychology, Philosophy,* 181–83.

62. Walter F. Prince, "Two Cures of 'Paranoia' by Experimental Appeals to Purported Obsession Spirits," Proceedings, Third Int'l Congress, 36–38.

63. Ibid., 38–42.

64. Ibid., 55–58. See also Colin Wilson, *Beyond the Occult* (New York: Carroll & Graf, 1988), 265–66.

65. D. Scott Rogo, *The Infinite Boundary* (New York: Dodd, Mead & Co., 1987), 198–99.

66. E. Lee Howard, *My Adventure in Spiritualism,* cited in D. Scott Rogo, *The Infinite Boundary* (New York: Dodd, Mead & Co., 1987), 161–62.

67. Carl Wickland, *Thirty Years Among the Dead* (Van Nuys: Newcastle, 1974) (1924), 114–15.

68. Ibid., *passim.*

69. John Pierce-Higgins, "Poltergeists, Hauntings and Possession," in J. D. Pierce-Higgins and (the) Rev. G. Stanley Whitby, eds., *Life, Death & Psychical Research* (London: Rider, 1973), 175.

70. Crabtree, *Multiple Man,* 63–64.

71. Ibid., 160–65.

72. Edith Fiore, *Unquiet Dead: A Psychologist Treats Spirit Possession* (New York: Ballantine Books, 1987), 21–22.

73. Moody, *Reflections,* 18–22.

74. Fiore, *Unquiet Dead,* 28–33.

75. Ibid., 34, 37.

76. Ibid., 119–23.

77. Ibid, 110–12, 119–21.

78. Ibid., 79.

79. Ibid., 32; Crabtree, *Multiple Man,* 120–24.

80. Gauld, *Mediumship,* 150–51.

81. Ibid., 151–54.

82. Rogo, *Boundary,* New York: 50–51.

83. Gauld, *Mediumship,* 155.

84. Griffin, *Parapsychology, Philosophy,* 192–93.

85. Stevenson, *Twenty Cases,* 16–17, 322.

86. Ibid., 97.

87. Ibid., 91.

88. Ibid., 101.

89. Ibid., 91–92, 98–99.

90. Ibid., 99–100.

91. Ibid., 100.

92. Ibid., 102.

93. Ibid., 102.

94. Ibid., 93.

95. Ibid., 96–100.

96. Ibid., 96–97.

97. Ibid., 95, 101.

98. Ibid., 94, 334.

99. Ian Stevenson, "A New Look at Maternal Impressions: An Analysis of 50 Published Cases and Reports of Two Recent Examples," **J. of Scientific Exploration** 6, No. 4, 353–73, 1992.

100. Ian Stevenson, personal communication to Griffin, cited in Griffin, Ibid.

101. Griffin, Ibid., 206–07.

102. Karlis Osis, "In Search of Evidence for Life After Death—Science, Experience or Both," **Proc. of the Academy of Religion and Psychical Research** (1995), 12–13.

103. Hornell Hart, *The Enigma of Survival* (Springfield, Ill: Chas. C. Thomas, 1959), 133–34. See also Gracia Fay Ellwood, "The Soal-Cooper-Davis Communal 'I'," **Int'l J. of Parapsychology** (Winter, 1968), 392–408.

104. Hart, *Enigma,* 135.

105. Ibid., 21.

106. Mrs. Henry Sidgwick (Eleanor Balfour Sidgwick), "Discussion of the Trance Phenomena of Mrs. Piper," **PSPR** 36, pp. 23, 26–27.

107. Ibid., 35–36.

108. Ibid., 37–38.

109. William James, "Report on Mrs. Piper's Hodgson-Control, Part II" in Murphy and Ballou, *James on Psychical Research,* 204–207.

110. Hart, *Enigma,* 201–02.
111. Ibid., 203.
112. Griffin, *Parapsychology,* 152.

Eleven: Agnostic Interpretive Frameworks
1. John Wren-Lewis, "Darkness of God," **Anabiosis**, 51–64.
2. Wren-Lewis, "Avoiding the Columbus Confusion: An Ockhamish View of Near-Death Research," **JNDS** 11, No. 2 (Winter, 1992), 77–78.
3. Ibid., 78.
4. Ibid., 80.
5. Ibid., 79–80.
6. Zaleski, *Otherworld Journeys,* 187–90.
7. Ibid., 190.
8. Ibid., 195.
9. Ibid., 190–91.
10. Ibid., 197–98.
11. Ibid., 198–99.
12. Ibid., 198–201.
13. Ibid. 157, 180–81.
14. Carol Zaleski, *The Life of the World to Come,* New York: Oxford Univ. Press, 1996, 36–50.

Twelve: Multi-World Frameworks
1. This summary is based on innumerable sermons and catechism lessons in my own upbringing as an orthodox (Christian Reformed) Calvinist.
2. *To Hell and Back* (Nashville: Thomas Nelson, 1993), *passim.*
3. Robert S. Ellwood, personal communication, January 1996.

Thirteen: One-World Frameworks: Gradualist
1. Radhakrishnan and Moore, *Sourcebook,* 600.
2. Aurobindo, *The Life Divine,* Vol. 1 (Calcutta: Arya Publishing House, 1939), 130.
3. *Life,* Vol. 1, 281.
4. Ibid., 132.
5. Ibid., 281.
6. Ibid., 293–99.
7. Ibid., 709.

8. *The Life Divine,* Vol. 2 (Pondicherry: All India Press, 1973), 759.
9. Ibid., 778–781, 798–99.
10. Ibid., 799.
11. Ibid., 815.
12. Ibid., 759–60.
13. Ibid., 802.
14. Ibid., 801.
15. Ibid., 762–63.
16. Ibid., ppp. 914–15.
17. Ibid., 972.
18. Radhakrishnan and Moore, *Sourcebook,* 607–09.
19. Ibid., 588.
20. Ibid., 604–08.
21. Ibid., 972.

Fourteen: One-World Frameworks: Projectionist
1. Robert Ellwood, *Many Peoples, Many Faiths* (Englewood Cliffs, NJ: Prentice-Hall, 1976), 144–45.
2. Ibid., 135.
3. Ring, *Life at Death*, 234–39.
4. Ibid., 240–43.
5. Ibid., 246–48, italics in original.
6. Ibid., 246–50.
7. Kenneth Ring, "Solving the Riddle of Frightening Near-Death Experiences: Some Testable Hypotheses and a Perspective Based on *A Course in Miracles,*" **JNDS** 13, No. 1 (Fall 1994), 15–16.
8. Kenneth Ring, *Toward Omega*, 47–48.
9. Kenneth Ring, personal letter, November 2, 1996, 2.
10. Ring, "Solving the Riddle," 21–22.
11. Christopher Bache, "A Perinatal Interpretation of Frightening Near-Death Experiences: A Dialogue with Kenneth Ring," **JNDS** 13, No. 1 (Fall 1994), 40; Kenneth Ring, "Frightening Near-Death Experiences Revisited: A Commentary on Responses to My Paper by Christopher Bache and Nancy Evans Bush," ibid., 57–58.

Fifteen: One-World Frameworks: Initiatory

1. Carl G. Jung, "Visions / Life After Death" in Bailey and Yates, *Reader,* 109–10.
2. Jung, *Memories, Dreams,* 308–09, 315–16.
3. C. G. Jung, *The Archetypes and the Collective Unconscious* (New York: Pantheon Books, 1959), 287–88.
4. Ibid., 180.
5. Northrop Frye, *The Secular Scripture: A Study of the Structure of Romance* (Cambridge, MA: Harvard Univ. Press, 1975), 3.
6. Ibid.
7. Ibid., 23–24.
8. Ibid., 15.
9. Ibid., 187.
10. Gen. 1:31, KJV.
11. Frye, 188.
12. Ibid., 97–99.
13. Ibid., 99–100.
14. Ibid., 101–02.
15. Ibid., 3–4.
16. Ibid., 102–03.
17. Ibid., 104.
18. Ibid., 104–11.
19. Ibid., 107–08.
20. Ibid., 111.
21. Ibid., 113.
22. Ibid., 114.
23. Ibid.
24. Ibid., 120–21.
25. Ibid., 123.
26. Ibid., 124–25.
27. Ibid., 129–31.
28. Ibid., 131–32.
29. Ibid., 149.
30. Ibid., 151–55.
31. Joe Geraci, cited in Ring, *Toward Omega,* 54.
32. Jayne Smith, cited in Ring, Ibid., 63.
33. Frye, *Secular Scripture,* 124–25.
34. Zaleski, *Otherworld Journeys,* 187–205.
35. Grosso, *Final Choice,* 181–84. See also Grosso, "The Myth of the Near-Death Journey," **JNDS** 10, No. 1 (Fall 1991), 49–60.
36. Grosso, *Final Choice,* 181–83.
37. Ibid., 184–94.
38. F. Gordon Greene, "Motifs of Passage into Worlds Imaginary and Fantastic," **JNDS** 10, No. 4 (Summer 1992), 205–31.
39. F. Gordon Greene, "Homer's Odysseus as an Ecstatic Voyager," **JNDS** 14, No. 4 (Summer 1996), 235–36.
40. Ibid., 242–43.
41. Stanislav Grof, *Beyond the Brain: Birth, Death and Transcendence in Psychotherapy* (Albany: SUNY Press, 1985), 30–31.
42. Stanislav Grof and Christina Grof, *Beyond Death: The Gates of Consciousness* (London: Thames & Hudson Ltd., 1980), 8–13, 90.
43. Ibid., 93–94; Stanislav Grof, *Realms of the Human Unconscious* (New York: Viking Press, 1975), 34–43.
44. *Beyond the Brain.,* 94–95.
45. Ibid., 96–98.
46. *Realms,* 83, 179.
47. *Beyond the Brain,* 33.
48. *Realms,* 72, 92–93.
49. Ibid., 102–06.
50. *Realms,* 105–06.
51. Ibid., 107.
52. *Beyond the Brain,* 102–06.
53. *Realms,* 109.
54. *Beyond the Brain,* 111–12.
55. *Realms,* 119.
56. Ibid., 118.
57. *Beyond the Brain,* 112.
58. *Realms,* 118.
59. Ibid., 144.
60. Ibid., 116–20.
61. Ibid., 120.
62. *Beyond the Brain,* 112, 113.
63. Ibid., 119–20.
64. *Realms,* 144.
65. Ibid., 124, 25.
66. Ibid., 129–30.
67. Ibid., 121.
68. *Realms,* 130–31.
69. Ibid., 126–27.
70. *Beyond the Brain,* 122–25.
71. *Realms,* 138–39.
72. Ibid., 126.
73. Ibid., 143–44.

74. Ibid., 48–49; see also Bache, "Perinatal Interpretation," 37.

75. *Beyond the Brain*, 139–40.

76. Ibid., 186–90.

77. Ibid., 179.

78. Ibid., 181–84.

79. Ibid., 183–84.

80. Ibid., 185.

81. Ibid., 191.

82. Ibid., 173–77.

83. Ibid., 127–29.

84. Ibid., 194–96.

85. Ibid., 196–97.

86. Ibid., 198–200.

87. Ibid., 203–04.

88. Ibid., 204–05.

89, Ibid., 202–03.

90. Atwater, *Coming Back,* 36.

91. Ibid., 40–441.

92. *Realms,* 196–97.

93. Ring, "Solving the Riddle," 21.

94. Ibid., 22.

95. Bache, "Perinatal Interpretation," 30.

96. Ibid., 27.

97. Ibid., 30.

98. Ibid., 35–36.

99. Christopher M. Bache, "Expanding Grof's Concept of the Perinatal: Deepening the Inquiry Into Frightening Near-Death Experiences," **JNDS** 15, No. 2 (Winter 1996), 118.

100. Ibid., 128.

101. Ibid., 138.

102. Ibid., 123.

103. Grof, *Realms,* cited in Bache, Ibid., 120.

104. Bache, "Perinatal Interpretation," **JNDS,** 42–44.

105. Robert S. Ellwood Jr., *Mysticism and Religion* (Engelwood Cliffs, NJ: Prentice-Hall, 1980), 174–88

106. Margaret Smith, *An Introduction to Mysticism* (New York: Oxford Univ. Press, 1977), 42–45; William Ralph Inge, *Christian Mysticism* (London: Methuen, 1933) (1899), 9–14.

107. Evelyn Underhill, *Mysticism* (London: Methuen, 1911), 203–05.

108. Ibid., 205.

109. M. Diepenbrock, ed., *Heinrich Susos Leben und Schriften* (Regensburg: n.p., 1825), cap. iii (no page given), cited in Underhill, ibid., 227.

110. E.T. Starbuck, *The Psychology of Religion* (London: n.p., 1901), 120, cited in Underhill, ibid., 231.

111. Underhill, 233–34.

112. Ibid., 240–41, 244, 249, 252, 255.

113. Ibid., 260.

114. Ibid., 257–59.

115. Ibid., 261.

116. Ibid., 267, 270, 269.

117. Ibid., 271.

118. Ibid., 267.

119. Ibid., 266.

120. Ibid., 273–74.

121. Ibid., 288–89.

122. Ibid., 296, 295

123. Ibid., 304, 311.

124. George Fox, *Journal,* Vol. 1 (London: editor, publisher and page number not given), 1901, cited in Underhill, ibid., 309; italics Underhill's. (In the J. Nickalls, ed., Cambridge Centennial edition, 29.)

125. Underhill, 317.

126. Ibid., 319–21, 325, 323.

127. Ibid., 324.

128. Ibid., 457, 459, 487.

129. Ibid., 465, 459, 467, 480, 479, 472, 471.

130. John Tauler, *The Inner Way* (A. W. Hutton, tr.) (London: n.p., 1909), 97, cited in Underhill, *Mysticism,* 404.

131. Maurice Maeterlinck, "Introduction" to John Ruysbroeck, *L'Ornement des Noces Spirituelles de Ruysbroeck l'admirable* (Bruxelles, n.p., 1900), v, cited in Underhill, Ibid., 405.

132. John of the Cross, in C. H. Steuart and R. Steuart, eds., *The Mystical Doctrine of St. John of the Cross* (Kansas City, MO: Sheed & Ward, 1946), 7, 10, 22–24, 53, 81, 102–03.

133. Bache, "Perinatal Interpretation," 42–44.

134. J. J. Stoudt, *Jacob Boehme: His Life and Thought* (Long Island City, NY: Seaburn, 1968), 115.

135. Jacob Boehme, *The Way to Christ* (Mahwah, NJ: Paulist, 1978), 18–19, 238, 248, 56–62.

136. Underhill, *Mysticism,* 468–69.

137. George Fox, *Journal,* J.L. Nickalls, ed. (New York: Cambridge Univ. Press, 1952), 571. Note that the Nickalls edition is to be preferred over the better-known one edited by Thomas Ellwood, who tampered with the text in the interests of downplaying both the paranormal deeds and flaws of George Fox.

138. C. Bernard Ruffin, *Padre Pio: The True Story* (Huntington, IN: Our Sunday Visitor Publishing Division, 1991), 101–02.

139. Underhill, *Mysticism,,* 467–69.

140. Ibid., 474–77.

141. Gracia Fay Ellwood, "Distressing Near-Death Experiences as Photographic Negatives," **JNDS** 15, No. 2 (Winter 1996), 83–112.

142. Underhill, *Mysticism,* 479–81.

143. Ibid., 499, 503, 508.

144. Ibid., 509–12.

145. Ibid., 526–27, 512–17.

146. David Farmer, *The Oxford Dictionary of Saints* (Oxford: Oxford Univ. Press, 1992) (1978), 51–52; Suzanne Noffke, "Introduction," *Catherine of Siena: The Dialogue* (New York: Paulist, 1980), 5–6.

147. H. Larry Ingle, *First Among Friends: George Fox and the Creation of Quakerism* (New York: Oxford Univ. Press, 1994), 234–36.

148. Judith Cressy, *The Near-Death Experience: Mysticism or Madness?* Hanover, MA: Christopher Publishing, 1994.

149. Bache, "Perinatal Interpretation," 42–44.

150. P. M. H. Atwater, *Coming Back,* 64–73; Barbara Harris and Lionel Bascom, *Full Circle* (New York: Pocket Books, 1990), 37; Flynn, *After the Beyond,* 34–44; Farr, *What Tom Sawyer Learned,* 94, Ring, *Toward Omega,* 123.

151. George Ritchie, presentation at Pasadena, California, May 1995.

152. Ring, *Heading Toward Omega,* 150–53.

153. Atwater, *Coming Back,* 109.

154. Farr, *Tom Sawyer Learned,* 34–35, 126–28; Atwater, *Coming Back,* 74; Ring, *Toward Omega,* 124–25; Sutherland, *Transformed,* 155–57.

155. Rawlings, *To Hell,* 75.

156. Grey, *Return,* 68, 70, 71.

157. Smith, *Introduction,* 41–44; Bernard McGinn, ed., "Introduction," and Johannes Eckhart, "Sermon 52," in *Meister Eckhart: The Essential Sermons, Commentaries, Treatises, and Defense* (New York: Paulist, 1981), 30–57, 200–03.

Conclusion

1. Sallie McFague, *Metaphorical Theology* (Philadelphia: Fortress, 1982), 145–64.

2. Rosemary Radford Ruether, *Theology and God-Talk: Toward a Feminist Theology* (Boston: Beacon, 1983), 72–82.

3. Ruether, *God-Talk,* 178–80; Jim Alsdurf and Phyllis Alsdurf, "Wife-Beating and the Christian Home," in *Daughters of Sarah,* July–August 1987, 10; cited in Ellwood, "Batter My Heart," 26–27.

4. Ruether, *God-Talk,* 259–66; *Gaia and God* (San Francisco: HarperSan Francisco, 1992, 194–201.

5. Griffin, *God and Religion,* 129–35.

6. Rawlings, *To Hell, passim.*

INDEX

The use of "n" in the page number indicates the information will be found in the note on that page.
Experiencers' stories are found in the index by subject or by name.